A quick guide to grammar rules
(Incorrect examples are in italics)

Rule	Example	Page
Agreement of pronouns and antecedents	The team won its opener. The Bears won their opener.	46
Agreement of subjects and verbs	GM and Ford are on strike. GM, along with Ford, is on strike.	48
Active or passive verbs?	Brown hit a homer. A homer was hit by Brown.	50
Capitalizing quotes	He called them "creeps." He yelled, "Creeps!"	75-80
Clauses, independent and dependent	The police arrested him. *While he was eating.*	44, 55
Clauses or phrases?	After swimming, he rested. After he swam, he rested.	44-45
Collective nouns	The jury announced its verdict. The college fired its president.	41, 45-46
Conjunctions	And, or, but	43
Dangling modifiers	*Driving fast, the trip took an hour.* Driving fast, she made the trip in an hour.	72
Either/or, neither/nor	Either the league or the players are right. Either the players or the league is right.	49
Infinitive form of verbs	To see, to be seen, to have seen	42
Lie, lay	He lay in bed all day. He laid the book on the bed.	51
Perfect tenses	He has seen the movie twice. He had seen the movie twice. He will have seen the movie twice.	42, 51-52
Nouns	General Motors, John Brown, apples, dogs, station wagons	41, 44, 45
Only, placing properly	The city bought only the arena. The city bought the only arena.	71
Parallelism	*He enjoyed reading books and flowers.* He enjoyed reading books and growing flowers.	74
Prepositions and prepositional phrases	In the play, by the judge, over the divorce, throughout the day	45
Participles and participle phrases	Driving a Porsche, he outran the police. *Driving a Porsche, the police couldn't catch him.*	43, 72
Pronouns	He, him, she, her, they, them, which, that	41-42
That, which and who	The firm that lost the suit paid dearly. Ace Autos, which lost the suit, paid dearly. Brown, who lost the suit, paid dearly.	55-56
Transitive or intransitive verbs?	His confidence dwindled. He pumped up his confidence.	44
Who or whom?	He could choose whom he wanted. He could choose who would be his wife.	52-54

A quick guide to punctuation

Rule	Example	Page
Adjective in series	The tired, old man The green station wagon	62
Appositives and commas	His play *My Friend* was terrible. His first play, *My Mom*, was good.	56-57
Colons	He bought weapons: knifes, guns and swords. He made one promise: He would be faithful.	65-66
Colons in headlines	Brown: 'I am innocent'	154
Comma splice	*He doubted the Bulls would win, they always choke in the playoffs.*	60
Compound modifiers	His front-page story	64
Dashes	Attorney Bill Brooks—he's the district attorney now—represented Bruno Klein	65
Dashes in headlines	'I'm innocent'—Brown Disney raises prices—again	154
Essential and nonessential clauses and phrases	The man who saw the crime said Jones did it. Brown, who saw the crime, said Jones did it.	55-56
However	They played hard; however, they lost.	66
Hyphens and adjectives	The front-page story won a prize. The 5-year-old law was repealed.	63-65
Hyphenated words	The traffic tie-up lasted hours. Police investigated the holdup.	63-65
Introductory clauses and phrases	After his dogs attacked him, he bought a cat. After winning the U.S. Open, Brown retired.	60-61
Lists	Red, white and blue Bill Jones, Houston, Texas; Sally Jones, Memphis, Tenn.; and Sue Brown, Tipton, Ind.	61-62, 66
Periods inside quote marks	He read the short story "The Killers."	66
Quotes	"If I win," Brown said, "I will retire." Brown said, "If I win, I will retire."	75-80
Quote marks and partial quotes	He called Brown "a stupid weasel."	77
Single quote marks inside double quote marks	The officer said, "His exact words were 'I done it.'"	67
Semicolons	Jones lost his rent money; however, he continued to bet.	65-66

EDITING TODAY

SECOND EDITION

EDITING TODAY

SECOND EDITION

RON F. SMITH
LORAINE M. O'CONNELL

Iowa State Press
A Blackwell Publishing Company

About the Authors

Ron F. Smith is a professor of journalism at the University of Central Florida in Orlando. He has worked for newspapers in Indiana, Ohio, and Florida. Smith has published numerous articles in *Journalism Quarterly, Newspaper Research Journal, Collegiate Journalist, Quill,* and *Journalism Educator.* He was a research fellow at the Poynter Institute. He co-authored *Groping for Ethics in Journalism* with Gene Goodwin and assumed sole authorship on the fourth edition.

Loraine M. O'Connell is the Deputy Lifestyles Editor at *The Orlando Sentinel*, where she has worked since 1985. Her other positions have included metro and national copy editor, wire editor for the Newsfeatures Department, and columnist and feature writer. Her work has been published in newspapers across the country, including *The Dallas Morning News, The Boston Globe,* and *The Washington Post.*

© 1996, Iowa State University Press
© 2003, Iowa State Press
A Blackwell Publishing Company

Iowa State Press
2121 State Avenue, Ames, Iowa 50014

Orders:	1-800-862-6657
Office:	1-515-292-0140
Fax:	1-515-292-3348
Web site:	www.iowastatepress.com

ISBN 978-0-8138-1306-6

First edition, 1996
Second edition, 2003

Library of Congress Cataloging-in-Publication Data

Smith, Ron F.
 Editing today/Ron F. Smith, Loraine M. O'Connell.—2ⁿᵈ. ed. p. c.m
Continues the evolution of Martin L. Gibson's classic Editing in the electronic era.
Includes index.

 1. Copy—reading. 2. Newspaper layout and typography. 3. Journalism—Data processing. I. O'Connell, Loraine M. II. Gibson, Martin L., 1934- Editing in the electronic era. III. Title.
 PN4784.C7 S65 2003
 070.4'1—dc21

                                                                          2002009723

CONTENTS

CONTENTS

INTRODUCTION

I ncreasingly, copy editing demands a strange mix of skills.
Some skills expected of today's editors are as old as printed newspapers themselves. The first printer-journalists recognized that the
quality of the writing and trustworthiness of the information were vital
if their publications were to succeed. They worried about the clarity of
the information, the grammar and the style of presentation.

In addition to needing these traditional skills, copy editors are at
the center of most developments in journalism. Computers made their
first appearances in newsrooms on the copy desk. They soon prolifer-
ated onto the desks of reporters, followed by those of photographers
and designers. When the production of the newspaper shifted entirely
to computers, the copy desk bore the burden of learning the software
to create pages.

Life on the desk continues to change. Newspapers no longer produce one product: the daily paper. They produce Web pages and radio
news programs. They provide news for TV stations, and some even
produce news on their own cable channels. Convergence, as this trend
is called, is beginning to broaden the demands on editors. They can no
longer concentrate on the wording of a story for print. They must consider the visual aspects of the story for television and the capabilities of
enhancing the information for the Web.

Iowa State Press has been at the forefront of providing textbooks
that deal with both the traditional skills and the new demands on the
desk. In 1979, Iowa State Press began publishing a series of editing
texts. As did most editing texts, the first one emphasized grammar,
clarity and headline writing. But even the book's title signaled that it
was looking ahead at the changing role of the copy desk. *Editing in the
Electronic Era* by Martin "Red" Gibson was published before IBM
marketed its first personal computer, before Steve Jobs and friends
invented the Apple computer, and even before the term *word processing* entered our vocabulary.

This second edition of *Editing Today* is the latest in this series of
editing texts. Basic word skills are still fundamental. A few years ago,
a survey was done to find out what skills newspaper editors expected
new copy editors to have. Grammar, spelling and punctuation topped
the list. The editors also were asked what skills journalist graduates
were lacking. Unfortunately, the editors answered grammar, spelling
and punctuation. The editors complained about the shortage of journalism students who wanted to be—or were capable of being—copy
editors.

We hope that we have beefed up these areas so that you can identify and begin to overcome any problems you may have. The chapters on grammar, punctuation and syntax are larger and, we think, better organized. We hope that by using this text and the *Editing Today Workbook*, a new crop of journalism graduates will prove to editors that today's graduates can handle deskwork.

Many newspapers—even larger papers such as the *South Florida Sun-Sentinel*—now expect new copy editors to design some pages. The job title at many papers is now copy editor/designer. In keeping with this expectation, we have enlarged the design and typography chapters. We think this section of the book now offers a solid overview of contemporary design practices. We hope it provides you with enough background to competently design a page—without panicking.

Presenting the news has become a team operation. We show you how copy editors, reporters and graphic journalists work together to cover a story at the *South Florida Sun-Sentinel* and the contributions of content editors, copy editors and designers to a story at *The Tampa Tribune*.

The new edition introduces you to the latest development in journalism: convergence. In the first chapter, we take you to *The Tampa Tribune* and follow a story through its preparation for the paper, the Web site TBO.com and WFLA-TV, a Tampa TV station. We have also added a chapter on editing for the Web.

Many people have helped with this book. We were fortunate to have the cooperation of three excellent newspapers. Managing Editor Elaine Kramer of the *Orlando Sentinel* allowed us to make extensive use of her paper and its staff. Darryl Owens provided excellent examples of feature writing, and state editor Mike Griffin provided guidance, as did other *Sentinel* staffers.

Tampa Tribune Managing Editor Donna Reed allowed us access to the news operations. Staffers from the *Tribune*, TBO.com and WFLA-TV, including Michelle Bearden, Penny Carnathan, Carlos Albores, Kevin Barnard, Kiely Agliano and Peter Howard, let us follow a story as they produced it for the three news outlets. They also talked to us about the impact of convergence on their jobs.

We are greatly indebted to Jeff Glick, deputy managing editor/creative director of the *South Florida Sun-Sentinel*, who provided guidance throughout the writing of this book. Glick also allowed us access to the *Sun-Sentinel* newsroom, where David Horn, Charles Jones, Jim Rassol, Scott Horner and Noreen Marcus allowed us to look over their shoulders as they worked.

We benefited from e-mail interviews with designers at several newspapers including the *Detroit Free Press*, *Cleveland Plain Dealer*, *Savannah Morning News*, *Daily Breeze* (Torrance, California), *Star Tribune* (Minneapolis), *Jacksonville Courier-Journal* (Illinois), *Seattle Post-Intelligencer*, *San Jose Mercury News*, *Virginian-Pilot*, *News &*

Observer (Raleigh, North Carolina), and *Courier & Press* (Evansville, Indiana).

My students, present and past, have been extremely helpful in revising the book. They made it clear which sections they thought were helpful and which ones put them to sleep. Many professors who used the first edition were kind enough to critique it and offer valuable advice on how to improve the book.

We would like to thank Iowa State Press Director Gretchen Van Houten, who gave us the opportunity to write this book. We benefited from the expertise of journalism acquisitions editor Mark Barrett, production editor Judi Brown and designer Justin Eccles.

Co-author Smith wants to give special thanks to Rene Stutzman, who did double duty. As an accomplished journalist at the *Orlando Sentinel*, she provided insights that strengthen almost every section of the book. And as my wife, she forgave me for hiding out in my office while I was working on this book.

We alone accept blame for any mistakes that might have crept into the book. We are sure you will find grammar flaws, goofs or typos in this book. Send them or any comments you want to make to us at rsmith@Pegasus.cc.ucf.edu. It's embarrassing to make editing mistakes in an editing book. We have only one consolation: The aim of the book is to produce a crop of first-rate editors. When you find mistakes, maybe it's a sign we're achieving our goal.

Ron F. Smith, Professor
University of Central Florida

Loraine O'Connell, Deputy Lifestyles Editor
Orlando Sentinel

I. THE COPY EDITOR'S JOB

THE EVOLUTION OF A NEWS STORY 1

So here you are, about to enter the world of editing. Odds are, you're wondering just what editors do. *Everybody* knows what reporters do. But few people know what editors do, and there's no shame in admitting that you're among the clueless.

Not to worry. In this book, we explain not only what editors do but how and why as well.

The best way to explain the role of editors is to give you an overview of the whole process of getting a story into print so that you can see assignment editors, copy editors and designers at work.

You'll also get a view of what may be the newsroom in your future. Today it's not unusual for a newspaper reporter to write for the Web and TV. Perhaps nowhere is this media convergence more visible than in The News Center in Tampa. The first floor houses the news operation of NBC affiliate WFLA, a perennial leader in news ratings in the Tampa Bay area. The award-winning Web site, TBO.com, is on the second floor. *The Tampa Tribune*, a daily with a circulation of 225,000 on weekdays and 290,000 on Sundays, fills the top floor. WFLA, TBO.com, and the *Tribune* are all owned by Media General.

We follow Michelle Bearden, a reporter for the *Tribune* who, since 1998, has been a key player in that paper's goal of "converging" print, TV and online coverage. Her beat is religion, and she's a whirlwind of activity in producing copy and TV packages related to all aspects of her subject, from the serious think piece to the lighthearted look at a man who calls himself the "Gator Crusader."

Bearden produces the weekly "Faith & Values" page that runs Saturdays in the *Tribune*. Her work for that page includes a column and often the main story.

In addition, Bearden writes cover stories for the *Tribune*'s Bay Life section, covers breaking news for the paper's Metro section, and prepares a weekly package called "Keeping the Faith" for WFLA-Channel 8. And, of course, her stories make their way to TBO.com (Tampa Bay Online).

"I do a lot more stories for the newspaper" than for TV, Bearden says. "Not all of them work for TV." TV is all about visuals, and Bearden has come to know instinctively which stories will provide good video, and those are the ones she pitches for her TV packages.

Not all of them meet with the approval of her *Tribune* assignment editor, Penny Carnathan, whose responsibility is making sure Bearden's stories are newsworthy enough to make the *Tribune*. But the vast majority of Bearden's ideas do pass muster with Carnathan.

"Penny trusts my judgment," Bearden says.

And Bearden trusts Carnathan's instincts as well.

COACHING

They've built this mutual trust through the process of "coaching," an idea developed by Roy Peter Clark and Don Fry of the Poynter Institute for Media Studies in St. Petersburg, Fla.

Clark and Fry believe that assignment editors and reporters should work together as a team rather than work around each other in an adversarial relationship. It may not sound revolutionary, but for a lot of veteran reporters and editors, it's nothing short of life-changing.

Before coaching caught on in newsrooms, a reporter might throw out an unformed story idea, and the editor might say, "Well, what are you waiting for? Get me 25 inches by 3 p.m." Then, when the story was turned in, the editor might very well go ballistic: "This isn't what I expected! What were you thinking?"

Of course, that's the problem: The reporter and editor didn't give the story any thought before the reporter left the building; they didn't discuss its possibilities. And after the reporting was done, they didn't discuss what the reporter had found. The reporter wrote; the editor read; neither was happy with the results.

Today, coaching—which very often is nothing more than informal chitchat—is a mainstay of many newsrooms because it serves both the editor and the reporter. The editor has a good idea what the story will look like and doesn't fear a nasty surprise; the reporter knows the story will meet with the editor's approval and doesn't fear being ambushed with demands for a total rewrite.

At its most basic level, coaching is conversation.

The reporter and assignment editor begin weighing a story's possibilities as soon as the idea is presented. They talk about what to look for in the reporting, and they kick around possible angles the story might take.

When the reporter returns to the office, the two discuss what the reporter actually found; they discuss good quotes, good anecdotes and themes that the reporter came across. By simply talking, the assignment editor can help the reporter unearth the key ingredients for a focused, compelling story.

The *Tribune*'s move toward convergence has added another thing for reporters and editors to consider: Might this story be one that WFLA-TV and the TBO Web site would want?

Bearden has particularly well-honed multimedia instincts because of her experience juggling TV and newspaper stories.

When she heard about the "Gator Crusader," a guy who uses alligators to teach Bible lessons, she knew immediately that she wanted a video photographer, as well as a *Tribune* still photographer, to accompany her to the Christian school where he would be demonstrating his ministry.

The idea for the story originated with Channel 8 video photographer Carlos Albores, who knew of the "crusader's" upcoming appearance at the school and passed word along to Bearden.

In their brief discussion of the story, Bearden apprised Carnathan of her intended approach to the story: watching him in action, getting the kids' reactions, explaining how he meshed his passion for gators with his love of the Gospel. They also agreed that it would be an excellent TV piece.

"Because Carlos found the story, he was given the opportunity to shoot it with me, and they made sure he could edit it," she says.

That's not a typical aspect of convergence at the *Tribune*. "A photographer may shoot a piece for you," Bearden explains, "but if he's sent to a fire, it goes into the editing pit," and another WFLA video editor will do the job.

On the Tuesday that Bearden and Albores shot their TV piece, they met at 7 a.m. at the *Tribune*. Bearden drove them to the 8 a.m. presentation that "crusader" Michael Womer was giving at Northside Christian School in St. Petersburg. On the way, the two discussed what Bearden hoped to capture in her TV package.

Whereas in print, a photographer "often parachutes in and then he's gone," Bearden notes, "in TV we're more team-oriented." Reporters preparing TV pieces have to know exactly what they want so that their shooters come back with video that matches the scripts written by the reporters.

Obviously, both reporter and photographer must remain flexible.

"Sometimes you see something else—another element," she explains. "Things can change, but you and the photographer are a team."

As part of the convergence operation, photographers for Channel 8 and the *Tribune* are being given both still and video digital cameras and quick courses in how to use them. Then they "job-shadow" each other for hands-on learning.

It was a good thing that Albores had a still camera. The *Tribune* photographer assigned to the "Gator Crusader" story got stuck in traffic and couldn't be there. Albores shot some stills, one of which the paper used. But he soon was completely involved in shooting video of Womer, his alligators, and the kids, and in getting good "natural sound" of the goings-on.

"He throws the camera to me!" Bearden says. And her photo of Womer showing an alligator to the schoolkids ended up on the cover of the Bay Life section.

Then, while Albores shot random scenes of the children for general use during the broadcast (what TV photographers call B roll), Bearden got her print interviews.

"You need tons more detail for the print interview," she says, because the print reporter paints with words, whereas the TV package will have video.

Indeed, she called Womer three more times after his St. Petersburg presentation to gather more information and detail for her *Tribune* story.

She and Albores were headed back to The News Center by 9:45 a.m. Bearden began to log in the tapes Albores had shot, meaning that she reviewed them on a monitor, selecting good sound bites and also scanning for good quotes for her print story.

"TV is the appetizer, the newspaper is the main course and TBO is dessert," she says of multimedia.

Because she tries to work a week ahead on her TV packages, the print version of her "Gator Crusader" story wasn't scheduled to run as the *Tribune*'s Bay Life cover until the Friday of the following week; it would air that same day on Channel 8 at 5:30 p.m. and again on Sunday at 9 a.m.

"We try to keep the TV and print versions on either the same day or within a day of each other," Bearden says.

With so much lead time, Bearden waited a week after the interview to write her TV script. She started on the script around 11 a.m., took a lunch break, and wrapped it up by 2 p.m.

"It's the thinking process that takes longer, not the writing" for TV scripts, she finds.

She sent this script to one of the Channel 8 producers. The capitalized words are the ones she will record in a sound studio at the station. A video editor puts her words with the video, sounds and words of Mike Womer.

Start with footage of school, with music underneath.
IT'S TIME FOR CHAPEL . . . IN THE SCHOOL AUDITORIUM.
Bring up kids reciting either prayer or patriotic stuff, some nat [natural] sound here.
AND TODAY'S GUEST SPEAKER . . . MIKE WOMER.
Show him getting gator out of cage.
WHO BROUGHT ALONG A FEW OF HIS FRIENDS.
Nat sound of Mike introducing Goliath to audience.
MEET THE GATOR CRUSADER . . . WHO PROVES THAT BEAUTY IS IN THE EYE OF THE BEHOLDER.
Use either as a voiceover or up full, Tape 2, 00:39:30.
Mike Womer: I mean, I look at this alligator and I know most people are like, auggh! Look at that! But I really think this is one of the most beautiful things I've ever seen.
THE LOVE AFFAIR BEGAN AS A CHILD.
Tape 2, 00:34:22.
Mike: Like any kid, I was really into dinosaurs. Then I was very disappointed when I found out dinosaurs weren't around anymore.
Footage of him with gator.
Keep up footage with this voiceover: Tape 2, 00:34:32.
Voice of Mike: Then I saw pictures and heard about alligators, and I thought, that's the next best thing.

SO WHEN A GATOR GUY GROWS UP, WHAT DOES HE DO FOR A LIVING?

Tape 2, 00:35:19.

Mike: My dream was to work at a gator farm and wrestle alligators. I chose that over college. Looking back 10 years later, I'm not sure that was a good idea. Kids, go to college!

HE GOT HIS JOB AT GATORLAND . . . AND SOMETHING ELSE.

Tape 2, 00:43:58.

Mike: I got married actually in the alligator pit at Gatorland.

Tape 2, 00:45:13.

Mike: My wife came out there in her white dress, I was in my tuxedo, then we said our wedding vows—with the 18 alligators as our guests of honor, so to speak.

Show him with gators and kids watching in audience, with nat sound.

NOW HE TEACHES THE GOSPEL, ACCORDING TO THE GATOR.

Tape 1, 00:26:03.

Mike: It doesn't take long for an alligator to go from small to really big to even bigger! You know what? Your little sins, they can grow like that, too.

Pop in another Bible lesson here, or use this bite as a voiceover while he talks to kids: Tape 2, 00:38:01.

Voice of Mike: They may have heard a Bible story or heard a certain verse a hundred times in their life, but when you've got a living example, it kind of brings the Bible to life.

Footage of him with kids crowding around: Tape 2, 00:28:34.

Mike: Watch his eye when it opens. Did you see that thing slide? That's God's built-in swimming goggles. Isn't that cool? That way he can see underwater.

IT CAN BE DANGEROUS WORK.

Tape 2, 00:43:23.

Mike: I have been bitten probably about 6 or 7 times. I've never lost any fingers. All still in one piece. I must not taste very good.

GATOR LOVE . . . IT'S NOT FOR EVERYBODY.

Voiceover: Tape 2, 00:43:13.

Voice of Mike: They look like a monster. They eat people, yet I know how to handle them. That's just the most amazing thing to me.

End with kids clapping enthusiastically in auditorium.

MICHELLE BEARDEN, OF THE TAMPA TRIBUNE.

Afterward, Bearden went downstairs to the Channel 8 newsroom to record her part of the script. Then she placed her voice tape and the two tapes Albores had shot in a mailbox and left a note asking the assignment desk editor to allow Albores time to edit the Gator piece.

THE ASSIGNMENT EDITOR'S ROLE

Tribune editor Carnathan wanted Bearden's print version filed by 8 a.m. Wednesday morning. After finishing the TV package, Bearden went home to write the newspaper version. She e-mailed it to Carnathan Tuesday evening.

"I'm a very fast writer," Bearden says. "TV teaches you to be fast. I probably wrote 40 inches in 2½ hours. Penny probably cut 5 inches."

Here's the unedited version of the story Bearden filed:

1. Some people find true love at a tender age.

2. Take the tale of Michael Womer, aka "The Gator Crusader," and his deep and abiding affection for the reptile that defines Florida.

3. It began 23 years ago, when he was just a 5-year-old tyke. He fell in love with dinosaurs. When he learned he could never own or even touch one, he transferred that love to the next best thing: alligators. He filled his pockets with rubber imitations, lined his bedroom shelves with them.

4. When his parents took the family to Disney World, he remembers passing Gatorland billboards along the way. Drop me off there, he begged. It didn't work, but the pictures on those advertisements inspired a dream. When he grew up, he resolved, he would work at an alligator farm and wrestle the mighty creatures.

5. Not only would Womer fulfill that dream, he's gone on to bigger ones. A man of deep faith, he's found a way to combine his love of God and gators into one gig. In 1996, he launched his "Gator Crusader" ministry, teaching biblical principles in Christian schools, churches and religious gatherings. His props: two of his four pet gators, Samson and Goliath, and a colorful king snake named Fluffy.

6. "You get their attention with these guys," he says. "Maybe they've heard the Scripture story dozens of times, but when you use a living example, it paints a different picture, and they see it in a different light."

7. The Gator Crusader is part comic, part educator. He weaves in jokes ("What does an alligator have to do with the Bible? If he bites me, I'll be a lot more holy!") and sprinkles in gator facts ("The record length is almost 20 feet long"). But his real goal is to imprint a message of faith by the time the 40-minute presentation ends.

8. It may seem like a bit of a stretch, but Womer does it in such a natural way, it works. One example: He brings gators that are a year apart in age, showing how fast they can grow in that time span. Then he compares just how fast a small sin can grow into a larger one. With Fluffy, he talks about how the snake routinely sheds its skin. In the same vein, "when you give your heart to Jesus, you become a brand-new person, and everything you've done wrong can go away."

9. At a recent presentation at Northside Christian School in St. Petersburg, his alma mater, Womer let the kids come up and pet the gators, whose mouths were taped shut as a safety precaution. While he's quick to point out that gators can be dangerous, he also uses this time to promote their positive attributes, and how humans need to respect these creatures in their own environment.

10. "Everybody, come here for a second. I want to show you something neat about this alligator," he says, as elementary students clamor around him and a mellow Samson. "Watch his eye when it opens. Did you see that thing slide? That's God's built-in swimming goggles. Isn't that cool? That way he can see under water."

11. Reaction from the kids ranged from "Nice teeth!" to "What a cool tail. Can I touch it?"

12. "What Mike is doing is fabulous," says Northside principal Mark DeBee. "He's using one of God's own creations to teach about the wonders of faith. This connection he's making in the community will have a lasting impact on the kids."

13. He takes his show on the road on weekends and evenings, charging a small fee to offset travel expenses and gator upkeep. One day, Womer would like to produce a television show, something along the lines of Steve Irwin's "Crocodile Hunter" on the Animal Planet network. He envisions going deep into the alligator's own natural habitat, while teaching Bible lessons along the way.

14. "We're put on this earth to bring people to Christ," he says. "Well, I have this unbelievable passion for alligators. And I've found out how to use it for the Lord."

15. A little boy's dream came true in 1992, when Womer landed the job at Gatorland after graduating with honors from Northside Christian School in St. Petersburg. He didn't even consider the scholarship offers for college. He just wanted to be with the gators.

16. "Looking back 10 years, I would probably advise kids against that," he admits. "But there was no stopping me."

17. They loved Womer at Gatorland. At 5 feet four, he was dwarfed by the big and beefy fellow wrestlers beside him. But when Womer tangles with a reptilian opponent, his small stature only makes the gator look that much larger, giving the audience an even bigger thrill.

18. He found another love at Orlando's popular tourist attraction. A woman named Carolyn working in the souvenir booth caught his attention. To those who knew them, it came as no surprise when they got married in the gator pit, surrounded by 18 alligators in a moat.

19. "We had all the wrestlers standing by, just to be on the safe side," he says. Afterwards the newly married couple—he in his tuxedo, she in her white wedding gown—posed for their official wedding portrait atop one of the gators.

20. They came back to the Tampa Bay area in 1996 to be closer to family. Womer got a job running a warehouse for a Largo medical supply company. That pays the bills. Launching the "Gator Crusader" ministry was a natural progression.

21. Carolyn gave him full support, even putting up with several gators living in their Seminole garage in their early years of marriage. She didn't even raise an eyebrow when her husband came up with the idea of "Gator Art"—putting wet paint on their tail and feet and letting them walk around on poster board, creating colorful abstract paintings.

22. "It's not like any of this was a big shock," says Carolyn, who quit work to stay at home with their 4-year-old daughter. "This is who Mike is. He definitely has a gift with gators and he's using it in a good way."

23. With a small child, two cats and a Shih Tzu dog living at home, the Womers decided it was best to moe the gators to the Suncoast Primate Sanctuary in Palm Harbor. Womer goes there several times a week to feed them and clean their cages. Although his affection for the reptiles is as strong as ever, he knows his place in their life.

24. "Their brain is so small—the size of a thumb, really—they never really think of me as a friend or a buddy," says Womer, who's been bit about seven times. "I admit, after a hot summer day, when I've just spent three hours cleaning up after them, and one tries to bite me as I'm leaving, it's a little frustrating."

25. But not enough to end the relationship. After all, this is unconditional love— yet another lesson he imparts upon his young audiences. When you give freely, do it out of love, and don't expect anything in return.

26. Still, he can't explain his enduring connection with these prehistoric-looking, sometimes man-eating animals. He thinks he and Irwin, the Crocodile Hunter, are in a "very small club" that few would understand.

27. "I look at this alligator and I know most people are like, 'Ugh, look at that,' but I think this is one of the most beautiful things I've ever seen," he says, stroking Samson's scaly back. "To me, he's really a work of art."

As Carnathan read Bearden's story, she automatically made various grammatical and style corrections that have become second nature to her.

For example, in paragraph 17, "5 feet four" became "5-foot-4" in accordance with the Associated Press Stylebook; in paragraph 19, "afterwards" became "afterward"; in paragraph 21, "tail" became tails, in keeping with the plural "gators"; and in paragraph 23, "life" became "lives," again based on the plural "them"; and in paragraph 24, "bit" became "bitten."

Carnathan also added subheads where she thought they were appropriate—and pounced on incidents of wordiness.

"I do a lot of tightening with Michelle because she writes like she talks"—a tad verbosely. For instance, "deep and abiding" in Paragraph 2 became simply "deep." And paragraph 8 went from 94 words to 77.

The original:

> It may seem like a bit of a stretch, but Womer does it in such a natural way, it works. One example: He brings gators that are a year apart in age, showing how fast they can grow in that time span. Then he compares just how fast a small sin can grow into a larger one. With Fluffy, he talks about how the snake routinely sheds its skin. In the same vein, "when you give your heart to Jesus, you become a brand-new person, and everything you've done wrong can go away."

The condensed version:

> It seems like a stretch, but Womer pulls it off. Example: He points out the big difference in size between Samson and Goliath born just a year apart. That's how fast a small sin can grow into a larger one.
>
> With Fluffy, he talks about how the snake routinely sheds its skin. In the same vein, "when you give your heart to Jesus, you become a brand-new person, and everything you've done wrong can go away."

Carnathan, whose ungainly title is Team Leader for Personal Life, has been Bearden's editor for two years, after having worked as a reporter, editor, copy chief and bureau chief in her 21 years at the *Tribune*.

Bearden's copy is generally clean, Carnathan says. "She knows how to organize a story."

However, Bearden's TV writing sometimes seeps into her print writing.

"What you run into occasionally is that, in newspapers, you want the lead up very high, and in TV you bury the lead," Carnathan explains. "If Michelle hasn't shifted entirely out of TV gear, we'll sometimes get a buried lead."

Not in the Gator Crusader story, though. The lead was fine; however, the offhand tone of TV writing did find its way into the story.

"In TV you're a lot more flip; you tend to use clichés," Carnathan said. "That slips into Michelle's copy."

Thus, the alliterative "love of God and gators into one gig" in paragraph 5 had to go, especially that word "gig."

Bearden's original:

Not only would Womer fulfill that dream, he's gone on to bigger ones. A man of deep faith, he's found a way to combine his love of God and gators into one gig. In 1996, he launched his "Gator Crusader" ministry, teaching biblical principles in Christian schools, churches and religious gatherings. His props: two of his four pet gators, Samson and Goliath, and a colorful king snake named Fluffy.

Carnathan's rewrite:

Womer fulfilled his boyhood dream, and moved on to bigger ones. A man of deep faith, he's found a way to share the Gospel—using alligators.

In 1996, Womer launched Gator Crusader, a ministry that teaches biblical principles in Christian schools, churches and at religious gatherings. His props: two of his four pet gators, Samson and Goliath, and a colorful king snake named Fluffy.

In paragraph 7, Carnathan thought Bearden's last sentence was slightly stilted, particularly her use of the word "imprint."

So the paragraph went from:

The Gator Crusader is part comic, part educator. He weaves in jokes ("What does an alligator have to do with the Bible? If he bites me, I'll be a lot more holy") and sprinkles in gator facts ("The record length is almost 20 feet long"). But his real goal is to imprint a message of faith by the time the 40-minute presentation ends.

to:

The Gator Crusader is part comic, part educator. He weaves in jokes ("What does an alligator have to do with the Bible? If he bites me, I'll be a lot more holy!") and sprinkles in gator facts ("The record length is almost 20 feet"). But at the heart of his 40-minute presentation lies a message of divine love and redemption.

A key storytelling element Carnathan has worked on with Bearden is imagery.

In some of her TV stories for print, "she didn't have descriptions because she's thinking, 'I have the camera.'"

But storytelling in print requires a lot of description and detail, and Bearden has made a point of working those into her stories, as in her reference to the painted gators walking around "on poster board, creating colorful abstract paintings" in paragraph 21.

Carnathan injects more detail into paragraph 3 by using "T-rex," which conjured up a more concrete image than "dinosaurs" or "one."

In paragraph 17, Carnathan noted Bearden's use of "was dwarfed by the big and beefy fellow wrestlers."

"I try to get her away from passive sentences," Carnathan said.

So paragraph 17 went from:

They loved Womer at Gatorland. At 5 feet four, he was dwarfed by the big and beefy fellow wrestlers beside him. But when Womer tangles with a reptilian opponent, his small stature only made the gator look that much larger, giving the audience an even bigger thrill.

to:

They loved him at Gatorland. His fellow wrestlers—a beefy crew—dwarfed Womer, who stands 5-foot-4. That gave audiences a thrill—when he tangled with the gators, they seemed even bigger.

After reading the whole story, Carnathan came back to paragraph 24:

Their brain is so small—the size of a thumb, really—they never really think of me as a friend or a buddy," says Womer, who's been bitten about seven times. "I admit, after a hot summer day, when I've just spent three hours cleaning up after them, and one tries to bite me as I'm leaving, it's a little frustrating."

Said Carnathan: "Time for this story to be over. It's come to its natural conclusion." But Bearden made a case for maintaining Womer's "work of art" quote, so they agreed to condense the ending, taking the story from:

But not enough to end the relationship. After all, this is unconditional love—yet another lesson he imparts upon his young audiences. When you give freely, do it out of love, and don't expect anything in return.

Still, he can't explain his enduring connection with these prehistoric-looking, sometimes man-eating animals. He thinks he and Irwin, the Crocodile Hunter, are in a "very small club" that few would understand.

"I look at this alligator and I know most people are like, 'Ugh, look at that,' but I think this is one of the most beautiful things I've ever seen," he says, stroking Samson's scaly back. "To me, he's really a work of art."

THE COPY EDITOR'S ROLE

Kevin Barnard, team leader for Features Copy Editing—also known as "copy chief" in print newsroom parlance—tries to read all of the centerpiece stories going on Bay Life covers.

He pulled Bearden's story out of the queue and began editing it. He worked quickly, knowing that Carnathan is both a good assignment editor and a first-rate copy editor. He expected that any story edited by Carnathan would be "clean," meaning it would have few errors. This proved to be the case.

Barnard's first read-through of the Gator Crusader led to several grammatical changes. For instance, "he's found" in paragraph 4 of the edited version became "he has found" because "he's" is the contraction for "he is," not "he has." Similarly, "who's been bitten" in paragraph 29 became "who has been bitten." He changed "moe the gator" to "move the gator" in paragraph 23.

Barnard also verified names and titles, ensuring that Bearden identified Steve Irwin correctly—he checked out the Animal Planet host on google.com—and that the theme park mentioned in paragraph 4 was identified by its full name, Walt Disney World.

And he changed T-rex to T. rex, after looking it up in a dictionary.

Barnard also reworded some sentences slightly to make the copy easier to understand.

For example, in paragraph 5, he tweaked the opening sentence from:

> In 1996, Womer launched Gator Crusader, a ministry that teaches biblical principles in Christian schools, churches and at religious gatherings.

to:

> In 1996, Womer launched Gator Crusader, a ministry that teaches biblical principles in Christian schools and churches and at religious gatherings.

And he added a comma in paragraph 8:

> "He points out the big difference in size between Samson and Goliath, born just a year apart."

Barnard was given the pictures that will be used with the story and some notes about what is in them. He then wrote the cutlines (captions) for the pictures. He would also write the words for the headline. But the headline would not be written until the page designer had decided how she wanted the headline to look—how big, how many words, how many decks. For this story, the designer used an "art head," so Barnard's task was to come up with a couple of words that would tell the story and entice readers. He considered "Gator Crusader" but decided on "Gator Gospel." The layout also called for a deck that gave Barnard a chance to explain the story a little more. Unlike most decks, which are directly below the headline, this deck ran alongside the picture over the headline (see Fig. 1.1).

THE PAGE DESIGNER'S ROLE

By this point, the print version of the story was ready for Kiely Agliano, who would be designing the Friday Bay Life cover.

Agliano became a designer after going to art school. But after working at *The Atlanta Journal-Constitution* for a while and at the *Tribune* for five years, she considers herself a journalist rather than an artist—a journalist who uses design to help report the news.

Agliano began to arrange the pictures and text on her computer. The *Tribune* uses the software program In Design for pagination, having switched recently from QuarkXpress. The page on her computer screen has an 11-column grid that the *Tribune* uses for feature pages.

In choosing which photographs to use, designers listen to the suggestions of reporters and editors, of course. "But our job is to read the story and decide what will summarize it," says Agliano, team leader for features design.

The wedding picture of Womer and his bride in a gator pit caught Agliano's eye. The happy couple smiles brightly as the bride is perched atop a gator. It was good, she said, but she would put it on the jump page because the story was about this guy's presentations in religious schools, not his wedding. Instead she chose two other pictures for the cover of the section. She picked one that showed Womer, a gator and lots of schoolkids. (See Figure 1.1.) The picture told the main elements of the story. She decided that a cutout of Womer pointing a gator into the text of the story would be visually exciting.

Because Bearden's story was the centerpiece for the page, Agliano decided to use an "art headline." She tinkered with the typography but left the wording of the headline to the copy desk.

GETTING THE STORY ONLINE

As Team Leader for News and Special Projects with TBO.com, Peter Howard has to know what WFLA and the *Tribune* are covering so that he can plan TBO.com's coverage. His daily routine involves lots of meetings. At 9 a.m. he attends a news meeting at WFLA. At 10:15 a.m., he gathers with news chiefs from the *Tribune*, WFLA and TBO.com for the morning "converged news" meeting. He also attends the *Tribune*'s news meetings at 10:30 a.m. and 4:30 p.m.

Throughout the day, of course, he's talking to his producers about the stories to highlight on TBO.com and briefing them on what WFLA and the *Tribune* are working on. Howard's staff manages the news sites for the TV station and the newspaper, www.tampatrib.com and www.wfla.com, as well as TBO.com, which serves as a regional portal.

Howard has been a reporter and an editor at the *Tribune*. When the newspaper announced plans for a Web site, Howard interviewed for the job and got it.

Although WFLA, the *Tribune* and TBO have the same owner and are in the same building, "we're all independent, separate companies," Howard notes. So independent is the online operation, in fact, that "original reporting is 10–15 percent of a TBO producer's job," Howard says.

Because the newspaper's computerized production system is set up to interact with TBO.com,

Figure 1.1. Gator Gospel package on front page of *The Tampa Tribune's* Bay Life features section.

stories filed by *Tribune* staff writers are automatically "dumped" into the online operation's queues. However, the online producers make the call as to which print stories get the "multimedia" treatment. For some stories, they can add additional pictures and links to related sites. If the story has been both in the *Tribune* and on WFLA, they may decide to work the text, pictures and video into one multimedia package.

Bearden hoped her package about the Gator Crusader might be chosen for a multimedia package on TBO, but it wasn't. Instead, producers used her story as part of TBO's local news coverage. They combined Bearden's story with one of Albores' pictures. (See Figure 1.2.)

CHANGING ROLES OF EDITORS

There you have it. Our story has gone from conception through reporting and editing and into production. You now have a sense of how all the parts fit together and of the roles of each player—reporter, assignment or content editor, copy desk chief, layout editor, and copy editor. In broad terms, this book emphasizes the work of three kinds of editors:

- *Assignment or content editors,* who supervise reporters and work with them as they gather information and write their stories, helping them

Figure 1.2. Bearden's story and a picture by Albores were used on the TBO.com Web site.

make sure the stories are accurate, fair and well-written. Some people call this process "coaching writers."

• *Editors on the copy desk,* who perfect the writing of stories; check for accuracy, fairness and libel; and write the headlines.

• *Designers and editors with design responsibilities,* who lay out pages, order and sometimes produce graphics, and edit photographs.

In many newsrooms, the roles of these editors are being redefined. At one time, editors saw themselves as specialists. Assignment editors and copy editors saw themselves as "word people," who cared about how well the news was reported and written but wanted nothing to do with design and graphics. Designers, artists and photographers were "visual people" who didn't know anything about writing and cared only about how well the news was packaged.

Newspapers today are encouraging journalists to forget these labels and think of themselves as members of a team. Each member of the team shares two fundamental responsibilities: making sure that the news is reported clearly and that it's presented so well that people will want to read their newspapers.

Word people must try not only to make the writing as strong as possible but also to think about graphics and photographs that would help explain their stories and entice people to read them. Visual people need to become visual *journalists,* who recognize that their role is to help tell the news.

Newsgathering is becoming a team event. The idea for the Gator Gospel story came from TV photographer Carlos Albores. He and *Tribune* reporter Michelle Bearden plotted the coverage together. Both of them took pictures that were used in the *Tribune.* His pictures were used on both WFLA-TV and TBO.com.

The team concept is also evident in the relationship between Bearden and Penny Carnathan, the assignment editor who handled the Gator Gospel package. Carnathan sees herself as a coach. Her mission is to draw the best work possible out of her reporters.

CONVERGENCE MAY BE THE FUTURE

Tampa's combining of a newspaper, TV news and a multimedia Web site is not unique. The *Sarasota Herald-Tribune, Orlando Sentinel* and other papers have teamed with local cable companies to provide their communities with 24-hour local cable news. Many papers have cooperative arrangements with local TV stations to share coverage. If the FCC drops its rules against a media company buying a TV station and a newspaper in the same city, the movement toward convergence will accelerate.

Already, some free-lancers consider themselves "backpack journalists." They carry digital cameras, video cameras, tripods and laptop computers. They write stories and take pictures that they sell to newspapers, magazines, Web sites and TV.

Many expect this to be the future of journalism. Jeff Glick, deputy managing editor/creative director of the *South Florida Sun-Sentinel,* foresees a day when "print reporters will be expected to do TV, and TV reporters will be expected to do print. This is an evolutionary process that is going to bring about a change in the newsroom culture."

The *Sun-Sentinel* is one of the few newspapers that have converged into radio. It produces a local newscast with a public broadcasting station in Palm Beach. The broadcast includes both professional announcers and reporters from the *Sun-Sentinel* newsroom. The paper also shares coverage with TV stations in both Palm Beach and Miami. The news also makes its way onto www.sunsentinel.com. The paper's Web site is a leader in using animated graphics to explain the news. To Glick, the paper's newsroom is "a news-gathering engine that feeds several methods of presentation of the news." He expects the newspaper's involvement in TV and on the Web to continue to grow.

Today you may envision yourself as a die-hard reporter who never wants to spend a minute of your career as an editor. Remember, though, that you'll be working with a *team* of editors and designers. If you understand—dare we say, appreciate—their work, you'll become a more valued member of the newsroom team.

And if you think you might want to be an editor, now's the time to begin picturing yourself in that role. As a copy editor, you'll design pages; examine stories for organization, syntax and grammar; cut stories to fit the space available; combine wire stories to produce a coherent, informative story; and compose headlines that both inform and entice readers. And you'll work with photographers, graphic artists and designers to produce news packages that tell the news in a compelling way.

LIFE ON THE COPY DESK 2

Think about the backgrounds of reporters at most midsize daily newspapers. Nearly all of them are college-educated and most have taken several courses in reporting and newswriting. They must know their jobs or their bosses wouldn't keep them on the payroll. So, why would these professional reporters need copy editors?

We suggest five reasons.

1. Sometimes reporters don't have the time to do the job well. Perhaps they couldn't find the sources they needed until minutes before deadline. Or they may have been assigned too many stories. So, to meet their deadlines, they end up throwing together their stories with no time for revision.

2. Sometimes even the best of us have bad days. Just as professional athletes go into slumps, reporters go through periods when they have trouble putting words together. Even worse, good writers occasionally get carried away with their own verbal abilities and produce copy that is overwritten and wrongheaded. Editors have the task of convincing them that what the reporters saw as Pulitzer Prize material is really just purple prose.

3. Sometimes good reporters get buried in their own information. They collect so many strong facts and so much interesting detail that they lose sight of the story. Editors who are less involved in the project are in a better position to judge what needs to be in the story and what can be left out. An even more frequent problem occurs when reporters become experts on the areas they cover and pick up the jargon of their sources. This expertise helps them while they're gathering information, but often they end up writing stories that are over the heads of average readers or that emphasize insider gossip that readers couldn't care less about.

4. Let's be honest. The sad truth is that some reporters are lousy writers. At nearly every paper, you'll find people who excel at gathering information. They cultivate sources easily and have uncanny instincts about where to go and what to ask. Editors value them for their reporting, which is always accurate and thorough. But when these poor souls sit down to write their stories, they're lost. Their style ranges from overwrought to boring. Their narratives are disjointed and their grammar is appalling.

5. The most common problem for writers is that they read over their own mistakes. They know what they want to say, so when they check over their own copy, their eyes see what's supposed to be written there, not what they actually typed. You may have done this in your own newswriting classes.

The lesson to be learned? Every writer needs a good editor. This chapter will start with a discussion of the daily life of copy editors. Then we give you some advice on how to do the job.

WHAT LIFE IS LIKE ON THE DESK

Life on the desk varies considerably, depending on the size of the paper. Copy editors on small papers might not only edit local copy and write headlines but also design pages and handle the wire services. At larger papers, editors specialize in page layout and wire editing.

A truism in journalism is that the number of tasks handled by a copy editor or reporter is directly related to the circulation of the paper. Reporters on a large paper might write two or three stories a week, whereas small-town reporters could lose their jobs if they don't produce that many every day. Another truth: Salaries are also related to the size of the paper. The bigger the paper, the bigger the paycheck. But no matter what size the paper is and what responsibilities copy editors have, they experience the same pleasures and pressures.

PRESSURES OF THE DESK

Perhaps the most obvious pressure comes from deadlines. Copy editors often must do their work quickly. They'd like to spend the time reading through a story one more time, searching for a better verb for the headline or improving the layout of the page. But they can't. They have to get the work done. If they fail to meet the deadline, the paper will be late getting into production and late getting into delivery trucks, therefore late getting to readers.

If you watch a copy desk in action, you may be surprised by the fluctuations in the level of activity. At times, copy editors are reading newspapers and gabbing. Then as a deadline nears, the pace picks up dramatically. Copy editors focus single-mindedly on their computer screens, and copy chiefs' voices rise a notch. When the deadline has passed, the desk quiets down again while awaiting the surge before the next deadline.

Time pressure isn't the only pressure copy editors deal with. Copy editors are the last people to see a story before it's set in type. They must make sure that every *i* is dotted and every *t* crossed. Having to be right every time is a burden that copy editors carry every day.

THE COMING OF PAGINATION

Unfortunately, on many newspapers copy editors are feeling even more pressure these days. Although computers have improved newspapers in many ways, they've also shifted more work and more responsibility to the desk.

Before computers, copy editors did their jobs with paper and pencils. They edited copy that reporters had typed on sheets of cheap paper, wrote headlines on slips of paper and drew their page layouts on dummy sheets. They then sent all these pieces of paper off to the composing room, where the actual production of the newspaper was done. Linotype operators retyped the stories on typesetting machines. Proofreaders reread all the stories, checking for errors made by typesetters and, in the process, correcting errors that copy editors had missed. Composing room personnel built the pages following the editors' layouts and sometimes suggested improvements. But today, linotype operators and proofreaders are history at most papers. Technology has allowed newspapers to eliminate their jobs.

Getting rid of high-paid, unionized back-shop employees may have helped the company's bottom line. But in most newsrooms, it meant more work for copy editors. Copy desks were now expected to do the pagination—the newspaper term for producing pages on computers with programs such as Quark Xpress, In Design, or a system specially designed for larger newspapers. Even though more work was dumped on the copy desk, many papers were reluctant to hire enough additional copy editors to deal with the increased load.

The result? Copy editors' jobs became even more pressured. Creating pages on computers takes time. That's time they can't spend editing copy. And no longer are there any backup proofreaders to catch errors. Copy editors are expected to know more, do more, and make fewer mistakes.

THE PLEASURES OF THE DESK

Let's not dwell on the negative. A person trying to choose between a reporting career and an editing career will find that each has its advantages and disadvantages.

Editors don't enjoy the excitement that reporters experience in tracking down and reporting on the activities of the mighty. They don't experience the pleasure of piecing together a story from several sources that will allow readers to understand their communities. An editor's job satisfaction comes from other things. Assignment editors know they were the ones who found inaccuracies in the reporter's first draft and suggested additional sources for the reporter to check. They were the ones who helped shape the story into something readable. And copy editors know that they sharpened the writing and used their expertise to design pages and write headlines that encouraged people to read the story.

Also, copy editors don't have to put up with many of the frustrations that reporters encounter. For example, copy editors never face the anxiety of tracking down a source on deadline or of wrangling with people reluctant to part with information.

Many people prefer life on the desk to life on the streets as reporters. There's often more camaraderie among copy editors than among reporters. Editors are more likely to see themselves as members of a team. They know the quality of a colleague's work; they know when to seek help and when to offer it.

Finally, editing almost always provides a chance to be creative and make a contribution to the quality of the newspaper.

NEW CHALLENGES ON THE DESK

You're preparing to enter the newspaper profession at one of its most turbulent times. Increasingly, Americans are abandoning news. Newspaper circulations are not keeping pace with population growth. TV newscasts, both local and network, are getting lower ratings. Cable news has its die-hard news junkies. But, unless there's a major news event, the audience for cable news is relatively small.

Newspaper editors recognize that they must try to produce papers that will overcome this trend. Their concern is not just for the financial health of newspaper owners: They understand that democracies such as ours depend on having an informed citizenry. Newspapers are one of the best sources of in-depth information. But a newspaper can't inform unless people are willing to buy the paper and spend some time with it.

Newspapers and TV stations are searching to find ways to attract readers. Some research suggests that high-quality, exciting journalism can bring back readers and viewers. That means:

- News stories that are more thoroughly reported.

- Improved writing and new approaches to storytelling.

- Pages that are better designed.

- Photographs and graphics that help readers understand the news.

The copy desk plays a key role in achieving each of these goals. Exciting days are ahead in journalism. You'll be there to help shape the news product as newspapers find ways to appeal to today's readers. And you may be part of the teams of journalists who will create new kinds of news delivery systems for tomorrow's readers.

Also, online journalism is becoming a multimedia mix of the best of broadcast and print journalism. Web sites can handle breaking news much the same as TV does. Also as with TV, they can use video and animation to explain the news more clearly. Online journalism also allows for the depth of traditional print journalism. But to achieve these goals, online producers will have to become copy editors, improving the writing, grammar, and graphics. Although they might not use the term, Web-based news sites will also need copy desks and fast, talented copy editors.

THE SHORTAGE OF COPY EDITORS

Managing editors will tell you that good copy editors are hard to find. Look through the classified ad section in *Editor & Publisher* magazine, you'll find lots of ads for copy editors, particularly for people who want to work on sports and business desks.

Hmmm . . . You've been told that newspaper jobs are scarce. Why are there so many openings on the desk?

Two possibilities:

- Desk work has a bad reputation. Many people believe that desk work is nothing but pressure and boring routine.

- Lots of journalism graduates don't have what it takes to do the work. They've spent too many hours watching television and attending high schools that stuff 40 students into English classes. They never developed the language skills required for the job.

Some newspaper editors would prefer to hire copy editors who have at least five years of reporting experience. They figure that people ought to be able to produce good copy of their own before they start hacking on someone else's. Also, having been a reporter helps editors understand that some information is hard to get and that sources aren't always cooperative.

As much as newspapers want to hire experienced people, many have had to settle for beginners. Some papers make an effort to give these novices reporting experience. They arrange "job swaps" in which the newly hired copy editors work as reporters for six months or a year. Or they vary the new editors' weekly schedules so that they work three or four days on the desk and then a day or two as general assignment reporters.

That's not to say that all editors need reporting backgrounds. Many successful editors started their careers on the copy desk and have done no reporting. They would point out that the skills and personality traits needed to be a good reporter differ from those needed to be a good copy editor. Good reporters often are very individualistic people. They like the challenge of working on stories by themselves or with only minimal assistance and supervision. Typically, good reporters have outgoing personalities that make it easy for them to develop sources quickly and be aggressive in getting the information they want. These traits are less important on the desk. The routine of the copy desk requires team players who are willing to spend considerable time working at their computer terminals. The job requires an appreciation for getting the details right.

LANDING AN EDITING JOB

Reporters can send editors clips of their stories to show they can report and write. Copy editors can send clips of headlines they've written and pages they've designed. But how do they show an editor that they really can edit copy?

Surveys of editors indicate that recommendations of former employers are key when they decide which applicants to interview. Internships and college newspaper experience are the best ways to get those recommendations. Editors also go over your cover letter and résumé closely, looking for errors. If they find grammar or spelling mistakes, they're unlikely to trust you on the desk. Recruiters say they are shocked by the number of letters they get with the names of their newspapers misspelled.

Your scores on copy editing tests are also going to be a consideration. Most midsize and larger papers give written copy editing tests. Often applicants are given error-riddled stories and asked to edit them and write headlines. Some papers add spelling, grammar, and current-events sections. Joe Grimm, development editor at the *Detroit Free Press,* recommends that prospective editors call and ask to take the test. He recommends against sending examples of edited copy. Grimm says that few editors take the time to look at before-and-after examples.

Pagination and convergence have changed what editors expect. Jeff Glick, deputy managing editor/creative director at the *South Florida Sun-Sentinel*, said, "Several years ago we stopped hiring people who were purely copy editors or just designers. We're able to get multitalented, very versatile individuals on the desk. We don't have a design desk that does nothing but design. We hire copy editors/designers who can do both jobs."

At most papers, the final stage in the job search is the tryout. At some papers, this is a one-day affair. But many papers require several days of work on the desk. Some employers pay applicants who are taking tryouts.

SLOTS, MAESTROS AND RIMS

At some newspapers, nearly all the copy is edited at one large copy desk, often called a *universal desk*. Many editors prefer universal desks because the paper is edited more uniformly. All the copy editors work under the same guidelines, so business stories are edited much as local news or features are.

At other newspapers, each section—national news, state and local news, sports, business news, features, and so on—has its own *specialized desk.* Many editors believe that if copy editors handle only one kind of news, they can do a better job of recognizing problems in stories. They concede, however, that the paper will have less consistency among its sections and that there's a greater chance of the same story appearing in different sections of the paper on the same day. Hey, it happens.

Many papers, especially smaller papers, have specialized desks for sports (they fear that a non-sports fan wouldn't understand the intricacies of zone defenses) and features, whereas the rest of the copy goes through one main desk.

The editor in charge of a desk is usually called the copy desk chief. At other papers, this editor is called the *slot,* and copy editors are said to be *on the rim.* These peculiar terms come from the days when stories were typed on paper. Copy desks were U-shaped to make it easier for the copy desk chief to hand stories to copy editors. Copy editors sat on the outside rim of the desk, so they became *rim men* (women editors were rare in those days) or, more derisively, rim rats. Copy desk chiefs sat inside the U, in its slot. Few newsrooms have U-shaped copy desks anymore, but the jargon remains.

In traditional newsrooms, the reporter and the assignment editor would work on the newsgathering and writing of the story. They would then pass the story along to the copy desk. Editors there might decide that the story needed some graphics or other art. If time was available, artists and photographers were called in. The stories, graphics, and photographs would then land on the desk of the person who was going to design the page. The stories would be passed along to copy editors to edit while the page was being designed.

Many newspapers are trying to increase the amount of coordination between editors, reporters, photographers, artists, and copy editors. Some use what they call *pod systems*, in which a copy editor, designer, reporter, and photographer may be asked to work together to produce a story or to cover a certain topic.

Other papers, including large ones such as *The Oregonian* in Portland and *The Tampa Tribune* and smaller papers such as *The Sun Herald* in Biloxi, Miss., use a *maestro* system. The maestro is an editor who conducts meetings at which reporters, editors, photographers and graphic artists discuss how each of them can contribute to telling a news story. Often the photographers and artists can help the reporter see the visual elements in the story while they gain a better understanding of the information and point of the story. The result of these meetings frequently is a better-thought-out story. And, because the photographers, artists and designers have more time to work on the story, they can produce a better news package.

To further the spirit of teamwork in the newsrooms, many newspapers no longer have feature editors and copy desk chiefs. They have feature team leaders and copy desk team leaders.

DAILY ROUTINE ON THE DESK

Most copy editors don't work 9-to-5 schedules. Within your own state, it's likely that copy editors are reporting to work every hour of the day. That's because newspapers have lots of deadlines. Obviously, deadlines will differ between papers printed in the morning (called, appropriately enough, A.M.s) and those printed in the afternoon (P.M.s). Deadlines also vary by the circulation of the paper, the amount of computerized equipment in use, and the size of the area the paper covers.

Larger papers print several editions each day. Some are zoned editions. Editors tailor these editions to specific communities so that subscribers can get more news from their own communities and less news from more distant places. Because these towns and cities may be many miles from the printing plant, their editions usually have earlier deadlines so that the papers can be printed and trucked to readers on time. The copy desk will then "make over" these editions, taking out news aimed at one community and putting in news about another. Later editions are delivered to the paper's hometown readers and sold in news boxes. The *South Florida Sun-Sentinel* publishes 33 zoned editions each day. Because single-copy sales are a large part of its circulation, the paper also publishes a special edition that is sold on the streets by hawkers and in news boxes. It has huge front-page headlines that shout the news.

News developments can also alter deadlines. Some papers set the deadline for the final edition late enough to print the scores of late-night ballgames (for morning papers) or the closing numbers on the stock market (for afternoon papers). In basketball-crazy Indiana, papers give sports later deadlines on high-school basketball nights and compensate by setting earlier deadlines for news in order to have those pages finished before the sports copy starts pouring in.

The various sections in a newspaper also have their own deadlines. Usually, the front section and sports section have the latest deadlines. Business sections and editorial pages may have deadlines several hours earlier and, as we said previously, deadlines for feature sections (often called *Lifestyles*, *Style*, *Living*) may be a day or two earlier.

Smaller papers may have only one or two editions and therefore have fewer deadlines—often around midnight for morning papers and noon for afternoon papers.

So what's the daily routine like for copy editors? We can make some general observations about life at a midsize morning paper.

Long before the final deadline, some copy editors will be at work handling advance material, including whole sections that must be preprinted. But the work on the next day's paper picks up dramatically in the early afternoon when the news editor comes in. That person's first task is to examine the news hole for the next day's paper. The news hole is the amount of space for the news. The number of pages has already been decided, and the ads have already been placed on the pages.

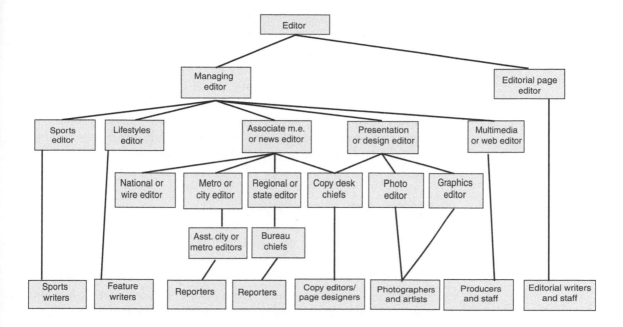

Figure 2.1.

Organizational chart of a typical newspaper. Larger papers will have more staff positions; smaller papers fewer. Titles will vary from paper to paper.

Shortly after arriving at work, the news editor meets with the various assignment editors and the managing editor. The assignment editors and wire editor discuss the stories they expect to have that night, and they make decisions about where the stories will appear in the paper. At these so-called "budget meetings," editors outline what is likely to be on the front page.

(For reasons unknown, newspapers are not very consistent when it comes to assigning titles. At some papers, the person we're calling "news editor" may have a grander title such as "night managing editor" or "assistant managing editor," or a less impressive one such as "night editor" or even "city editor." As we just mentioned, a more recent trend is to replace the term "editor" with "team leader." One title is consistent: The "managing editor" at nearly every paper is the person in charge of the daily newsgathering. For most of your life as a newspaper journalist, the m.e. will be your boss (or your boss's boss). See Figure 2.1 for an organizational chart of a typical midsize paper.

Soon copy editors are assigned stories to edit. When they finish their editing and have written a headline, they send the story back to the copy chief, who second-guesses the copy editor's work. The chief may ask for a new headline or suggest improving some wording in the story.

This movement of copy from the reporters to the desk and eventually to the printing press is called *copy flow*. It presents a kind of balancing act for news editors. They know they must keep copy flowing and not hold everything until the last minute, yet they also must save space in case an important story breaks late. Fortunately, most news is announced ahead of time. (The wire services keep editors posted on stories they plan to cover, and the various assignment editors in the newsroom know what stories their reporters are likely to produce.) A little experience will tell a news editor how much space should be saved through the work shift.

At most newspapers, the copy editors also do the proofreading. Before a page is sent to the presses, the desk receives a photocopy of it. That gives copy editors one more chance to correct any errors. Don't confuse copy editing with proofreading. When you're "proofing" a page, you usually fix only glaring typographical errors, misspellings, serious factual problems, and the like. You don't tinker with the writing. So, you ask, what's copy editing? Read on.

HOW TO EDIT COPY

Books on copy editing usually suggest reading every story three times: once for familiarization, once for editing, and a third time for double-checking. That's good advice, especially for novices. Seasoned copy editors may compress those three readings on many stories, but until you've developed the concentration that's required of good editors, stick with the three-step advice.

Beginners sometimes start editing the story the second they get it. You see them struggling with punctuation and worrying over the phrasing of a clause. Then a few minutes later, you see them rewriting the phrases they just labored over—or deleting them altogether. That's why, during your first reading of the story, you probably shouldn't do any heavy editing. The first time through the story, just try to understand it. Watch for any inconsistencies or confusing passages. You have to know what the story is about before you begin serious editing.

If the story has no glaring problems and you understand it, you're ready to edit. On the second pass, be concerned with spelling, grammar, punctuation, concise expression, smooth writing, general accuracy and comprehensibility. Make sure that the lead is understandable and interesting. And make darn sure that the lead adequately summarizes or sets the stage for the rest of the story.

Whatever you do, don't skip the third step: Always check your own work. Nothing embarrasses a copy editor and angers reporters more than when an editor *puts* errors in a story.

TOP 10 TIPS FOR EDITORS

If copy editing sounds like a frustrating exercise in perfectionism, relax. Martin Gibson, who taught editing both on college campuses and in newsroom seminars, put together some tips that have helped many beginning editors. We've taken many of his and added a few of our own to create this Top 10 list that just might make you a better editor.

1. *Mumble.* No doubt you've turned in a paper to your English or newswriting professor that you slaved over. You were convinced

you had caught every error. Then when the paper was returned, you were embarrassed by all the things you had missed. Your problem was that you read over your mistakes. Instead of reading every word and seeing every letter, you saw only what was supposed to be there. The same thing can happen when you edit other people's copy. Silent mumbling—reading so that you can hear yourself with your mind's ear—forces you to hear the wording. It makes poorly worded phrases become more obvious.

While you're mumbling, say to yourself every name you run across in copy—names of people, names of organizations, names of places. Fix them in your mind. It's easy for reporters to foul up names while working hard to turn their notes into a story. Often they get them right on first reference—when they're concentrating on getting the name right—but get them wrong later in the story because they're concentrating on other details. For instance, a copy editor at the *Chicago Tribune* once "slept through" a story that gave a man's name and address and then in all subsequent references called the guy by the name of his street.

2. *Read slowly.* From elementary school onward, your teachers rewarded the students who read the fastest. The emphasis on speed continues when students enter college and receive those hefty reading lists. You may even have taken a speed-reading course to help you cope. But those courses may work against you when you become a copy editor.

Copy editors need to read slowly. They must look at every letter in every word and every word in every sentence. Remember that you're the last person in the newsroom who will see the story. If you let a misspelled word get by, it comes out misspelled in the newspaper.

Looking at every word will help you in other ways: (1) You can weigh sentences and decide whether they carry unnecessary words. You can decide whether one word would do the work of the four words the reporter used. (2) You can scrutinize each word to see whether it's the best choice for the substance and style of the story.

Yup, we're talking major nit-picking here. You can't be a successful copy editor without paying attention to details. You absolutely must learn to go back over the material you've edited. You say that you're positive your work contains no errors? Go over it again anyway. Go over every word, every letter, every punctuation mark.

3. *Verify or duck.* The opportunities for error in a daily newspaper are staggering: thousands of facts, spellings, dates, quotations, figures. Editors must view everything as a source of potential error—and be willing to express their concerns. Copy editors, especially

beginners, often leave questionable material untouched, thinking the writer must know the facts. Wrong move. Even the most astute writers occasionally misstate a fact. Copy editors who don't ask enough questions soon become former copy editors. Ask reporters where they got the facts for their stories. Ask veteran copy editors who may be able to confirm facts. If your paper has them, ask librarians for help. Check the facts on the Internet or in your paper's archives.

Wise editors also know that sometimes it pays to duck. They'll worry if a reporter writes that an event was "the largest gathering of Democrats in the history of the county." They can already hear the phone calls after the story appears: "What about when Truman's train paused at the station during his whistle-stop tour in '48?" or "What about the funeral for Mayor Boss Jones back in '32?" Rather than face a flurry of phone calls, the wise editor ducks and changes the copy to "one of the largest gatherings of Democrats in the history of the county."

4. *Compress.* One of the copy editor's key missions is to weed out unnecessary words. In these fast-paced times, readers are too busy to spend time reading bloated, overly long sentences when more concise alternatives are readily available.

5. *Cultivate a dirty mind and watch for double meanings.* Check the back page of *Columbia Journalism Review* if you want a good laugh. *CJR* collects newspaper foul-ups. Many are statements and headlines that have two meanings, one of which is nothing like what the poor journalist meant to say. Here are two headlines that appeared in midsize papers: "Disney keeps touching kids" and "Lay position proposed by bishop for women." Not all double-meaning heads have risqué interpretations, of course. There's nothing sexual about "Convicted S&L chief donated to UT" and "Clinton visits hurt soldiers," but they can be read two ways. You don't want readers chuckling at (or getting offended by) your serious headlines.

6. *Be alert for repetition.* You'd be astonished at the number of times people say something in one sentence and then repeat it, in different words, in the next. Many writers merely change words around from one sentence to the next and offer the same thought.

Good copy editors recognize that flaw in writing because they read the material carefully and grasped what the writer said. Then the idea is familiar when it comes back in other clothes. The editor who is paying attention will see that the same thoughts and information have been offered once before.

If you didn't notice all the repetition in the preceding paragraphs, you must learn to pay closer attention when you start taking money for editing. However, don't get carried away with your newly found skill of deleting repetition. Writers should reinforce their main points. For example, they might include statistics in support of a point already made or use an anecdote to illustrate a fact.

8. *Avoid procrastination.* Don't trust your memory to bring you back to a place that you've mentally marked for re-examination. Don't say to yourself, "I'll check the spelling of that word when I finish editing this story." It's better to do it now than to see an error in the paper and say, "Oh, yeah; I meant to look that up."

9. *Edit; don't rewrite.* It's been said that the strongest drive in the human soul is not sex, hunger, or greed—it's the urge to change someone else's copy. Good editors fight off that urge. They preserve the writing style of the reporter rather than substitute their own. They make the sentences smoother, polish the transitions, and clean up the grammar. But they try to keep as much of the original wording as they can. And they leave good copy alone.

   We know one copy editor who was given a miserably written piece of copy. He spent lots of time getting it to make sense while keeping the reporter's writing style. He turned a hopeless story into something very readable. The next day the reporter asked the copy editor why he had spent so much time editing the story and yet hadn't made a single change to it. The copy editor took the question as a compliment.

10. *Most important, always think about the readers.* After all, these are the people you're really working to serve. Could the story be easier to understand? Might a graphic or a picture or a chart make the information more accessible? Does the story need more examples or anecdotes? Could the writing be improved to make the story more interesting?

So, will following those 10 tips make you a great copy editor? Maybe not. There are only nine tips in that list (go back and check). Here's the 10th tip:

Never trust a reporter with numbers. A standard joke in many newsrooms is that journalists would have obtained legitimate jobs if they could do math. But journalists, particularly those on the copy desk, need to know some math basics. *The New York Times* once ran a story noting that 900 cases of lead poisoning had been found in 27,000 children tested, which it said was 0.03 percent of the total. The copy editor should have known a little more about percentages or at least have checked the arithmetic. A headline in another paper reported that the sales tax may go up 2 percent. The story said the tax was going from 4 percent to 6 percent. If that happens, sales tax will be going up 50 percent, not 2 percent. Many readers will notice these errors and laugh, whereas other readers will be misled by them. Those are not the outcomes editors want.

Another example: A story lists 49 students from eight local high schools who have been named National Merit Scholars. How will good copy editors handle those numbers? They'll count the number of schools listed to make sure that all eight are named. Then they'll count the number of scholars in hopes of finding 49 names. Chances for error abound. The reporter could have mistyped the numbers—maybe it was 39 winners. Or worse, the reporter could have left one out. The copy desk has to be on guard. Check. Count. Add things up. If they don't come out right—and they won't always—the copy must go back to the reporter.

Perhaps because copy editors are insecure about numbers, they sometimes let silly errors pass. A major newspaper recently reported that 267,961 people were married in Britain the previous year. Many readers wrote the paper, expressing concern for that one lonely soul. The paper corrected the record to say that 267,961 marriages took place.

Most editors have handled enough stories with botched numbers that they call every phone number. If a story says readers can get tax advice from the IRS by calling 1–800—829–1040, the editor will dial that number to see whether tax people answer. Web addresses deserve the same diligence. The official site for the White House is www.white-house.gov. Mistype it as www.whitehouse.org, and you get a site that pokes fun at the president. Worse, www.whitehouse.com is a pornography site.

BASIC TOOLS FOR EDITING FACTS

From this chapter, you've learned that copy editors are expected to check the grammar, spelling, and facts in the stories they edit. Are you supposed to become a walking encyclopedia? No, but you should know how to use one, as well as all the other reference works at your disposal.

- *Dictionaries.* Nearly every copy desk has well-worn dictionaries, and they're not used just to check spelling. Is it correct to use *truck* as a verb? Is *accidently* a word? What's the preferred spelling: *catalog* or *catalogue*?

- *Thesauruses.* Reporters sometimes jump at the first verb that comes into their minds. Thesauruses can help editors freshen up the stories they edit, replacing dull verbs with more vivid ones. For copy editors, dictionaries and thesauruses play another role. When editors write headlines, they must find the right words both to tell the story and fit the space. Dictionaries and thesauruses are mother lodes of colorful, short words for them to use. In addition, dictionaries typically list colloquialisms that can spark a headline idea. For example, after listing several definitions of the word *high*, *Webster's New World Dictionary* offers definitions of *high and dry* and *high and mighty*. One of those might be turned into a play on words that would work as a headline.

- *AP Stylebook*. In addition to answering style questions, the *AP Stylebook* is a concise guide to grammar and punctuation. It also has lists of useful information. For instance, what's the difference between Chapter 10 bankruptcies and Chapter 11 bankruptcies? Is the correct title for clergy in the Baptist Church pastor or minister? Was that a blizzard or just a heavy snowstorm? Is Notre Dame in the Big Ten? Is it Big Ten or Big 10?

- *Your newspaper's stylebook*. Most newspapers supplement the *AP Stylebook* with their own style guides. Those guides may explain, for instance, whether the local department store is Marshall Field, Marshall Fields, Marshall Field's or Marshall Fields'. They may spell out the paper's preferences for dealing with sensitive matters, such as whether to refer to people as "gay" or "homosexual," to use "black" or "African-American" or to describe pickets at an abortion clinic as "pro-life" or "anti-abortion."

- *Almanacs*. Almanacs are another good source of facts. A world almanac answers questions on everything from the population of Delaware County, Ind., to the amount of deposits in the nation's leading banks, the number of votes Bill Clinton got in Illinois in 1992, the correct spelling of the name of the president of Iowa State University and the differences between the flags of Italy and Mexico. Many states and even some cities have their own almanacs, which list names of local leaders and organizations, outline tax structures and give details about the larger industries. Some state almanacs even explain current political issues.

- *Atlases*. Maps and atlases are common tools for editors. You know that north-south U.S. highways usually have odd numbers whereas even-numbered ones go east and west. What happens if a report says a triple-fatality accident blocked the intersection of routes 434 and 436? It seems unlikely that two east-west roads would intersect. The editor can check the map. You also can use maps and atlases to verify spellings of the names of streets, cities and counties.

- *Phone books and city directories*. Don't confuse these two important resources. City directories contain much more information than phone books. Want to know who lives at 1316 Georgia Blvd.?

Check the city directory. It has a reverse listing that gives you the name of the person living at a certain address. Occasionally, police reporters use this trick to call neighbors when they hear about a serious fire. Reporters also use city directories' "reverse" or "crisscross" listing of phone numbers. The reverse phone directory will tell them whose phone number is 555-1234. City directories also can be used to confirm that Joe Jones is married to Betty Sue Jones. The spouse's name is often printed for each address. How up-to-date are these directories? That depends on where you live. In cities where people move frequently, city directories become obsolete quickly. In smaller towns and rural areas, people tend to stay put and the directories are more reliable. Polk Directories, the largest publisher of city directories, has books and CDs for more than 1,000 U.S. cities.

- *Other good books.* Other reference books common in newsrooms are *Bartlett's Familiar Quotations,* the Bible, *Book of States, Congressional Directory, Statesman's Yearbook, Statistical Abstract of the United States, U.S. Postal Guide* and *Who's Who.* Lots of newspapers have *Facts on File,* a good place to look for recent history (how many people were killed by the 1992 hurricane in South Carolina?) and other information.

- *Computer databases.* Computerized databases are now common tools for journalists. Many newspapers have previous editions of the paper computerized, making it easy for copy editors to call up earlier stories to check the facts as they edit. These computer databases are replacing the "morgues," where stories were clipped and filed away, and the more recent use of microfilm or microfiche systems.

- *A traditional source.* Long before computers, reporters and editors had already found reliable sources for all kinds of data: librarians. Most newspapers employ librarians, who are usually amazingly skilled at finding facts. Also, most public libraries have reference librarians who will look up information for callers. If you have a specific question, they'll often find the information while you wait.

USING THE INTERNET

The Internet has made life much easier for copy editors. It enables them to check facts in stories, to look up words in dictionaries and thesauruses and often to search public records and legal documents. Here is a list of sites that many copy editors have found to be useful. Keep in mind, though, that the Internet changes daily. New sites are created, some expand and many close up shop.

SEARCH ENGINES

Google (www.google.com) probably has the largest database of any of the search engines. Many Internet users consider it the best. Google's computers scour the Web looking for keywords. Because Google has several computers that are constantly searching the Web, sometimes if you wait a minute and then repeat the search, you will get different listings. Microsoft Network (www.msnsearch.com) and Wisenut (www.wisenut.com) are newer sites. Wisenut, in particular, is gaining in popularity, and some say it rivals Google for thoroughness.

Yahoo! (www.yahoo.com) began as a directory of Web sites. Researchers visited the sites and listed the ones they deemed appropriate. Today, Yahoo! still uses human research to create its data files. But it also uses computer programs to provide more thoroughness. In 2001, Yahoo! began to supplement its own materials with Google's.

Some search engines list only Web sites that pay to be included. A search about skin cancer may find several miracle vitamin cures but not information from legitimate sites such as the Mayo Clinic. Other search engines give priority to paying sites. In 2002, the Federal Trade Commission asked search engines to disclose which sites have paid to be listed. Google and Yahoo! already followed that practice. Google placed paid listings in a section called "Sponsored Links." It determines which sites will be first in its listings by using a formula based on two factors: the number of Web sites that link to it and the number of times the search words appear on the site. A newer search engine, www.alltheweb.com, claims to have an even more sophisticated formula for rating sites.

Dogpile (www.dogpile.com) and MetaCrawler (www.metacrawler.com) are two metasearch engines. They send your request to several search engines simultaneously. If you are looking for rather obscure information, these multiple searches can help. You need to be precise in your wording, however, because these metasearchers can find more sites than you can browse. Also, these engines often put at the top those sites that pay to be listed.

Findlaw (www.findlaw.com) has sources that explain the law and direct you to court rulings. Many state courts and most federal courts also post their decisions on the Internet. Lexis-Nexis is the standard legal research tool for lawyers. It is a rather expensive service found mostly at larger newspapers and libraries.

WebMD (www.webmd.com) has information about diseases, commonly prescribed drugs and everything else medical. Be careful when using the Internet for medical stories. Some very elaborate sites are filled with fake research and phony miracle cures. Stick to sites such as WebMD or the Mayo Clinic's extensive offerings (www.mayoclinic.org).

For business-related information, try www.business2.com, which, although not strictly a search engine, can direct you to useful sites.

An easy guide to the stock market is the Motley Fool at www.fool.com. Many brokerages and mutual fund companies also have useful sites.

Search Bug (www.searchbug.com) ties into several search engines for information about people. You can find someone's name if you know an address or phone number. You also can locate area codes and ZIP codes.

The Journalist's Toolbox (www.journaliststoolbox.com) is a great list of information useful to journalists. It offers links to Web sites and lots of helpful information about how to track down information.

GOVERNMENT SITES

Firstgov.gov (www.firstgov.gov) is the official U.S. government search site. Its database is massive, so you need to be specific in your request. The site also allows searches of state government documents.

Thomas (thomas.loc.gov), www.house.gov and www.senate.gov report activities of Congress.

Depending on the strength of your state's public records laws, you can find lots of information online through state government sites. In most states, you can access the property assessor's records to get an idea of the value of someone's home. In states such as Florida, which has very strong public records laws, you can find out whether a doctor has been sued for malpractice or see mug shots and learn the criminal histories of everyone being held in state correctional facilities. Many county court records are also on file.

For information about state laws, courts and so on, Washburn Law School site (www.washlaw.edu) is a general directory to Web sites for every state.

Several Web sites, including http://www.pac-info.com and http://www.publicrecordfinder.com, provide lists of public-record sites. If the information you need is not listed in these sites, try a Google (www.google.com) search for the government body and the information you need.

NEWS SITES

Lexis-Nexis is the top site for searching news stories. But it's expensive, and only larger newspapers and libraries will have it. With Lexis-Nexis, you can search for news stories from thousands of newspapers, magazines and newsletters from around the world. You can target geographic areas and time periods. It's very useful in gathering background information, checking facts and spellings, and finding a broader context for stories. Many university libraries subscribe to an abbreviated version of Lexis-Nexis called Lexis-Nexis Academic.

Yahoo! News (http://news.yahoo.com/) is a free site that scans several major news sites including the AP and MSNBC. Some of its searches can go back a month; most go back the previous week.

Total-news (www.totalnews.com) is another free site that searches hundreds of newspapers. It claims it can access the previous two weeks of stories.

News Index (www.newsindex.com) provides access for hundreds of news organizations but seems limited to the news of the day of the search.

Most newspapers also have archives of stories, often going back to when the papers first computerized their newsrooms. A few still allow the public free access to the archives, but most now let you read the lead of a story and decide whether you want to pay to download the rest of it. Sometimes the information in the lead is all that you will need. Of course, you can access your own paper's archives without charge and probably those of other papers in the same chain.

SITES ABOUT WORDS AND LANGUAGE

Merriam-Webster's site (www.m-w.com) has a dictionary and a thesaurus. You can also listen to how the word is pronounced. Merriam-Webster has a site for children at www.wordcentral.com.

Wordsmyth at www.wordsymth.net (note that it ends with *net*, not *com*) combines a dictionary and thesaurus. It's also handy at correcting your spelling. Type *dawg* and you'll get *dog*.

You can find the *American Heritage* dictionary at http://www.bartleby.com/61/. This site offers etymologies of words and automatically lists words with similar meanings.

Several dictionaries are searched when you use www.dictionary.com. The site's Doctor Dictionary allows you to ask grammar and word usage questions.

The RhymeZone (www.rhymezone.com) can help headline writers looking for word plays. In addition to rhymes, it lists words with similar pronunciations and meanings and has a neat fill-in search of quotations from Shakespeare.

BE LEERY

All these reference materials and the Internet put a lot of information within easy reach. Approach all this information with skepticism. You can be led astray in a variety of ways. Here are a few:

- *Repeated errors.* One oft-repeated tale involves comedian Joan Rivers. *The New York Times* did an in-depth story about her and got her age wrong. Later, other reporters doing stories about her calculated her age based on the *Times'* erroneous report.

- *Information changes.* Phone books, city directories, Internet sites and all other references can be out of date. A 1997 atlas or a Web site that has not been updated might say that Miami is in Dade County. Since then, however, the name has been changed to Miami-Dade County. Or, if all you know is that fire trucks are being sent to 1316 Georgia Blvd., don't write that it's the Joe Jones residence just because the city directory says that's who lives there. The Joneses may have moved last week. But if the fire chief at the scene told the reporter that the fire destroyed the home of Mary Thompson but the city directory spells the name Thomson, you may have made a good catch. You'll want to do some more checking.

- *Hoaxes.* Everyone has heard stories of news organizations taking Internet reports too seriously. The Fox News Network in 2002 reported that an animal-rights group in Ohio was buying bullet-proof vests for deer to wear during hunting season. Fox had fallen for a bogus Internet story produced to look like an Associated Press dispatch. To avoid these errors, journalists need to approach the Web with the same skepticism they approach all sources. Just as well-dressed lawyers can lie, so can well-designed Web sites be bogus.

As you know, many readers and viewers don't trust the news media. Part of their distrust springs from their repeated observations of our errors. We can't eliminate all error. But we surely can cut down on the number of errors by double-checking information, names, titles and dates with reference materials, librarians and sources.

II. HELPING REPORTERS TELL THEIR STORIES

If you're tempted to tune out at the very mention of the word *grammar*, don't.

We've tried to make this as painless as possible. No long-winded lectures on grammar and all its glories. Just the most important rules and some examples of them.

We know from experience that we can assume one of two things: Either you never received a comprehensive education in grammar in 12 years of school, or you slept through it.

Whatever the case, consider this chapter a crash course.

(If you actually did learn grammar—including punctuation and syntax—consider this chapter a mere refresher course that you're destined to breeze through.)

And no matter which group you fall into, pay attention, because grammar is one of the fundamentals of editing. If you don't know your language, you can hardly judge someone else's.

Ready? Set. Go.

WHAT DO GRAMMAR TERMS MEAN?

PARTS OF SPEECH

NOUNS

Noun: The name of a person, place, or thing.
The *train* hit the *car*. (*Train* and *car* are nouns.)

Collective noun: A singular-sounding word that names groups of people.
The *jury* said the *team* should pay the man's medical bills. (*Jury* and *team* are collective nouns.)

Pronoun: A word used in place of a noun, such as *he, she, it, they, them, who,* and *that.*
He gave *her his* word about *that.* (*He, her, his,* and *that* are pronouns.)

A VARIETY OF PRONOUNS

Personal pronouns: I, you, he, she, it, we, you, they

Demonstrative pronouns: This, that, these, those

Indefinite pronouns: Each, either, any, anyone, someone, everyone, few, all, and so on

Intensive pronouns: Myself, yourself, himself, herself, ourselves, themselves

Relative pronouns: Who, whose, whom, which, that, and compounds such as whoever

Antecedents: The nouns or phrases to which pronouns refer. The *students* forgot *their* notebooks. (*Their* is the pronoun; *students* is its antecedent.)

VERBS

Verb: A word or phrase used to express action or state of being. Jane *runs* every day, but she *was* originally a walker. (*Runs* expresses action; *was* expresses state of being.)

A VARIETY OF VERBS

Helping (or auxiliary) verb: A verb that helps form another verb. The main helping verbs are *be, can, could, do, has, have, may, might, must, ought, shall, should, will, would.*

Active verb: A subject of an active verb does the action. Williams hit a home run. (Williams—the subject of the sentence—does the hitting.)

Passive verb: A subject of a passive verb receives the action. The ball was hit over the fence. (The ball—the subject of this sentence—gets hit.)

Linking verb: A verb that shows no action but just connects words. The various forms of *to be* are the most common linking verbs.
The book *was* old, but the words *were* still legible.

VERB FORMS OF *TO BE*

Present tense: I *am*; you *are*; he *is*; they *are.*

Past tense: It *was*; they *were.*

Present perfect tense: It *has been*; they *have been.*

Past perfect tense: They *had been.*

Future tense: I *shall*; she *will.*

VERBALS

Verbals: Forms of verbs often used as other parts of speech.

A VARIETY OF VERBALS

Infinitive: The "to" form of a verb.
The coach wanted *to win* his final game.
He seems *to have died* of natural causes.

Gerund: A verbal used as a noun.
Talking during movies should be illegal. (*Talking* is a gerund that is the subject of the sentence.) He banned *smoking* on airplanes. (*Smoking* is a gerund that is a direct object.)

Participle: A verbal used as an adjective.
Running this time as a Democrat, Burns won easily. (*Running* is a participle modifying Burns.)

MODIFIERS

Modifier: Words or phrases that change your image of other words.

Adjective: A word that modifies nouns and pronouns.
Five men in *blue* suits were the *last* ones to leave. (*Five, blue,* and *last* are adjectives.)

Predicate adjective: An adjective that comes after a linking verb.
Tuition is excessive. (The adjective *excessive* modifies *tuition*.)

Adverb: A word that modifies a verb, an adjective, or another adverb.
Jane walked *quickly*. (The adverb *quickly* modifies the verb *walked*.)
The president was *extremely* angry. (The adverb *extremely* modifies the adjective *angry*.)
The children ate *surprisingly* slowly. (The adverb *surprisingly* modifies the adverb *slowly*.)

CONJUNCTIONS

Conjunction: A word or phrase that connects words, phrases, or clauses.

Coordinating conjunction: Connects words, phrases, or clauses of equal rank. The coordinating conjunctions are *and, but, or,* and *nor.*

Correlative conjunction: Conjunctions consisting of two elements that are used in pairs; for example, *both . . . and; not only . . . but (also); either . . . or; neither . . . nor.*

Subordinating conjunction: Used to join a dependent clause to an independent clause; for example, *when, where, after, before, if.*

USES OF WORDS IN SENTENCES

Subject: A word, phrase, or clause that names the person, place, or thing about which something is said.
The *president* expelled the editor of the paper. (*President* is subject of the sentence.)

Compound subject: Two or more subjects joined by a *conjunction.*
Boston and Hartford received a foot of snow.

Direct object: The person or thing that is directly affected by the action of the verb.
The train rammed the *car*. (*Car* is the direct object of the verb *rammed.*)

In dictionaries, you will see verbs described as **transitive** and **intransitive.** Transitive verbs can have direct objects; intransitive ones can't.
Myriam *rejected* the job offer. (Transitive)
As the company's stock *tumbles*, layoffs *occur*. (Intransitive)

Indirect object: The person or thing indirectly affected by the action of the verb. The indirect object can be made the object of the prepositions *to* or *for.*
The president handed (to) the *students* their diplomas. (*Students* is an indirect object.)

CLAUSES AND PHRASES

Clause: A word group that has a subject and a verb.

A VARIETY OF CLAUSES

An **independent clause** expresses a complete thought and can stand alone as a sentence.
Brady will go to Northern State. (A complete thought)

A **dependent** (or **subordinate**) **clause** does not express a complete thought and cannot stand alone as a sentence.
Brady will go to Northern State (*independent clause*) if he receives a scholarship (*dependent clause*).

Clauses as modifiers: A clause can modify words much like adjectives and adverbs do.
Fans *who left the game early* did not see the touchdown. (The clause *who left the game early* modifies the noun *fans*.)
After he won the Maine primary, Butler thought he had a chance. (The clause *After he won the Maine primary* modifies the verb *thought*.)

Clauses as nouns: A clause can be the subject or object in a larger sentence.
Whoever wins the primary will face Jackson in the fall. (The clause *Whoever wins the primary* is the subject of this sentence.)
The gangster said he would shoot *whoever opened the door*. (The clause *whoever opened the door* is the direct object of the verb *would shoot*.)

Phrase: A grouping of words in a sentence that does not have a subject and verb.

A VARIETY OF PHRASES

Modifying phrases serve as modifiers much like adjectives and adverbs.

Watching his diet, Jones lost 10 pounds. (*Watching his diet* is a phrase that modifies the noun *Jones.*)

After winning the U.S. Open, Butler said he would retire. (The phrase *After winning the U.S. Open* modifies the verb *said.*)

Noun phrases function as nouns.

Writing obituaries is not her dream job. (*Writing obituaries* is a phrase that is the subject of this sentence.)

PREPOSITIONAL PHRASES

Prepositions: Connector words that show the relationship between a noun or pronoun and other words in the sentence. Some common prepositions are *from, to, in, of, at, by, for, with,* etc.

Prepositional phrases: Consist of the preposition and its object.

In Cleveland, students from several universities met with legislators for four hours. (*In Cleveland, from several universities, with legislators,* and *for four hours* are each prepositional phrases.)

A rule to remember: Do NOT use *off of* or *outside of.* Only one preposition is needed in these contexts, and it's NOT *of.*

Wrong: He fell off *of* the roof.
Right: He fell *off* the roof.
Wrong: The property lies outside *of* the city limits.
Right: The property lies *outside* the city limits.

NOUN-PRONOUN AGREEMENT

What do grammarians mean by "agreement"? Just that singular nouns should have singular pronouns, and plural nouns should have plural pronouns.

The *prosecutor* told the *defense attorney* that *his* client failed to answer *her* questions. (*Prosecutor* and *her* are singular; *attorney* and *his* are singular.)

The *department* assigned *its* best investigators to question the *terrorists* about *their* crimes. (*Department* and *its* are singular; *terrorists* and *their* are plural.)

Among the obstacles to proper agreement are collective nouns, which are singular-sounding words that name groups of people.

"Team," for example, is singular. You say "the team *is*," not "the team *are*." However, depending on the sport, 40 or more people may be on a team. Sometimes writers think about all those people and refer to them with plural pronouns:

> **Wrong:** The team ended their season by shutting out the Tigers.
> **Right:** The *team* ended *its* season by shutting out the Tigers.
> **But:** The *Broncos* ended *their* season by shutting out the Tigers.

Broncos is plural. You'd say, "The Broncos *are* on the field," not "The Broncos *is* on the field."

PRONOUN-ANTECEDENT AGREEMENT

An *antecedent* is a noun or noun phrase to which a pronoun refers. If an antecedent is singular, its pronoun must be singular.

> **Wrong:** The Acme Chemical Corp. announced that they lost more than $2 million last year.

Acme Chemical Corp. is the name of a company and is singular.

> **Right:** The *Acme Chemical Corp.* announced that *it* lost more than $2 million last year.

Or you can add a plural noun and keep the pronoun plural:

> **Right:** Acme Chemical Corp. *officials* announced that *their* company lost more than $2 million last year.

Again, watch out for collective nouns:

> **Wrong:** The jury deliberated for more than 10 hours before they reached their verdict.
> **Right:** The *jury* deliberated for more than 10 hours before *it* reached *its* verdict.
> **Right:** The 12 *jurors* deliberated for more than 10 hours before *they* reached *their* verdict.

Don't let prepositional phrases trick you into making a grammatical error.

> **Wrong:** The *jury* of five men and seven women told the judge *they* were ready to announce their verdict.

"Jury" is the subject of the sentence, and it's singular. So we need to refer to it with a singular pronoun:

> **Right:** The *jury* of five men and seven women told the judge *it* was ready to announce its verdict.

Pronouns and nouns must agree even when they're in different sentences.

Wrong: The suit contends that *Acme Chemical Corp.* did not respond to the woman's complaint that she was being sexually harassed. Instead, *they* transferred her to another plant.

The "they" in the second sentence refers to Acme Chemical Corp. Because Acme Chemical is singular, the pronoun must be singular too:

Right: The suit contends that *Acme Chemical Corp.* did not respond to the woman's complaint that she was being sexually harassed. Instead, *it* transferred her to another plant.

Or:

Right: The suit contends that Acme Chemical Corp. *officials* did not respond to the woman's complaint that she was being sexually harassed. Instead *they* transferred her to another plant.

INDEFINITE PRONOUNS

When used as antecedents, these pronouns—*no one, anyone, someone, everyone, nobody, anybody, somebody, everybody*—always take singular pronouns.

Wrong: Everybody knows they have to study for finals.
Right: *Everybody* knows *he* has to study for finals.

LOGICAL AGREEMENT

Look at this sentence:

Larry Bird gave the children an autographed picture of himself.

Was Bird so stingy that he gave all the kids one picture of himself to share? Probably not. Perhaps the reporter meant:

Larry Bird gave the children autographed pictures of himself.

If the reporter wants to avoid the impression that Bird gave several pictures to each child, he or she could write:

Larry Bird gave each of the children an autographed picture of himself.

Another piece of advice: Make sure readers know which people or things your pronouns refer to. Check out these sentences:

The deputy admitted to the sheriff that he had crashed his car. The way coaches treat their players has a direct effect on their chances of success.

Whose car was wrecked? The deputy's or the sheriff's? Whose chances of success will be affected? The coaches' or the players'? You can't tell from the way these sentences are put together.

Better wording might be:

The deputy admitted to the sheriff that he had wrecked the sheriff's car. (If, in fact, it was the sheriff's car that was wrecked.)

The way coaches treat their players directly affects the coaches' chances of success. (If, in fact, the writer meant the coaches' chances, not the players' chances.)

SUBJECT-VERB AGREEMENT

In any sentence, the verb and the subject must agree in number. A singular subject takes a singular verb; a plural subject takes a plural verb.

The tricky part is figuring out what the subject is. Here are some tips:

1. *And* connects equal things. Subjects that include things connected with the word *and* are plural and need a plural verb.
   Dick and Jane are playing baseball. The subject is "Dick and Jane"—two people. So, we need "are playing," not "is playing."
      Naturally, there are two exceptions to the "and" rule:
   a. When a compound subject is considered a single unit, use a single verb:
      Research and Development *plans* to expand its staff.
   b. When the items in the subject are modified by *each* or *every*, use a singular verb.
      Each reporter and copy editor *needs* a good background in grammar.
      Every boy and girl who *attends gets* a ticket to the movies.

2. The rule doesn't change with the addition of phrases such as the following: *in addition to*; *as well as*; *along with*; or *not to mention*. Phrases beginning with these words are parenthetical. They modify the simple subject, providing additional information, but they don't make the subject plural.

   Wrong: Brown, as well as Franklin and Vickers, plan to attend.
   Right: Brown, as well as Franklin and Vickers, plans to attend.

   Brown is the subject. It's singular, so it takes a singular verb.

Wrong: Cleveland, along with five other Northern cities, have asked for more federal aid.
Right: *Cleveland*, along with five other Northern cities, *has asked* for more federal aid.

"Cleveland" is the singular subject, so it takes a singular verb.

But what about:
A better training course for firefighters and a new fire station downtown are high on his list of goals for his administration.

The sentence is correct because the subject consists of two items—a course and a fire station—making it plural. So, the verb needs to be plural, too.

3. Watch out for those annoying phrases that begin with the word "of." They often disguise the true subject.

Wrong: Every one of the 12 jurors are going home.
Right: Every one of the 12 jurors is going home.

The subject in this example is "one." "Every" is an indefinite adjective, and "jurors" is part of the prepositional phrase that beings with "of." So: "One . . . is going home."

4. The following indefinite pronouns always take a singular verb: *no one*; *anyone*; *someone*; *everyone*; *nobody*; *anybody*; *somebody*; *everybody*; *each*; *neither*; *either*; *another*; *everything*; *anything*.

Wrong: Neither of the candidates are ready for a debate.
Right: Neither of the candidates is ready for a debate.

5. When the parts of a compound subject are joined by *either/or*, *neither/nor*, *not only*, or *but also*, the verb must agree with the subject nearest to the verb.

Wrong: Neither the coach nor the players was confident.
Right: Neither the coach nor the players were confident.
Right: Neither the players nor the coach was confident.

6. Auxiliary, or helping, verbs may be omitted, but only if they are in the same form as the other auxiliary verb(s) in the same sentence.

Wrong: Six sailors were injured, and one killed in the explosion.

This sentence is saying that six were injured and one were killed.

Right: Six *sailors were* injured, and *one was* killed in the explosion.

7. The pronoun *none* can be singular or plural. *None* is singular when you could easily insert the words "not one" for "none" in the sentence.

None (not one) of the candidates *gets* my vote.

However, when the meaning of "none" is "no two" or "no amount," use a plural verb.

Although we interview many candidates, *none* but the best *are invited* for tryouts.

PASSIVE AND ACTIVE VERBS

Let's refresh your memory about active and passive voice.

• With verbs in the active voice, the subject of the sentence is doing the activity, as in "Brown hit a home run."

• With verbs in the passive voice the subject of the sentence receives the action: "A home run was hit by Brown."

You should shun passive voice for two reasons. First, passive voice makes sentences wordy. Notice in the examples that the sentence with an active verb has five words. The passive version has seven. Second, passive voice makes writing lifeless. Reporters want readers to be able to picture the event in their minds. Active voice usually does a better job:

Active: According to witnesses, the police officer clubbed the man on the head with his nightstick and then yanked his arm behind his back.
Passive: According to witnesses, the man was clubbed on the head by the police officer, and then his arm was yanked behind his back.

Although trading active for passive voice usually improves sentences, we don't support a complete ban on passive voice. Sometimes the person or thing receiving the action is the key element in a story:

Mayor Carl Weaver was charged Tuesday with 14 counts of embezzling city funds.
Eighteen children were killed Tuesday when a tornado ripped through Southside Elementary School.

That the person arrested was the mayor is probably more important than who arrested him, and that 18 children are dead is more important than a tornado.

LIE AND LAY

Make sure you understand the meanings of these words. *Lie* means to be in a state of rest; to be doing nothing.

The book lies on the table.

The book is lying on the table.

I lie in bed reading.

We also use forms of *lie* in expressions showing that someone or something is inactive, such as "to lie down on the job" and "won't take the penalty lying down."

Lay, however, has a different meaning. It has action to it. If the sentence would sound right with action words such as *put* or *place*, chances are you should use *lay*:

The teacher lays the book on the table.

The man is laying new carpet in his den.

We also use *lay* in many expressions that indicate action, such as "to lay out pages," "to lay off employees," "to lay to rest our fears," and "to lay away birthday presents."

Bankrupt factories are laying off their workers.

Here are the correct verb forms for *lie*.

Lie (present tense):

I lie in bed and read.

He lies in bed and reads.

They lie in bed and read.

Lie (past and perfect tenses):

I lay in bed and slept last night.

I have lain in bed many hours reading.

I have been lying in bed all day.

Here are the correct verb forms for *lay*:

Lay (present tense):

I lay the book on the table.

She lays the book on the table.

They lay their books on the table.

Lay (past and perfect tenses):

I laid the book on the table.

I have laid the book on the table many times.

I have been lay*ing* the book on the table each day.

Quickie reminder:

To lie (to rest; to do nothing): lie, lay, lain, lying

To lay (to put something somewhere): lay, laid, laid, laying

When the verb *lie* means "to tell a falsehood," the verb forms are the following.

The Liar Lie (present tense):

I lie about my age.

He lies about his education.

They lie about their criminal records.

Past and perfect tenses:

I lied about my age.

I have lied about my age many times.

I have been lying about my age since I was 17.

WHO AND WHOM

The trick for remembering which one of these to use is simple: Read the sentence twice. The first time, replace the *who* with *he*. Then read it a second time, replacing *who* with *him*. If the sentence sounds correct with *he*, use *who*. If *him* sounds correct, use *whom*.

Let's try one:

Who answered the phone?

OK, now which sounds better: "He answered the phone" or "Him answered the phone"? Big duh, right? *He* sounds better, so *who* in the original sentence is correct.

Try this one:

You gave the money to who?

Subbing gives you either "You gave the money to he" or "You gave the money to him." Obviously, the second substitution is the one that works:

You gave the money to *whom*?

It's more difficult when you have longer sentences. You have to dig out the clause (subject and verb combination) or phrase with the who/whom problem to do your substitutions:

The man who bought the drugs was later found murdered.

In this sentence, "who" is the subject of the clause "who bought the drugs." Now do the substitution:

"He bought the drugs" or "Him bought the drugs"?

Right: "He" is correct, so the sentence is fine as it stands.

The election will be won by whoever is able to win the farm vote.

The who/whom choice is in the clause "whoever is able to win the farm vote." Do your substitutions:

"He is able to win the farm vote" or "Him is able to win the farm vote"?

Exactly: "He" is correct, so the sentence is correct with "whoever."

Occasionally, identifying the clause with the who/whom problem takes some thought, and you may have to rearrange words a little before you can try the he/him substitution. For example:

The reporter refused to say who he called before he wrote the story.

This sentence has three clauses: "the reporter refused"; "who he called"; and "he wrote the story."

We want to look at "who he called." It's easier to make the substitutions if we rearrange this clause in the order of subject-verb-direct object: "he called who." With the substitutions, we have "he called he" or "he called him." No question about that one: "Him" equals "whom," so the sentence should read:

The reporter refused to say *whom* he called before he wrote the story.

Some books that can help you with your grammar:

George T. Arnold, *Media Writer's Handbook: A Guide to Common Writing and Editing Problems*, McGraw-Hill, 1999.

William A. Sabin, *The Gregg Reference Manual Ninth Edition*, McGraw-Hill, 2000.

Buck Ryan and Michael O'Donnell, *The Editor's Toolbox*, Iowa State University Press), 2001.

William Strunk Jr., E.B. White and Roger Angell, *The Elements of Style* (4th Edition), Allyn & Bacon, 2000.

No, we're not going to drill you in *all* the punctuation marks.

We figure that if you've managed to get to college, odds are you know how to use periods, question marks and exclamation marks. Instead, we focus on the more troublesome punctuation marks.

COMMAS

The comma is probably the most abused of all punctuation marks. However, after you understand the difference between *essential* and *nonessential* information, you'll have an easier time using commas.

PHRASES AND DEPENDENT AND INDEPENDENT CLAUSES

First, a refresher course on clauses.

A *clause* is a word group that has a subject and a verb. An *independent clause* can stand alone; it's a complete sentence that makes sense without any additional information:

> The reporter reads *Editor & Publisher*.

"Reporter" is the subject and "reads" is the verb. The clause is a complete thought.

A *dependent clause* cannot stand alone because it relies on the rest of the sentence to make sense:

> The reporter reads *Editor & Publisher*, which lists job openings.

The phrase "which lists job openings" is a dependent clause. It doesn't make sense without the rest of the sentence. "Which" is the subject of the dependent clause, and "lists" is the verb.

Phrases are groups of words that do not have subjects and verbs. In the following sentence, "making the delivery" is a phrase:

> A truck driver making a delivery found the body.

ESSENTIAL AND NONESSENTIAL INFORMATION

After you identify phrases and dependent clauses, you are confronted with a question: When should you set them off with commas? The answer depends in part on whether the phrase or dependent clause has essential or nonessential information. Take this sentence:

55

He wants to attend Northern State University.

As it is, this sentence is straightforward. It tells us where the guy wants to go to college. Now let's add some information to the sentence:

He wants to attend Northern State University, which has a tremendous music school.

The clause "which has a tremendous music school" explains why the guy picked NSU. But it isn't needed to identify the university he wants to attend. We knew he wanted to go to NSU before we read the clause. Thus, the information in the clause is nonessential because it isn't required to help identify the university. So the rule to remember is this:

Nonessential information is set apart by commas.

So we must put a comma between "University" and "which."

What if the sentence had said "He wants to attend a university"? From that sentence, we would have an idea where he wanted to go to school. There must be thousands of universities. Now look at this sentence:

He wants to attend a university that has a tremendous music school.

The clause "that has a tremendous music school" certainly narrows his choices. Only a few universities would satisfy his needs. Because the clause helps identify the kind of school he wants to attend, that clause is essential. So, the other rule to remember is this:

Essential information is *not* set off by commas.

That's why there's no comma between "university" and "that."

COMMAS AND APPOSITIVES

Appositives are phrases that mean the same thing as or explain the word(s) they follow. To decide whether to set appositives off with commas, you apply the rule for essential and nonessential information. In this sentence, *Macbeth* is an appositive:

Shakespeare's tragedy *Macbeth* will highlight the fall theater program.

Shakespeare wrote a lot of tragedies. The appositive *Macbeth* is essential to telling the reader which of the Bard's tragedies will be presented. Because it's essential, it is not set off by commas. Let's try another sentence:

Baron Williams, a rookie outfielder, slammed the ball
into the upper decks.

A rookie outfielder is not essential to understanding who hit the homer.
It was Williams. That he is a rookie is interesting—and may be important
for readers to understand the writer's point. But it is nonessential information to identify Williams and therefore is set off by commas.

Use common sense when deciding whether something is essential.
Here are two sentences punctuated correctly:

Jackson's novel *Down By the River* is considered a
masterpiece.

His latest novel, *Up Near the Creek*, has been panned by
critics.

Jackson has written several novels. In the first sentence, the name of
the novel is essential so that readers can know which of his books is
considered a masterpiece. But in the second sentence, the name of his
novel is not essential because he can have only one "latest novel."

THAT AND WHICH

Now that you know the difference between essential and nonessential
information, you can solve the mystery of when to use *that* and when
to use *which*. The rule to remember is this:

That usually is used in essential clauses (the kind WITH-
OUT commas), and *which* is used in nonessential clauses
(the kind WITH commas).

The rule applies to the following two similar sentences:

Sen. Carl Smith said he will accept the support of any
group *that opposes strict gun controls.*

Sen. Carl Smith said he will accept the support of the National
Rifle Association, *which opposes strict gun controls.*

In the first sentence, the dependent clause is essential for us to
understand what groups might support him. Because it is essential, the
clause starts with *that* and is not set off by commas. In the second sentence, *National Rifle Association* identifies the group. The clause may
explain the senator's motive, but it is not essential to identifying the
NRA. The clause begins with *which* and is set off by commas.

Here's another pair of sentences that follow the *which/that* rule:

The Society of Professional Journalists, *which* has
fought efforts to close records on other campuses, has
pledged to help pay the editor's legal expenses.

> A professional journalism society *that* has fought efforts to close records on other campuses has pledged to help pay the editor's legal expenses.

You probably noticed the word "usually" in our last rule. That's because there are two exceptions related to the *that/which* rule. The first exception is easy to remember:

Use *who,* not *that* or *which,* when referring to people.

Wrong: Students *that* live in dorms are not allowed to park in commuter lots.

Right: Students *who* live in dorms are not allowed to park in commuter lots.

The second exception is the kind of thing that gave grammar a bad name back in elementary school:

> If a sentence already has the word *that,* you can substitute *which* for variety.

> *Overkill:* He feared that any accounting firm that used the software program that he has written would make mistakes that would be overlooked in a normal audit.

> *Better:* He feared that any accounting firm using the software program he has written would make mistakes which would be overlooked in a normal audit.

Alas, this second exception doesn't work the other way around. No matter how many times *which* appears in a paragraph, you can't change one of them to *that.*

COMMAS AND THE MEANING OF A SENTENCE

Commas can be the sole determinant of meaning:

> The family sold the property for $10,000 more than its appraised value.

Because it has no comma, this sentence is saying that the family received $10,000 more than the property's appraised value. The sentence doesn't tell the actual price.

> The family sold the property for $10,000, more than its appraised value.

Because of the comma, this sentence is saying that the property's appraised value was less than $10,000 but that it sold for $10,000.

> Professor Jacques Malala, a vice president of the
> statewide teachers union and an official in the American
> Federation of Teachers opposed the salary offer.

Because of the comma, this sentence is saying that Malala wasn't alone in opposing the salary offer. A veep of the statewide teachers union and an official with the national union also opposed it.

> Professor Jacques Malala, a vice president of the
> statewide teachers union and an official in the American
> Federation of Teachers, opposed the salary offer.

Change the commas and you change the meaning of the sentence. This version is telling us two things: Malala opposed the offer and Malala is a veep in the state union and an official in the national union.

> City police officers, who make less than $30,000 a year,
> will be given special pay increases in the fall.

Because of the commas, this sentence is saying that all city police officers make less than $30,000 a year, and all of them will receive pay increases.

> City police officers who make less than $30,000 a year
> will be given special pay increases in the fall.

Because there are no commas, the sentence is now saying that *only* those police officers who make less than $30,000 a year will receive pay increases. The better-paid cops won't get the special raises.

> The Democrats, say the Republicans, are sure to win the
> next election.

This sentence is saying that the Republicans are predicting a Democratic win.

> The Democrats say the Republicans are sure to win the
> next election.

Without the commas, the sentence is saying that the Democrats are predicting a Republican victory.

COMMAS AND CONJUNCTIONS

Remember that an independent clause is a word group with a subject and a verb and can stand alone as a complete sentence. A sentence can have two independent clauses:

> Democrats won every seat on the city council, but
> Republicans swept the races for county offices.

This sentence is really two short sentences—two independent clauses—stuck together with a conjunction (connecting words such as *and, but, or* and *yet*). The rule to remember here is this:

> When a conjunction such as *and, but* or *for* links two
> clauses that could stand alone as separate sentences, use a
> comma before the conjunction.

You need a comma before *but* because the sentence has two independent clauses. You should understand why the rule doesn't apply to this sentence:

> The Democrats won in the city but lost in the county.

What's the difference? "The Democrats won in the city" is a complete sentence; however, "lost in the county" is not. Because the sentence does not have two independent clauses, there is no comma before *but*. Another example:

> The man was wanted by city police for failure to pay
> parking tickets and by the FBI for questioning about a
> bank robbery.

There's only one independent clause: "The man was wanted by city police for failure to pay parking tickets." The rest of the information is provided by a series of prepositional phrases: "by the FBI"; "for questioning"; "about a bank robbery." The sentence needs no commas.

COMMA SPLICES

A comma splice occurs when two independent clauses are separated *only* by a comma. One way to fix a comma splice is to add a conjunction. Sometimes it is better to break the sentence into two sentences:

> **Wrong:** Residents were told they could return to the island, the
> hurricane had changed course.

> **Right:** Residents were told they could return to the island
> because the hurricane had changed course.

> **Or:** Residents were told they could return to the island. The hurricane had changed course.

COMMAS AND INTRODUCTORY INFORMATION

The rule is simple:

> Introductory phrases and clauses are followed by commas.

These sentences are correct:

> Having seen his brother shot down in the streets,
> Johnson decided to dedicate his life to stopping crime.

> Although the coach had a winning record, his off-court
> antics caused many alumni to want him fired.

> During the first two hours of intense cross-examination,
> Johnson seemed amazingly confident.

Naturally, this rule has an exception. If the introductory clause or phrase is very short, the comma is optional, as in this sentence:

> After he quit he felt better.

Remember, we're talking about *introductory* clauses and phrases. If we move the same information to the *back* of the sentence, the commas aren't needed:

> While Hernandez was an undergraduate at Harvard,
> she published two essays in prestigious legal journals.

> Hernandez published two essays in prestigious
> legal journals while she was an undergraduate at
> Harvard.

> After the Eagles gave up 120 points in their opener, the
> coach decided to switch to a zone defense.

> The coach decided to switch to a zone defense after the
> Eagles gave up 120 points in their opener.

COMMAS IN A SERIES

Commas are used to separate elements in a series:

> The Rev. Burton Brown told the mayor the city needed
> honest police, clean streets and safe playgrounds.

Newspaper style is to omit a comma before the conjunction—in this case, "and." This rule has one exception, and fortunately you will not encounter it very often. Commas must be used to separate elements in a series when two of the elements naturally require a conjunction. In this sentence, "research and development" refers to one unit. So, a comma appears after "sales" so that the reader can readily understand that "research and development" refers to one item.

> The new owner plans to combine marketing, sales, and
> research and development.

Commas are also used to separate adjectives—words that describe nouns or pronouns—when the adjectives are equal in importance and could be connected with a conjunction such as *and*.

The long, gray days of winter are followed by warm, revitalizing days of spring.

If the reporter had written "long and gray days," the sentence would have been correct, just wordy. "Long" and "gray" modify "days" equally. So, when you take out the "and," you need the comma. But commas are not used when the last adjective before a noun is part of the name of an object:

He threw away his tight blue jeans.

All they had to eat was a cold hot dog.

The words "blue jeans" and "hot dog" jointly name the objects, so no comma appears after "tight" or "cold."

Commas are used to separate items in a series that would confuse readers without the punctuation:

He was charged with fleeing the scene of a crime, attempted murder of a store clerk, and child and spousal abuse.

Omitting the comma after "clerk" might cause readers to think for a moment that he had also attempted to kill a child.

COMMAS AND ATTRIBUTION

Attribution names the sources of information. It tells who said something. Commas are used to separate the quote from the person who said it, as in the following two sentences with direct quotations:

"The Democrats are a bunch of numskulls, and we need to chase them out of the Legislature," Jones said.

"What you must understand," the witness said, "is that I didn't mean to kill him."

Commas are usually needed to set off attribution in sentences with indirect quotes:

The man was also wanted on fraud charges, according to police.

According to his attorney, Jones was in Spain when the crime was committed.

The city can't afford to pay police more, the mayor said.

An exception is when attribution with "said" comes at the beginning of the sentence:

> President John Kennedy said life is not fair.

> The mayor said the city is running out of money.

COMMAS WITH AGES AND ADDRESSES

Commas are used to separate ages, birth dates, and cities and states:

> Fong was born in Dayton, Ohio, in 1954. (*Notice the comma after Ohio.*)

> Fong was born in Dayton in 1954.

> The company has plants in Longwood and Sarasota.

> The company plans to open plants in Vicksburg, Miss., and Lexington, Ky.

> Brown was born on March 5, 1972, and died on Jan. 15, 1999. (*Notice comma after 1972.*)

> Jones was arrested in Columbus, Ohio, on Jan. 10, 1990, on fraud charges. (*Notice comma after 1990.*)

> Smith was born in Long Branch, N.J., in October 1944 and died in Pueblo, Colo., in May 2002. (*Notice comma after N.J. but not after 1944*).

> Jackie McKinley, 38, of Chicago gave the opening address. (*Usually no comma when "of" is used with an address.*)

> José Martinez, 23, Terre Haute, Ind., was the valedictorian.

HYPHENS

Even the most admired grammar manuals disagree on when hyphens are needed. And when the manuals do agree, it's hard to figure out why some nouns and adjectives are hyphenated whereas others aren't.

We can't solve all the mysteries of the hyphen, but we can offer some tips that will serve you well.

> Don't use hyphens with the word "very" or with any of the –*ly* adverbs.

> **Wrong:** The newly-elected mayor thanked his supporters.

> **Right:** The newly elected mayor thanked his supporters.

> **Wrong:** She brought a very-overweight friend along.

> **Right:** She brought a very overweight friend along.

Use hyphens when two or more words in front of a noun work together to describe the noun. Those words also are known as *compound adjectives*.

Wrong: A three alarm fire gutted the abandoned warehouse.

Right: A three-alarm fire gutted the abandoned warehouse.

A simple way to determine whether two adjectives form a compound adjective requiring a hyphen is to look at them separately. You wouldn't say, "A three fire gutted the abandoned warehouse." Nor would you say, "An alarm fire gutted the abandoned warehouse." But, used together, the words "three" and "alarm" form a unit with a singular meaning: "a three-alarm fire." The hyphen links the two adjectives into a unit.

Wrong: He wanted to write a front page story.

Right: He wanted to write a front-page story

Wrong: She was tired of playing for a last place team.

Right: She was tired of playing for a last-place team.

The AP uses hyphens even when a compound adjective follows a linking verb (also known as forms of the verb *to be* such as *is, are, was, will be*).

Wrong: Judge Harris is well known.

Right: Judge Harris is well-known.

Use hyphens with compound nouns.

Wrong: Clint Eastwood is a skilled actor director.

Right: Clint Eastwood is a skilled actor-director.

Use hyphens when ages are used to modify a noun.

Wrong: The 13 year old girl looked forward to her bat mitzvah.

Right: The 13-year-old girl looked forward to her bat mitzvah.

Wrong: The girl is 13-years-old.

Right: The girl is 13 years old.

Use hyphens when ages are used in place of nouns.

Wrong: The 15 year old had a fake ID.

Right: The 15-year-old had a fake ID.

Certain words that are hyphenated as adjectives or nouns are broken into two words when used as verbs.

Noun: The traffic tie-up lasted for five hours.

Verb: The parade will tie up traffic for hours.

Adjective: The robber handed the teller a hold-up note.

Verb: The robber decided not to hold up the bank after all.

The best way to use words like this correctly is to get into the habit of looking them up in the Associated Press Stylebook. If you can't find the answer there, try a dictionary or reference guide.

DASHES

Use dashes for emphasis. Because they are more dramatic in signaling an interruption or a shift in tone, you may use dashes to replace commas, semicolons, colons or parentheses.

There's nothing wrong with using dashes—as long as they don't become a habit. Writers who lace their copy too liberally with dashes end up with choppy copy. Also, many editors contend that using two sentences is often clearer than combining ideas with dashes. If you want to use dashes, here are some grammatically correct ways to do that.

Instead of a comma:

> The mayor praised the City Council—including the three Democrats—for supporting her budget.

Instead of a colon:

> The arrangement between the partners is simple—Brooks was the brain who made the loans, and Jackson was the muscle who collected when they were not repaid.

Instead of a semicolon:

> The mayor did the work—the City Council got all the credit.

Instead of parentheses:

> Attorney Bill Brooks—he's the district attorney now—represented Bruno Klein in his first trial.

COLONS AND SEMICOLONS

Semicolons can be used to separate independent clauses—word groups that can stand alone as separate sentences—when the second clause is related to the first clause. Some editors prefer two sentences. In this sentence, a semicolon is used when there is no conjunction (such as *and*, *but*, *or*):

> Jefferson saw the humor in the remark; Wilson did not.

Use semicolons to separate independent clauses that are linked by words such as *however, accordingly, for example, then, thus,* and so on:

> The Democrats are ahead in the polls; however, they
> have already spent most of their campaign money.

Use semicolons to separate a series of items that are already punctuated. Unlike commas, semicolons are used before the conjunction ("and" in this example):

> The candidate made stops in Rye, N.Y.; Sioux City,
> S.D.; Portland, Ore.; and New Orleans, La.

Use colons to separate independent clauses when the second clause explains the first clause. The clause after the colon begins with a capital letter when it's a complete sentence but not when it's just a sentence fragment. You can also use colons to introduce a list. Words in the list are not capitalized.

> George Bush made one promise repeatedly: He would
> not increase taxes.

> George Bush made one promise repeatedly: no tax raise.

> Adams says Americans are guided by three principles:
> democracy, freedom and capitalism.

QUOTATION MARKS

In case you've forgotten: Commas and periods always go inside quotation marks.

> **Wrong:** He likes Stephen Crane's short story "The
> Veteran".

> **Right:** He likes Stephen Crane's short story "The
> Veteran."

> **Right:** He likes "The Veteran," a short story by Stephen
> Crane.

QUOTATION MARKS AND QUESTION MARKS

The meaning of the sentence determines whether the question mark goes inside or outside the quotation marks. If the whole quote is a question, the question marks go inside the quotation marks:

"Who does he think he is?" Wright asked.

"Are common-law marriages legal in this state?" the attorney was asked.

If only the last few words of a question are in quotation marks, the question mark goes outside the quotation marks:

Have you heard the term "common-law marriage"?

Who wrote the short story "The Veteran"?

QUOTATION MARKS AND COMMAS

As you know, one of the purposes served by commas is to separate quoted material from the person who said it (attribution):

"I know I can win," the candidate told the convention.

However, the comma is dropped when the quoted material ends with a question mark or exclamation point.

Wrong: "You must be joking!," she exclaimed.

Right: "You must be joking!" she exclaimed.

Wrong: "How much will it cost?," the mayor asked.

Right: "How much will it cost?" the mayor asked.

QUOTATION MARKS WITHIN QUOTATION MARKS

In American English, the only time we use single quotation marks is to set off quoted material within other quoted material.

"I would like someone to explain the word 'cyber-space,'" Morgan said.

The crash survivor said, "I knew we were in trouble when the pilot said over the intercom, 'If you want to smoke a cigarette, now is your last chance.'"

"Did you hear her say, 'How much longer will he live?'" Snyder asked.

"Have you heard the term 'common-law marriage'?" the lawyer asked the witness.

*I*diom and *syntax* refer to the way words usually are arranged in sentences and to the subtle meanings given to words and word combinations. If editors make sure stories are written in idiomatic English and with standard syntax, readers will find them easier to understand.

IDIOM

Try this experiment: Define the words *on*, *up*, *down*, *around* and *play*. Now use your definitions of these words to explain what the following sentences mean:

> He played on the crowd's emotions.
>
> She played on despite the heavy rain.
>
> He played up to the professor.
>
> She played up to her ability.
>
> He played down his involvement in the crime.
>
> She played around with computers in college.

Your definition of *around* probably doesn't mean much when *around* is combined with "played." Yet each of these examples makes sense to people who understand idiomatic English.

And if writers use sentences that aren't in idiomatic English, readers won't understand them or will wonder about the writers' ability to use the language.

Try these idiomatic expressions on for size:

Wrong: His novels revolve on events that happened in his life.

Right: His novels revolve *around* events that happened in his life.

Wrong: The union says its new proposal is different than the one it offered last week.

Right: The union says its new proposal is different *from* the one it offered last week.

Wrong: His thesis compared working conditions at small newspapers to those of large newspapers.

Right: His thesis compared working conditions at small newspapers *with* those of large newspapers.

69

> **Wrong:** I read where Jones Hardware is closing after 50 years in business.

> **Right:** I read *that* Jones Hardware is closing after 50 years in business.

Here are some quick tips for mastering idiomatic English:

1. If you aren't completely sure of a word or phrase, check it out. Check *The Associated Press Stylebook* or your newspaper's stylebook first. The *AP Stylebook*, for instance, explains the difference between "compared to" and "compared with." And it tells you that "different" takes the preposition "from," not "than."

2. Become familiar with other guides, too. There are many good books about the language and its use. Among the classics are *The Elements of Style* by Strunk and White and several books by Theodore M. Bernstein, especially *The Careful Writer*, *Headlines and Deadlines* and *Watch Your Language*. More contemporary guides include *The Gregg Reference Manual* by William A. Sabin and *Media Writer's Handbook* by George T. Arnold. *The Gregg Reference Manual* firmly warns against substituting *where* for *that*.

3. Use your dictionary for more than just spelling. For example, if you had checked *Webster's New World Dictionary*, the standard dictionary at most news organizations, you would have found an entry using "revolve around" that applies to the example above. *Webster's New World* also has entries explaining the meanings of "play around," "play on" and other idioms.

SYNTAX

Even the order of the words in sentences, or syntax, plays a key role in understanding a language. Look at these sentences:

> The city twice paid the list price for computers that are normally discounted.

> The city paid twice the list price for computers that are normally discounted.

Where we put that word "twice" makes a big difference. Reporters and editors need to worry about where they place words, phrases and clauses.

MODIFIER PLACEMENT

Modifiers are adjectives and adverbs—words that change your image of other words.

When you hear the word *car*, you have an image of a car in your mind. If you hear *rusty car*, you have a different image. The word *rusty* has modified your image of the car. Because *rusty* modifies a noun, it's an adjective.

When you hear the words *he ran*, your mind conjures up some images. But if you hear *he ran slowly*, your images change. Because *slowly* modifies a verb, it's an adverb.

Not all modifiers are one word long. Look at this sentence:

He ran slowly through the forest.

The phrase "through the forest" modifies your mind's picture of a man running slowly. So the entire phrase is a modifier.

Check out this sentence:

He found the car that was stolen.

The clause "that was stolen" changes your image of the car. Therefore that clause is also a modifier. Here's the incredibly simple rule about modifier placement:

Modifiers should be near what they modify.

To illustrate this rule, grammar books often use the example of "only":

Only the mayor thought the city had enough money to rent the arena.

The mayor thought only the city had enough money to rent the arena.

The mayor thought the city only had enough money to rent the arena.

The mayor thought the city had only enough money to rent the arena.

The mayor thought the city had enough money only to rent the arena.

The mayor thought the city had enough money to rent only the arena.

The mayor thought the city had enough money to rent the only arena.

The mayor thought the city had enough money to rent the arena only.

As you can see, where you put "only" makes a big difference in sense. Our minds are wired in such a way that we automatically apply the rule about modifier placement to help us determine the meaning of a sentence.

Maybe you're wondering, If this rule is so ingrained in us, why do we need to discuss it? Unfortunately, reporters sometimes know a story so well that they forget to explain it clearly to their audience. So, editors have to be on the lookout, as in the following example:

> After the trial of the four gang members, the prosecutor said he was upset that Jackson only was sentenced to four years in jail despite the brutality of the crimes.

See where the modifier "only" is placed? What is it supposed to modify—"Jackson" or "was sentenced"? Is the prosecutor upset that only Jackson, and none of the other gang members involved, will go to jail? Or is he objecting to how little time Jackson is going to spend in jail? The editor must check the rest of the story or ask the reporter for the right interpretation. Here are the editor's options:

> If the prosecutor was complaining that Jackson, and no one else, was sentenced, the editor will make it "only Jackson was sentenced."

> If the prosecutor was upset that Jackson received such a short jail term, the editor will change the sentence to read "the prosecutor said he was upset that Jackson was sentenced to only four years in jail."

The placement of "only" isn't just a grammatical nicety; it's important to helping people understand what the sentence means.

DANGLING MODIFIERS

Participles are verbal adjectives—that is, they are verb forms used to modify nouns. They often end in *-ing*, such as *seeing*, *believing* and *knowing*. These words often are used in phrases, and these *-ing* phrases often are misplaced or left hanging without a subject, which is why they're sometimes called "dangling participles."

> Walking through the forest, the trees frightened the lost little boy.

It doesn't take much thought to conjure an image of a bunch of trees strolling through the forest and frightening the kid. Most of us would be frightened if trees began to walk. This is what the writer probably was trying to say:

> Walking through the forest, the lost little boy was frightened by the trees.

Remember: Put the modifier near what it modifies. In this case, "walking through the forest" is modifying "the lost little boy."

OTHER DANGLING PARTICIPLES

Not all participle phrases end in *-ing*. For instance, look at these sentences:

> Born in Michigan, Maunez began his career working for General Motors.

> Convicted of tax evasion, Miller was sentenced to four years in a federal prison.

The participial phrases "born in Michigan" and "convicted of tax evasion" are correctly placed near what they modify (Maunez and Miller), following the rule for modifier placement. What about this sentence?

> Mired in controversy within his own party, few observers thought Johnson could be re-elected.

The observers aren't the ones mired in controversy; Johnson is. We have to get Johnson closer to the opening phrase. One way to fix the problem is to rearrange the sentence. Either of these will work:

> Mired in controversy within his own party, Johnson was given little hope of re-election by many observers.

> Knowing Johnson was mired in controversy within his own party, few observers thought he could be re-elected.

Another way exists to correct this sentence as well. Sometimes you can change the *-ing* phrase to a clause. (Remember: Clauses have subjects and verbs; phrases don't.) The edited sentence would read:

> Because Johnson was mired in controversy within his own party, few observers thought he could be re-elected.

INFINITIVES

Another kind of verbal, the infinitive, begins with the word *to*. Infinitives can form phrases much like participle phrases. Once again, the only rule to remember is to place the modifier—in this case, the infinitive phrase—near what it's modifying.

Wrong: To win the primary, lots of money will have to be spent on TV ads.

The infinitive phrase "to win the primary" doesn't modify "lots of money." It modifies the candidates who want to win the primary.

Right: To win the primary, candidates will have to spend lots of money on TV ads.

PREPOSITIONAL-GERUND PHRASES

Verb forms called *gerunds* can also be used as nouns. Often they end in *-ing*. When we combine a gerund with a preposition, such as *by* or *in*, we get a prepositional-gerund phrase. As with infinitive phrases and participle phrases, these often are misplaced as modifiers.

Wrong: By concentrating on TV ads, many of the advantages of newspaper ads were lost.

"By concentrating on TV ads" is a prepositional-gerund phrase. It should be modifying who did the concentrating.

Right: By concentrating on TV ads, candidates lost many of the advantages of newspaper ads.

PARALLELISM

Suppose that you came across this sentence in a story about your old high school English teacher who retired last year:

Arranging flowers and opera occupy much of Meyers' time these days.

Hmm . . . you knew the old guy liked to discuss operas, but you always thought he had a tin ear. Now he's arranging operas!

Nah, not likely. Probably the reporter meant that your old teacher was attending operas or perhaps listening to them on CDs. The grammar is faulty. The reporter has violated the rule about parallelism:

Sentence parts connected by "and" and "or" should be of the same grammatical construction.

Arranging flowers and listening to opera occupy much of Meyers' time these days.

Look at this example:

Before voting on the measure, the commission wanted to know the proposed location of the plant and how many workers would be employed there.

If you read this sentence closely, you'll see that the sentence parts connected by "and" are not parallel. "Location" is a noun; "how many workers would be employed there" is a clause. We can fix this by turning both of the sentence parts into nouns:

Before voting on the measure, the commission wanted to know the proposed location of the plant and the number of workers to be employed there.

Or we can make them both clauses:

> Before voting on the measure, the commission wanted
> to know where the plant would be built and how many
> workers would be employed.

One more example: Sometimes you have to add "that" to keep things parallel:

Wrong: The mayor said he would fire the police chief and
that Capt. Barbara Moody will take control of the department.

You need a "that" before "he would" because you have one before "Capt. Barbara Moody." And you need the "that" before "Capt." so that readers won't think for even a second that both the chief and the captain got the ax.

Right: The mayor said that he would fire the police chief
and that Capt. Barbara Moody will take control of the
department.

Editors also need to pay attention to parallelism with verbs:

> The contractor said the repairs will be finished by Monday
> and the building would open Tuesday as scheduled.

Depending on the context of the sentence, the edited sentence could read:

> The contractor said the repairs will be finished by
> Monday and the building will open Tuesday as scheduled.

Or:

> The contractor said the repairs would be finished by
> Monday and the building would open Tuesday as scheduled.

ATTRIBUTION

Attribution in a sentence names who provided information or made a statement. Problems can occur when deciding when, where and whether to use attribution.

"SAID": THE JOURNALIST'S BEST FRIEND

Your thesaurus will give you dozens of synonyms for "said." You'll find "concluded," "conceded," "continued," "added," "indicated," "admitted," "stated" and "declared." When these words match the occasion, they're perfectly fine to use. However, reporters often throw them into their stories without regard for their special meanings, such as:

"I will love you forever," the bride expounded to her new husband at the altar.

"How would you feel if you lost your three best players the night before you play the top-rated team in the nation?" the coach queried.

"It's really cool. I want to ride it again," the teen stated after testing the theme park's newest ride.

"Expounded," "queried" and "stated" are good words, but they aren't suited to these sentences.

At other times, poorly handled attribution can make it sound as if a newspaper is taking sides, as in this sentence:

The senator explained why funding for the university should be cut in half.

Dictionaries define *explain* with phrases such as "to make understandable" or even "to make intelligible what is not immediately obvious." Therefore, the sentence seems to be saying that the senator is a wise man who "made understandable" the less-than-obvious truth that university funding should be cut.

More likely, the senator is explaining only his opinions about cutting the university budget. Careful editors will change the sentence to:

The senator explained why he believed funding for the university should be cut in half.

On other occasions, faulty attribution can incorrectly suggest how people feel about things, as in:

The mayor confessed that she did not have all the facts.

The senator admitted he was gay.

We often associate the words *confess* and *admit* with people who are telling us they've done something wrong—or at least something they're not proud of.

Editors shouldn't let such words pass unchallenged. They should check the context of the story. Is the mayor saying she erred by not having all the facts? Or is she just saying she doesn't have all the facts yet? Does the senator consider his homosexuality a failing? Or is he just acknowledging something about himself?

Unless the stories contain evidence that these people are, in fact, confessing and admitting, good editors will change them to:

The mayor said she did not have all the facts.

The senator said he was gay.

"Said" is a good, all-purpose word that carries no extra messages. And "said" doesn't jump out at readers. You can use it repeatedly without making readers grow tired of it. However, don't let this praise of "said" cause you to strike all colorful verbs.

Remember the words of the bride from a previous example: "I will love you forever." If the bride whispered those words of endearment, by all means use the word "whispered." If she shouted them as loudly as she could, say so. The lesson here is to pick your words carefully.

One more point on the use of "said": For the most part, use "Jones said" rather than "said Jones." Having the subject followed by the verb is normal English syntax. However, be sensitive to sentences such as this one:

> "Tuition must be held steady," Carl Rivers, vice president of
> financial affairs and development at Northern State
> University, said.

In this case and similar ones with wordy job titles, go ahead and write,

> "Tuition must be held steady," said Carl Rivers, vice
> president of financial affairs and development at
> Northern State University.

TYPES OF QUOTES

Reporters have three options when using other people's words. They can use a direct quotation:

> "The Democrats are a bunch of numskulls, and we need
> to chase them out of the Legislature," Jones said.

Or reporters can paraphrase what a person said, which is called "indirect quotation":

> Jones said voters need to get the Democrats out of the
> Legislature.

Or they can use a combination of paraphrase and direct quotation, called "partial quotation":

> Calling the Democrats "a bunch of numskulls," Jones said
> the voters need to "chase them out of the Legislature."

Although reporters have three options for handling quotations, editors have only two: paraphrase and partial quotation. Suppose a reporter wrote:

> "I think, unless something unexpected happens, that we,
> the city and the firefighters' union, will probably have an

> agreement by Friday that both sides, them and the city,
> can sign and point to with pride," the mayor said.

The editor immediately sees that the quotation is cumbersome and needs help. The editor might paraphrase it like this:

> The mayor said he believes the city and the firefighters'
> union will agree on a new contract by Friday.

A partial quotation might be:

> The mayor said he believes the city and the firefighters'
> union will agree to a contract by Friday that each side
> can "point to with pride."

But the editor cannot take a paraphrase or partial quotation and turn it into a direct quotation. Suppose a passage in a story said:

> The mayor said that he had not met with the leadership
> of the union to discuss the new contract and that he did
> not think any progress would come from such meetings.

An editor who considers this paraphrase too bland might be tempted to change it to:

> The mayor said, "I haven't sat down with the union to
> talk about a new contract, and I really doubt if it would
> do any good."

Foolish editors might argue that the colorful quote helps readers understand the story. The problem is that it's not accurate. Only the reporter and the other people present when the mayor was speaking know for sure what the mayor said. Editors were back in the newsroom, so they can't create direct quotations.

Which brings us to an argument that has become quite heated in many newsrooms: How much can you clean up a quotation and still use quotation marks?

Traditionally, editors have said that anything between quotation marks should be the exact words of the speaker. Nearly everyone would soften this rule to allow reporters to take out "uh" and other gruntlike sounds many of us make in normal speech. Many editors also see nothing wrong with correcting grammatical errors, especially if the speaker is normally quite literate.

PLACEMENT OF ATTRIBUTION

After reporters decide whether they will quote directly or paraphrase, they have to worry about where to put the attribution: before the quotation, in the middle of it or at the end. The choice should be based on common sense.

Often, the attribution is put at the end of a quotation or at the end of the first sentence if the quotation is two or more sentences long, as in this example:

> "Crime has become a major problem in our city,"
> Martinez said. "We need to hire more police officers
> and give them the tools they need to do their job."

Putting the attribution in the middle of a quote works well too:

> "I never took any kickbacks," the mayor said, "and I
> want the whole world to know that."

Sometimes you need to put the attribution first, especially when you change speakers.

> "Crime has become a major problem in our city,"
> Martinez said. "We need to hire more police officers
> and give them the tools they need to do their job."

> Steinberg countered, "But hiring more police will only
> create more problems for us. Arresting teenage offenders
> only hardens them. We need money for social programs
> to help them before they commit crimes."

WHEN TO USE ATTRIBUTION

It's essential to tell readers the source of your information so that they can judge its credibility. However, sometimes reporters go overboard, providing attribution for every sentence in a story. Editors need to know when attribution is necessary and when it's not. Let's look at some examples:

> Rain is forecast throughout the state.

Unless there's some controversy, no attribution is needed. The reporter has said rain is "forecast," which is sufficient qualification for the sentence.

> An unusual spring freeze in Brazil may double coffee prices.

Attribution is needed. Predicting effects is speculation in most contexts.

> North Dakota has been declared a disaster area after
> severe storms ripped through the state and left millions
> of dollars in damage.

An attempt at qualification has been made with the word "declared." But because county, state and federal governments can make official declarations in such cases, we need to say high in the story which governmental body made this pronouncement.

> Two thousand people were trapped for an hour today when a New York City subway train caught fire.

Attribution probably isn't necessary here. The reporter probably has solid sources for this kind of factual information. However, you'd want attribution if there were disagreements among sources.

> Federal income taxes must be paid by April 15.

No attribution is needed here. You generally can report accepted facts without attribution. If there's any reason to suspect that statements are controversial or are reporting new findings, attribute them.

> The trade agreement was the best the nation could make.

Attribution definitely is needed here. The statement represents a point of view.

WORDS TO WATCH OUT FOR

AFFECT/EFFECT

Affect means to influence or to change:
The disease will *affect* his balance.

Effect, as a verb, means to cause or to bring about:
He will *effect* many changes in the company.

Effect, as a noun, means result:
The *effect* of the attack was devastating.

ARRESTED FOR/CHARGED WITH

Arrested for suggests guilt. Don't write:
He was *arrested for* murder.

Charged with says only that a legal action has been taken. Use it:
He was *charged with* murder.

BIANNUAL/BIENNIAL

Biannual means twice a year and is a synonym for the word semiannual:
The *biannual* meeting of the teachers group will be held in Los Angeles.

Biennial means every two years:
Congressional elections are held *biennially*.

COMPRISE/COMPOSE

Comprise means to contain, to include all or embrace:
The United States *comprises* 50 states.

Compose means to create or put together:
The United States is *composed* of 50 states.

CONTINUAL/CONTINUOUS

Continual means regularly recurring:
Their marriage was marred by *continual* bickering.

Continuous means uninterrupted, steady, unbroken:
The sailor was driven insane by the *continuous* pinging of the sonar gear.

FARTHER/FURTHER

Farther refers to physical distance:
They found her car *farther* down the road.

Further refers to an extension of time or degree:
The officer will look *further* into the complaint if it will *further* her career.

FLAUNT/FLOUT

To **flaunt** is to make an ostentatious or defiant display:
He *flaunted* his knowledge of wine.

To **flout** is to show contempt for:
He *flouts* the law.

FLOUNDER/FOUNDER

A **flounder** is a fish; **to flounder** is to move clumsily or jerkily, to flop about:
Although graceful when swimming, the manatee *floundered* on land.

To **founder** is to bog down, become disabled or sink:
The company *foundered* after its founder died.

GRISLY/GRIZZLY

Grisly is horrifying:
The *grisly* murder scene upset the new police officer.

Grizzly means grayish or a grizzly bear:
The man's *grizzly* beard belied his relative youth.

HARDY/HEARTY

Hardy means daring, resolute:
Washington's *hardy* soldiers spent the winter in Valley Forge.

Hearty means extremely warm and friendly:
The French army received a *hearty* welcome when it entered Paris.

IMPASSABLE/IMPASSIBLE/IMPASSIVE

Impassable means that passage is impossible:
The bridge was *impassable*.

Impassible and **impassive** describe lack of sensitivity to pain or suffering. *Webster's New World* notes that impassible suggests an inability to be affected, whereas impassive implies only that no reaction was noticeable:
She was *impassive* throughout the ordeal.

IMPLY/INFER

Writers or speakers **imply** in the words they use:
Smith *implied* that presidential politics were to blame for the decision.

Readers or listeners **infer** something from the words:
The audience *inferred* that Jones was playing politics with the issue of new schools.

INTEGRAL/INTRICATE

Integral means necessary for completeness:
Research is an *integral* part of the doctoral program.

Intricate means hard to follow or full of elaborate detail:
The puzzle was too *intricate* for the 10-year-old to decipher.

ITS/IT'S

It's is the contraction for it is.
It's time to go.

Its is the possessive form of it:
The company fired *its* president.

NAUSEATE/NAUSEOUS

Nauseate means to cause to feel nausea:
Watching an autopsy was enough to *nauseate* the reporter.

Nauseous means sickening or disgusting:
The *nauseous* fumes caused people to run from the building.

NUCLEAR/"NUCULEAR"

Nuclear means related to atomic energy:
A *nuclear* reactor will never be built here.

Nuculear is not a word; *don't* use it as one.

ORAL/VERBAL

Oral refers to spoken language:
The teacher wants the class to give an *oral* presentation on the book.

Verbal is used to compare words with some other form of communication:
His tears revealed the sentiments that his poor *verbal* skills could not express.

PRINCIPAL/PRINCIPLE

Principal is a noun and adjective meaning someone or something in authority or with importance.
She is the school *principal*.
Money is the *principal* problem.
His monthly bill included *principal* and interest.

Principle is a noun that means a fundamental truth, law, doctrine or motivating force:
They fought for the *principle* of self-rule.

SEWAGE/SEWERAGE

Sewage is waste matter:
Raw *sewage* littered the streets of the devastated area.

Sewerage is the drainage system designed to carry away sewage:
The county commissioners debated whether to extend *sewerage* to the remote areas of the county.

THAN/THEN

Than is usually used in comparisons:
New York City is bigger *than* Iowa City.

Then usually refers to time:
First it was Buffalo, *then* Atlanta.

EDITING THE HARD-NEWS STORY 6

The last three chapters have dealt with editing on a very basic level. All editors worth having on the payroll will trim every bloated passage and check the grammar, syntax, punctuation, and word usage in every story they see. Editing becomes second nature to most copy editors. Eat lunch with them, and you'll see them correcting the grammar on the menu.

Now we're moving away from that kind of basic editing alone. In addition to correcting spelling and grammar, editors also judge the quality of the reporting and help reporters improve the way their stories are written. Some call this *content editing* or *first-read editing*. Just as your newswriting instructor returns your leads scarred with red ink and demands for rewrites, assignment editors often ask reporters to rework their stories.

Occasionally, assignment editors rewrite reporters' work themselves, although that's usually not a good idea. Rewriting stories does little to help reporters learn to write better. And it's unlikely to inspire them to put much effort into future stories.

What role does the copy desk play in improving the writing of stories? We wish we could give you a more definitive answer. But, honestly, it depends on where you work:

- You may work at a paper that is very editor-centered and encourages copy editors to make any changes they think will improve reporters' stories.

- You may work at a paper that is more reporter-centered. These papers limit what copy editors can do, often barring them from any rewriting. Instead, when they have questions about the merits of a lead or the organization of the story, they show it to the copy desk chief, who may kick it back to the assignment editor. The assignment editor may order another revision from the reporter, who by this time probably has had it up to here with the story.

- More likely, you'll work at a paper that falls somewhere between our reporter-centered and editor-centered models. At these papers, editors prefer to have their reporters do their own rewriting. But as deadlines approach, copy editors don't have the time to check with reporters, and the reporters might not have time to make the changes if they were asked. Under these circumstances, copy editors do what's necessary to improve the story and meet the deadline.

- Even at papers where you're not allowed to rewrite stories by your own reporters, you will be expected to rework copy from the wire services. Occasionally, you'll rewrite such copy completely, particularly when you combine stories from different wire services.

Here's what you need to remember: Although there are differences in how much authority you'll have to make changes, *no matter where you work, you'll be encouraged to make sure that poorly written stories are repaired before they make it into the paper.*

For years, newspaper people have broken news into two categories: hard and soft. Hard news includes stories about crime, politics, and the economy. Soft news consists of the lifestyle pieces, profiles, human-interest stories, and features. Traditionally, these two types of news were written in much different ways. In this chapter we deal with stories written in the traditional hard-news format; in the next, we look at other story formats and feature stories. But before we get too heavily involved with writing the news, let's take on a very fundamental question.

WHAT'S NEWS, ANYWAY?

Newsworthy is not an easy word to define, but most editors—and just about every newswriting textbook—agree that what we call news has a combination of *consequence, prominence, proximity, immediacy,* and *oddity.*

- The *consequences* of an event can make it important. If the legislature of your state passes a special 10 percent sales tax on new luxury cars costing more than $200,000, your paper might run a business brief about the tax. Not many people buy top-of-the-line Bentleys. But if that 10 percent sales tax were added to the cost of every new or used car bought in your state, you have an important story. The number of people affected by the news and how strongly they're affected play big roles when editors decide what's newsworthy.

- *Prominence* can turn an event into a national story. When an accountant is accused of fooling around with his young secretary, the story doesn't get much play, if any. But when people involved are the president of the United States and a White House intern, it's big news in just about every newspaper in the nation.

- *Proximity* is a deciding factor in many news decisions. An editor once said that the farther something happened from his hometown, the less newsworthy it was. That's an exaggeration, of course. But local names and local angles can add impact to otherwise so-so stories.

- *Immediacy* plays a role in many news decisions. There's truth in the old saying that "nothing's older than yesterday's news." That's particularly true at TV stations, where immediacy is king. Traditionally, newspaper editors have conceded that they can't beat TV's ability to report breaking news. Instead, their newspapers win readers by providing depth, background, and lively writing. Immediacy is taking on more meaning at newspapers with active Web sites that are updated throughout the day.

- *Oddity* rounds out the list. A man who loves his Porsche so much that he wants to be buried in it may be news. If the next day a woman wants to be buried in her Corvette, the coincidence may be news. If the next day another person opts for a four-cylinder coffin, editors will begin to bury the stories themselves. If a dozen people try to take their cars with them, a feature writer may use them as fodder for a trend story.

Don't be fooled by the simplicity of this list. News judgment is filtered through our life experiences. At most newspapers, decisions about what stories will appear on Page One are made at a meeting of top editors, all of them experienced journalists who should know news when they read it. Yet these meetings often become heated as editors argue over the relative value of the day's news.

News judgment also varies wildly from area to area. Editors must know their communities well if they are going to make sensible news judgments. They must know what kinds of things will affect the local economy. A change in the value of the yen may not be of interest to many Americans. But in states such as Michigan, where automakers compete with Japanese imports, and Washington, which exports lumber and farm products to Japan, changes in the value of the yen can be important news. News from Latin America is more important to papers in Florida, Texas and California than it is in Idaho, Montana and North Dakota.

Lifestyle and community issues also influence news judgment. Stories about young people may get more coverage in newspapers in college towns than they would in papers 20 miles down the road. Pronouncements by the AARP may be news in retirement areas. A meeting of Southern Baptists is likely to be bigger news in Charlotte than in Boston. The makeup of every community is unique. News judgment must be adapted to suit each community's needs.

AN EXPERIENCED EDITOR IN ACTION

Let's look at how an experienced editor does her job at a major newspaper. Because we are using a real story, we have changed the names of everybody involved.

The editor we are observing has worked at four newspapers during her 20 years in the news business. Along the way she picked up a law degree. Appropriately enough, she oversees the paper's legal-affairs reporters. Her job is to make sure the reporting is thorough and the stories are accurate, clear and well-written. During the course of a typical evening, she edits more than a dozen stories, ranging from briefs to front-page readers.

Earlier in the day, a reporter told her about a tip she had received. Reportedly, the mayor of a local community and members of the housing board had a major confrontation in an ongoing struggle over management of the housing authority. The editor agreed it was news and assigned her to write a 10-inch story. However, the tip led to a better story than expected, and the reporter's first draft was 15 inches long. Here's that draft of her story:

LAKEVILLE—Formal charges of inefficiency are being drafted against board members of the Lakeville Housing Authority after two of its members refused to resign Friday.

Mayor Bill Modano and the city's attorney privately met with chairman Woodrow Belfore and vice chairman Joe Madden on Friday afternoon urging them to gracefully leave the authority. The agency is being rocked by an FBI criminal investigation into the possible misuse of funds and mismanagement charges by the federal Department of Housing & Urban Development. It faces losing millions of dollars in funding.

Both Belfore and Madden, insisting the problems can be fixed, told Modano no.

So now Modano said he will announce charges against the board members at Tuesday's commission meeting to start the legal process of forcing them out.

"I'm disappointed they want to drag it out," Modano said.

Although city leaders aren't accusing the board members of wrongdoing, they have said that a drastic shake-up of the authority is needed. They also say that the volunteer board is forgiving of Executive Director Ralph Martin, who makes management decisions, and they hope a new board will replace him.

Florida law states that before authority members can be removed from office, they have to be given a copy of charges against them at least 10 days before a hearing.

The charges have to show proof of inefficiency, misconduct or neglect of duty. But city officials say the law allows for subjective standards, and they will likely point to a HUD report that uses terms such as "inefficiency" and "negligence" in referring to the authority.

Belfore, a well-known figure who was the city's first black firefighter and is also known for his famous cousin, former county commissioner Sylvia Belfore, said he's taking the issue personally.

"I've never really failed at anything I've tried to do," he said. "It's important I don't give this up. This is my watch. When they look back [and people say] they got rid of the housing members, they'll say, 'Who is the chairman? Belfore.' That's totally unacceptable."

"I haven't been able to rest good at night. And I'm not even paid a dime for this," he said. "It's crazy."

The last remaining authority member, Patricia Thomas, hasn't returned the mayor's telephone calls to even talk about resigning although Belfore said she has told him she likely will refuse to leave the board as well. She did not return a telephone call for comment.

"I know charges are going to be filed, that's what he told me," Belfore said. "We'll just tough it out. I'm going to get legal help. I'd be a fool not to get legal help. I ain't that brave."

But he'll stay until the end, he said. "I haven't done anything wrong."

As at most larger papers, content editors and reporters usually communicate by computer. The editor types comments and questions in notes and sends the story back to the reporter for revision. The reporter either makes the changes or sends a reply explaining why the story should remain as is. For this particular story, the reporter and content editor discussed the story together. The conversation was open and frank. Both people had the same goal: to improve the story. The discussion went something like this:

> LAKEVILLE–Formal charges of inefficiency are being drafted against board members of the Lakeville Housing Authority after two of its members refused to resign Friday.

EDITOR: So were these charges brought by the city? It's unclear from that lead whose charges we are talking about.
REPORTER: The city is drafting charges right now. They are the city's charges.

The editor revises the lead to indicate who is bringing the charges. She also shifts it from passive voice to active voice. It now reads:

> LAKEVILLE–The city is drafting formal charges of inefficiency against board members of the Lakeville Housing Authority after two of its members refused to resign Friday.

REPORTER: That's good. You know, there was one thing I didn't include in the story and I wanted to ask you about it: All three of the people who are being pushed out? Their terms expire in October anyway. I didn't write that. Do you think we should say that?
EDITOR: Well, we probably should.
REPORTER: They'll be gone in five months anyway.
EDITOR: Yes, but apparently the city thinks that's too long to wait.

They move on to the second paragraph.

> Mayor Bill Modano and the city's attorney privately met with chairman Woodrow Belfore and vice chairman Joe Madden on Friday afternoon urging them to gracefully leave the authority. The agency is being rocked by an FBI criminal investigation into the possible misuse of funds and mismanagement charges by the federal Department of Housing & Urban Development. It faces losing millions of dollars in funding.

EDITOR: I don't think we need "gracefully." (The reporter agrees and the word disappears from the screen.) It's unclear to me who's doing the investigation, the FBI or the city?
REPORTER: Well, you have two investigations here. You have

the FBI doing the criminal investigation and then you have charges by HUD about mismanagement. There are two issues.

EDITOR: Maybe it would be better to break that into two sentences to make it clearer. I don't think we can call them "mismanagement charges" yet. Maybe it would be better to say, "HUD is probing charges of mismanagement."

REPORTER: Probing? I don't know if probing is the right word. Can we call up the earlier story and see what word they used before? (The newspaper's computer system provides immediate access to the paper's archives. The editor begins to look for the previous story.)

EDITOR: Well, probing is another word for investigating. Are they looking into these charges?

REPORTER: No, they've finished with the investigation and have drawn their conclusions.

EDITOR: We need to make that clear.

She types in a proposed change and asks the reporter whether what she has typed is right. The reporter agrees that it is clearer. The editor then cuts the long paragraph into two paragraphs and moves on.

> Both Belfore and Madden, insisting the problems can be fixed, told Modano no.
>
> So now Modano said he will announce charges against the board members at Tuesday's commission meeting to start the legal process of forcing them out.
>
> "I'm disappointed they want to drag it out," Modano said.

EDITOR: I wonder whether that quote might be better following "told Modano no."

The reporter agreed and the quote was moved. They move on to the next paragraph.

> Although city leaders aren't accusing the board members of wrongdoing, they have said that a drastic shake-up of the authority is needed.

EDITOR: They aren't accusing board members of wrongdoing, right?

REPORTER: Well, no, not specific wrongdoing.

EDITOR: They're accusing them of general wrongdoing?

REPORTER: No. City officials say that the housing authority has a major problem. They want to shake them up. They aren't saying that individual board members have done anything wrong. They aren't saying, "Mr. Board Member, you pocketed $5 on June 5."

EDITOR: OK. I see. What if we say they aren't accusing the board members of any specific acts of wrongdoing? (She changes *wrongdoing* to *specific arts of wrongdoing*.)

They also say that the volunteer board is forgiving of Executive Director Ralph Martin, who makes management decisions, and they hope a new board will replace him.

EDITOR (pointing to the word *forgiving*): Forgiving?
REPORTER: They won't challenge him.

The editor replaces *is forgiving of* with *won't challenge*. Then she adds the information the reporter had suggested earlier: "The terms of the three remaining authority members expire in October."

After leaving several paragraphs untouched, they discuss this paragraph:

The last remaining authority member, Patricia Thomas, hasn't returned the mayor's telephone calls to even talk about resigning. She has told Belfore she likely will refuse to leave the board as well. Thomas did not return a telephone call for comment.

EDITOR (pointing to the second sentence): Did you get this from Belfore or the mayor or who?
REPORTER: Belfore.

The editor changes the sentence to "Belfore said she has told him that she likely will refuse to leave the board as well."

REPORTER: It's a good story, don't you think? It involves some of the most powerful people in Lakeville.
EDITOR: Yes, it is.
REPORTER: Do we have to cut five inches out of it?
EDITOR: No, I checked and we can use all 15 inches.

In the course of a five-minute conversation, the editor displayed the characteristics of good content editing. She made sure that the lead was supported by the story, that the information was presented clearly, and that the story was factual and fair. She did not rewrite the story. Most of the wording and the tone of the story remain just as the reporter wrote it.

After the content editor is satisfied with the story, it is sent to the copy desk. There, a copy editor/designer will edit the story again. Occasionally, a problem is discovered by the copy desk and the story is sent back to the content editor. This story, however, is in good shape. It is placed on an inside page in the Local section, and a headline is written. The content editor and the reporter rarely see the headline until they read the paper at home the next morning.

Here's the story as it appeared:

LAKEVILLE–The city is drafting formal charges of inefficiency against board members of the Lakeville Housing Authority after two of its members refused to resign Friday.

Mayor Bill Modano and the city's attorney privately met with chairman Woodrow Belfore and vice chairman Joe Madden on Friday afternoon urging them to leave the authority.

The agency is being rocked by an FBI criminal investigation into the possible misuse of funds. Also, the federal Department of Housing & Urban Development has found mismanagement and could cut off millions of dollars in authority funding.

Both Belfore and Madden, insisting the problems can be fixed, told Modano no.

"I'm disappointed they want to drag it out," Modano said.

So now Modano said he will announce charges against the board members at Tuesday's commission meeting to start the legal process of forcing them out.

Although city leaders aren't accusing the board members of specific acts of wrongdoing, they have said that a drastic shake-up of the authority is needed. They also say that the volunteer board appears unwilling to challenge Executive Director Ralph Martin, who makes management decisions.

City leaders say they want a new board to replace him. The terms of the three remaining authority members expire in October.

Florida law states that before authority members can be removed from office, they have to be given a copy of charges against them at least 10 days before a hearing.

The charges have to show proof of inefficiency, misconduct or neglect of duty. But city officials say the law allows for subjective standards, and they will likely point to a HUD report that uses terms such as "inefficiency" and "negligence" in referring to the authority.

Belfore, a well-known figure who was the city's first black firefighter and is also known for his famous cousin, former county commissioner Sylvia Belfore, said he's taking the issue personally.

"I've never really failed at anything I've tried to do," he said. "It's important I don't give this up. This is my watch. When they look back [and people say] they got rid of the housing members, they'll say, 'Who is the chairman? Belfore.' That's totally unacceptable."

"I haven't been able to rest good at night. And I'm not even paid a dime for this," he said. "It's crazy."

The last remaining authority member, Patricia Thomas, hasn't returned the mayor's telephone calls to even talk about resigning. Belfore said she has told him she likely will refuse to leave the board as well. Thomas did not return a telephone call for comment.

"I know charges are going to be filed, that's what he told me," Belfore said. "We'll just tough it out. I'm going to get legal help. I'd be a fool not to get legal help. I ain't that brave."

But he'll stay until the end, he said. "I haven't done anything wrong."

COACHING THE HARD-NEWS STORY

In the opening chapter of this book, we followed a feature story through the process of being edited and packaged at *The Tampa Tribune*. We watched as Penny Carnathan, the assignment editor, coached reporter Michelle Bearden as she was writing her story about the Gator crusader. The work of the content editor on the housing story is another example of successful coaching.

The performances of both editors show the characteristics that Roy Clark and Don Fry of the Poynter Institute consider elemental to good coaching: "asking good questions, preparing and debriefing the reporter, taking the story seriously, making good observations, offering alternative approaches, bouncing back the story to the writer and letting the writer know, now and over time, what you think is most important" *(Coaching Writers: The Essential Guide for Editors and Reporters.* St. Martin's Press, 1992: 11–18).

Clark and Fry distinguish between coaching and the traditional approach to editing, which they call "fixing." In extreme cases of fixing, editors may hack away at stories or rewrite them with abandon without bothering to consult the reporters. In fact, those hapless reporters have no idea what their finished products will look like until they open the next day's paper.

"Every editor must learn to fix stories, but fixing is not the same as coaching," Clark and Fry write. "Coaching is the human side of editing, fixing—the literary side. In other words, the editor coaches the writer but fixes the story.

"Editing serves the reader by making the story and the writer better at the same time. Editors accomplish both by helping the writer fix the story, rather than by repairing it themselves."

Coaching and fixing differ in lots of ways, Clark and Fry say. For example, coaching is part of an ongoing partnership between writer and editor; fixing occurs right on deadline. Coaching develops the writer, whereas fixing gets the story in the paper on time; coaching builds confidence, whereas fixing undercuts the writer; coaching builds on strengths, whereas fixing identifies weaknesses; coaching unites writer and editor, whereas fixing casts the two as adversaries; coaching fosters independence, whereas fixing creates resentment. And finally, coaching inspires risk taking, whereas fixing encourages "safe," often boring and clichéd approaches to stories.

EDITING HARD-NEWS LEADS

In your first newswriting class, instructors hammered you with the fundamentals of the hard-news story. You heard all about the summary lead and the inverted pyramid. You probably spent a couple of weeks being drilled in ways to perfect the 20 or so words that make up the first paragraph of a story. And you struggled to decide which facts were so important that they belonged in your lead.

It's not much different for reporters in the real world. They sometimes spend as much time writing the lead as they do the rest of the story, and despite all their effort, editors often see leads that need more work and stories that need rearranging.

THE CONTENT OF LEADS

Unsupported leads raise questions that are not answered in the story. They are a common problem. Editors should always check for them. The content editor did that with the housing board story we looked at earlier. The lead reported that "formal charges were being drafted," but the story never made it clear who was drafting the charges. After conferring with the reporter, the editor changed the lead to say that city officials were drafting the charges.

In the inverted-pyramid format, the point of the story ought to be in the lead, and the rest of the story should explain and amplify it. Sometimes reporters lose sight of the story's focus. They write leads that direct the reader's attention away from the point of the story. Look at this lead:

> Maria Santana, dean of students, addressed a joint meeting of the Faculty Council and the Student Senate at Northern State University Tuesday night.

This lead doesn't provide focus. It doesn't show us where the story is going. If you were a copy editor and confronted this lead, you might look through the story to see whether the reporter had anything interesting to say about the event. Perhaps the dean's message—and much of the reporter's story—is about the university's high tuition. If so, the lead might be:

> The dean of students at Northern State University asked the Faculty Council and Student Senate Tuesday night to demand that the Legislature cut tuition in half.

Usually what people say is considerably more important than where they say it. Instead of the bland "addressed a joint session," a strong lead might be:

> A top official at Northern State University wants NSU to abolish its football program after this season.

Her name and the location of her speech can go in the second paragraph:

> Addressing a joint session of the Faculty Council and Student Senate, Maria Santana, dean of students, said, "A university should be a place of learning, not a professional sports organization."

Some reporters have just the opposite problem. They don't want to write bland leads. So they pack their leads with punch. Too much punch. They may *hype* their leads by overstating the facts or sensationalizing them, as in the following:

> Police on Tuesday raided a major drug warehouse across the street from Northside High School on Tuesday and shut down the largest cocaine operation ever found in the county.
> "We think closing down this warehouse will deal a severe blow to the drug dealers in this city," Police Chief Cordell Jackson said.
> He said undercover officers had spent three months tracking down what he described as a "coke warehouse" in the Columbia U-Lock-It storage facility at 1256 N. Columbia St.
> "Big-time dealers were storing their stuff here," Jackson said. He said they were not using the site on the busy thoroughfare to sell drugs.

"They were using this facility the way any businessmen would," he said. "They would store it here and then distribute it all over the county."

Although no cocaine was found in the warehouse at the time of the raid, Jackson said police found indications that several hundred pounds of cocaine had been stored there recently.

"This warehouse probably held the biggest cache of drugs we've ever seen," he said.

No arrests were made Tuesday.

If this lead struck you as hyped and misleading, you're catching on. The reporter played up the proximity of the warehouse to Northside High School students. Many readers might get the impression that Northside students were involved either as dealers or customers of the cocaine ring. Yet, there's no indication of that in the story. Apparently, it was only a coincidence that the storage facility was near the school.

And what about the claim that the raid "shut down the largest cocaine operation ever found in the county"? It may be true. But the story doesn't really support that idea, either. The cops made no arrests and didn't find any cocaine. The police chief never claims they've "shut down" the ring; he contends only that they dealt it a blow. The drug dealers may have simply moved their stash across town. Clearly, the lead needs work—but first the story needs more reporting.

Many editors would also advise the reporter to be on guard for self-serving sources who try to make themselves look better by hyping the facts. That might be the case here. How would raiding a warehouse that the dealers aren't using anymore deal them "a severe blow"? The police chief may be able to answer that—or it may be just hype. The reporter needs to ask.

The police chief says that officers were able to look into an empty room and see "indications" that several hundred pounds of cocaine had been stored there. He then uses those indications to proclaim that it was the largest drug cache city police have "ever seen." The reporter needs to question the police chief a little more closely about those claims. For instance, how do you look into an empty room and determine how many pounds of cocaine were once stored there?

HOW LONG SHOULD LEADS BE?

There are no easy answers to question of how long to make leads. The personality of the newspaper itself plays a role in the length of its leads. Some editors want their papers to be serious and to appeal to the very literate. They encourage longer leads and allow reporters to display bigger vocabularies. For example the leads on the front page of a recent copy of *The New York Times* averaged 42 words. You'll also find editors who want their papers to be easy, quick reads. These editors may put a premium on conciseness. The average lead in the top stories of a recent *New York Daily News* had about 16 words.

Most editors want their papers to be somewhere between these extremes. They want their papers to seem lively and reader friendly. They encourage their staffs to write catchy leads and to inject as much fun into their stories as the subject matter allows. In these papers, you'll find some stories with very short leads and other stories with leads as long as those in the *Times*.

You'll even find editors who differ on the definition of *lead*. Many adhere to the traditional notion that the lead is the one-sentence-long paragraph that begins a story. But, as we discuss in more detail in the next chapter, some editors think the lead is the opening part of the story, in which the reporter explains what the story is about. To these editors, a lead can be several paragraphs long.

No matter what the personality of the paper and no matter how editors define *lead*, every lead must present the main points of the story without being so crammed that readers choke on the information.

SECOND-DAY LEADS AND STORIES

So far, we've concentrated on leads about fresh news: police raids, speeches and bureaucratic intrigue. In these *first-day leads,* reporters emphasize the news event itself. Suppose that a fire breaks out in a downtown store Thursday evening; the story in Friday morning's paper would be a first-day story, and its lead might be:

> A fire swept through Jensen's Department Store in Anderson-ville Thursday night, destroying the store and all its contents.

Reporters will then spend Friday looking for new details and will write a second-day story for Saturday's paper. Perhaps they'll report that fire officials have found the cause of the fire. Or maybe the company has decided to rebuild. Or maybe there's an investigation into why the fire alarms failed. *Second-day leads* will play the new angle to the story:

> Fire officials Friday said that arson may be to blame for the fire that destroyed downtown Andersonville's oldest depart-ment store Thursday night.

High in the second-day story, reporters need to repeat the details of the event. Not everybody reads the paper every day. Often a sentence or two of background goes in the second and third paragraphs, like this:

[Second-day lead]
> Mayor Paula Blake criticized the city's fire department on Friday for what she called a "ridiculously slow response" to Thursday's fire that destroyed a downtown department store.

[Background and new information]
Blake said the fire raced through Jensen's Department Store on East Main Street in for nearly 20 minutes before firefighters arrived.

[Background]
The store and all its contents were destroyed.

When you edit follow-up stories like these, keep two things in mind. First, make sure that reporters put the background high enough so that readers new to the story can understand it. Second, make sure that you don't cut out those details if you have to trim the story to make it fit.

AFTER THE LEAD

Good writers use *transitions* to make their copy flow from one paragraph to the next. When transitions are poorly handled, the story gives readers a choppy ride. They bounce from one idea to the next.

Suppose that a reporter is assigned to write about last night's storm. The story will focus on a tornado that heavily damaged one community. But because the story is a "roundup," it must include information about three other reported tornadoes and hail damage in some other areas of the state. The story may go something like this:

1. Four tornadoes plowed through Texas on Tuesday, including one that struck the hamlet of Lenorah, destroying a cotton gin and three of the town's 11 houses.

2. No deaths or injuries were reported from any of the tornadoes.

3. In Lenorah, the twister hop-scotched across town, hitting one house on the east side, skipping two blocks, and then ramming the cotton gin and two houses on the west side of town.

4. Central Cotton, owner of the gin, said it was too early to determine whether the plant would be rebuilt. The gin has about a dozen employees, according to Central Cotton spokesman James E. Brown.

5. Officials said families left homeless spent the night with friends.

6. Three other tornadoes were sighted in West Texas in a day of wild weather.

[The story continues with information about the other three tornadoes.]

Look at how connections are made between thoughts. The lead says four tornadoes hit Texas and singles out the destruction in the town of Lenorah. Paragraph 2 gives some additional information about the storms. Paragraph 3 starts with the transition "In Lenorah," which alerts readers that the next paragraph is going to focus on the one storm. Paragraphs 3, 4 and 5 describe the events in Lenorah.

Paragraph 6 moves us away from Lenorah to the sites of the other tornadoes. The words "Three other tornadoes" act as a transition, shifting the reader's attention to another facet of the story. We would get the same effect with, "Tornadoes were also seen. . . ." The word "also" can make an effective transition.

The weather roundup is a basic story. Sometimes hard-news stories are more complicated. Read this one:

1. A woman convicted of killing her parents was described Tuesday as "hurt and bewildered" by charges linking her to reported sex parties between women inmates and male guards at the Statesville Prison for Women.

2. The accusations against 23-year-old Mary Smith were made by other women inmates who said she recruited them to engage in sexual relations with top-ranking officials.

3. Prison sources said her accusers may be jealous of Smith's youth and good looks as well as her comparatively prestigious job as secretary to a prison official.

4. Her boss, Dennis Brown, 40, head of internal investigations at Statesville, is one of two men accused by inmates of having received the sexual favors. He and Denver Scott, 47, chief of security, face suspension from duty pending an investigation.

5. Wilban P. Morgan, Smith's lawyer, said Smith phoned him last week to disclose that she had been implicated in something she knew nothing about.

6. "She sounded hurt and bewildered and said she was being made a scapegoat by jealous inmates," Morgan told a reporter. "That is the general drift of our conversation."

7. Morgan said he is certain Smith is innocent and described the accusations against her as "a lot of bunk."

8. Prison sources said the accusations may stem from her secretarial job, a position rarely given to murderers.

9. "She walked around there like she owned the place," a former woman guard said. "I worked there for weeks before I realized she was an inmate. I thought she was a civilian employee."

10. Smith is serving 200 to 300 years in prison for the murder of her parents and younger brother. An appeal of her conviction is before an appellate court.

11. She has been in Statesville for about two years. She and her lover, Frank Donovan, were convicted of killing her parents after they disapproved of her relationship with Donovan, who was then 21 years older than Smith.

The lead brings up two ideas: First, an inmate has been accused of being involved in prison sex parties; second, she's hurt by the accusations.

The second paragraph begins with the words "The accusations," which serve as a transitional signal that the reporter is going to explain the charges mentioned in the lead. The third and fourth paragraphs continue the discussion of the accusations. Notice that in these paragraphs the reporter uses the words "accusers" and "accused," emphasizing the fact that these paragraphs are about the accusations.

Complicated stories such as this one may not be organized in the inverted pyramid style. They're often organized in blocks. In this story, paragraphs 2, 3 and 4 make up a block about the accusations against the woman.

The fifth paragraph is a transition. It moves the reader from the discussion of the accusations into the second part of the story—how the woman reacted to the charges. Paragraphs 5, 6 and 7 form a block about her reactions. Paragraph 8 shifts into a block of paragraphs that provide context to the story. Then the last two paragraphs offer background.

Transitions and clear organization are important to smooth writing. Editors insist that stories have them, and good editors try not to remove them when they trim the story.

MAKING THE WRITING CONCISE

Wordiness in a story makes for a sluggish read and stuffy tone. You won't have much trouble recognizing wordiness if you slow down and concentrate on what you're reading. Here are two examples:

> They had just purchased the New York home and were in the process of renovating it.

> He refused to comment on the fact that he had been indicted.

The first sentence is overwrought. The word "purchased" quickly can be replaced with the more common "bought." Next, we can ax "in the process of"—an unnecessary bit of verbosity most of the time.

They had just bought the New York home and were renovating it.

How about the second example? "The fact that" is right up there with "in the process of" when it comes to useless words. Our slimmed-down version:

> He refused to comment on the indictment.

PHRASES TRIMMED TO ELIMINATE WORDINESS

WORDY	CONCISE
Advance planning	planning
Advance reservations	reservations
At the intersection of Main and Maple streets	at Main and Maple streets
A period of three months	three months
Be offensive	to offend
Bring an end	to end
Climb up	climb
Completely destroyed	destroyed
Despite the fact that	although
Due to the fact that	because
Fall down	fall
File a lawsuit against	sue
For a period of six weeks	for six weeks
Foreign imports	imports
General public	public
Had knowledge of	knew
Impose a moratorium on	halt

WORDY	CONCISE
In order to obtain	to obtain
In the process of building	building
Is in favor of	favors
Is opposed to	opposes
Law enforcement officers	police
Make a final determination	decide
New construction	construction
On a permanent basis	permanently
Overcrowded	crowded
Place restrictions on	restrict
Provide insurance coverage for	insure
Produced definitive proof	proved
Take the case to trial	try the case
Whether or not	whether
With the exception of	except
Would be more costly to	would cost more

REPEATED WORDS

Most of the time, saying something once is enough. But reporters inadvertently repeat words, and copy editors, one hopes, clean up the wordiness. Editing teacher Martin Gibson coined the terms "double-verbing" and "double-nouning" to describe these types of verbal overkill:

1. The commission unanimously voted to turn down the proposal.

2. The last time the barn was painted was about four years ago.

3. The person who reportedly has the inside track to the job is a New Bern resident.

In sentence 1, if the commissioners "turned down" the proposal, they must have voted. Make it:

The commission unanimously turned down (or rejected) the proposal.

In sentence 2, we're using two verbs, "was painted" and "was," when only one is needed:

The barn was painted four years ago.

If we need to emphasize the idea of "the last time," we could write, "The barn was last painted four years ago."

In sentence 3, two nouns, "a person" and "a resident," refer to the same person. Make it:

A New Bern resident reportedly has the inside track to the job.

TRIMMING THE HARD-NEWS STORY

Stories have to fit the space allotted to them, so copy editors often have to lop off a couple of paragraphs. Let's quash two misconceptions you may have about trimming stories.

Rumor No. 1: You've probably heard horror stories about copy editors hacking a reporter's 1,500-word masterpiece down to 500 words. Sure, that kind of cutting happens, but not very often (except for wire copy).

In well-managed newsrooms, most local stories will be roughly the right size before they get to the copy desk. There are two reasons for this: First, assignment editors and reporters usually discuss the stories in advance so that each knows about how long the story should be. A reporter won't waste time writing a 1,000-word monster if the editor asked for a 100-word brief. Second, if stories do turn out to be too long for the space available, most assignment editors like to give reporters the first crack at trimming their own work. If they suspect the story will need to be cut, they may ask the reporter to mark the paragraphs that should be the first to go. If stories are still too long or if some development in the news changes the amount of space available, many assignment editors will make the cuts themselves before sending the story to the copy desk.

(Notice that we excluded wire stories from this discussion. That's because wire editors don't have the luxury of suggesting to the news services how long stories should be, and they can't bounce them back for rewrites. Wire editors often have to make massive cuts in stories. We discuss their plight in Chapter 8.)

Rumor No. 2: You may have heard that the inverted pyramid makes the job of trimming stories easy because the most important facts are at the top of the story and the least important at the bottom. If editors need to cut the story, they can chop off the last few paragraphs without fear of losing anything important.

On many stories, this approach just doesn't work. Take our story about the killer and the sex parties. The lead contained two ideas: the accusations against the woman and her reactions. If a copy editor had slashed away from the bottom, we might have lost the blocks that give background about her murder connections. That's bad editing. When good editors trim a story, they read it thoroughly. Then they shorten by cutting a few words here and a sentence there. The meat-cleaver approach has been replaced by something akin to a surgical procedure. Trimming a story tests editors' news judgment and writing abilities.

Computers have made the mechanics of trimming easy. First, computers tell editors how long the story will be in 10ths or even 100ths of an inch. There's no guesswork. Editors know exactly how long the story is after each cut. Computers also allow editors to tinker with the space between lines. If the story is a little too short, they can add a little more space between each line in the story to make it fit. This process is called *leading* (pronounced like the metal lead) or *leading out*. (Leading is discussed in Chapter 12.)

Now that we've destroyed some misconceptions you might have had about trimming stories, here's some advice on how it's done:

1. Read through the story, watching out for wordiness. You'll be surprised at how much easier finding wordy passages is when you know you have to trim 20 words.

2. Preserve as much information as possible. Often, good reporters raise an issue and then quote several people about it. Some of those people may be making the same point, so you might delete one of them without losing information. Or the reporter may present an idea and then explain it with statistics and anecdotes. Maybe the explanation can be shortened without losing the main idea.

3. We make this point several times throughout this book and we won't apologize for the redundancy: *Don't introduce error.* Nothing infuriates reporters and managing editors more than a copy editor who takes perfectly fine copy and screws it up. For example, some stories have sentences that serve as buffers between two ideas or two viewpoints. Remove those sentences and you lose context. Read this passage from a story:

    > "Councilman Summer is one of the dumbest people I've ever met in public life," the mayor said. "He does not have the slightest idea about how a city works."
    >
    > But the mayor said he agreed with Summer on some things.
    >
    > "Look at his idea for a summer school program for young children," the mayor said. "We've got a first-class program now."

Imagine that a copy editor needed to trim 10 words out of the story and decided to take out the second paragraph. Oh, come on, you think. Nobody would make that mistake. Guess again. Even well-edited newspapers run corrections for blunders exactly like that made by sloppy copy editors looking for a quick way to trim a story. Make sure that you aren't one of them.

OTHER WAYS TO TELL THE NEWS 7

So far, we've discussed the ins and outs of editing hard-news stories—that is, accounts of newsworthy events told in a straightforward, no-frills manner. These stories, told with summary leads followed by details organized in an inverted pyramid or in information blocks, have been the mainstay of American newspapers for more than 100 years.

Some editors argue that if newspapers are to survive in the 21st century, their stories will need to rely even more heavily on the summary lead and inverted pyramid. These editors contend that Americans prefer "quick reads," and there's no better way to write short, fact-filled stories than by using summary leads and inverted pyramids.

But other editors have come to a much different conclusion. They, too, are alarmed by reports that the percentage of people who regularly read newspapers is going down. But they point out that many people say they've stopped reading because they think newspapers are boring, hard to read and irrelevant to their lives. These editors believe that if the quality of newspaper writing is improved, newspapers can win back—or at least maintain—their share of readers.

Therefore, at scores of newspapers, editors are encouraging their reporters to think of themselves as storytellers and to write interesting accounts that involve readers in the news. Geneva Overholser, former editor of *The Des Moines Register,* wants reporters to write stories that make readers "laugh, weep, sing, hope and wonder how people can go on." She and other editors believe that if they make reading the news a pleasure, more people will be willing to try it.

These new ways of writing the news blur the line between hard-news stories and features. Stories about politics, government and crime are being written with the same voice and creativity that were formerly reserved for features. Instead of providing dry recitations of facts, reporters are presenting the news in more human terms. They want readers to visualize the problems they're reading about and be able to relate them to their own lives.

Many newspapers are allowing their reporters to experiment with writing styles. Reporters are encouraged to make their writing seem more like conversations between friends, to show more of their own "voice," to be more playful, and to use analogies to make their points. Editing such stories is more challenging than editing the traditional hard-news story. Editors must be sensitive enough to appreciate what the reporter is trying to achieve, yet wise enough to question writing that is overwrought or wrongheaded. Helping you develop that sensitivity is the goal of this chapter.

103

DELAYED AND ANECDOTAL LEADS

Many reporters now use delayed leads. Unlike traditional leads, these don't always state the news immediately. Instead, they may illustrate the news with an example before summarizing it.

These leads can be written in many ways. On some stories, reporters find that *anecdotal leads* work best. Anecdotes are very short stories that stir a variety of emotions. They can be funny, poignant, sad, frustrating, uplifting, scary, maddening. Here's an example from the *St. Louis Post-Dispatch:*

For weeks, Duane Honchak kept telling fellow drug addicts that he would kill Judith Kay Million, the director of their rehabilitation program in Alton.

On Friday, Honchak drank his usual dose of methadone from a paper cup, pulled a pistol from beneath a sweater draped over his arm and fatally shot Million almost pointblank, firing three times without uttering a word as she sat at her desk.

After failing to kick in the locked door of his own caseworker's office nearby, Honchak, 37, walked to his silver Mercury Sable parked outside and killed himself with a shot to the head.

(Reprinted with permission of the *St. Louis Post-Dispatch*)

This lead, which is three paragraphs long, seems more like the work of a storyteller than it does the work of a news reporter. Notice that the event itself is what most editors would consider hard news: a shooting at a methadone clinic. But the reporter tells the story with a highly readable, almost featurelike approach. Note, too, that the lead also hints at a bigger problem: Threats aimed at employees at the center aren't taken seriously. That angle is developed later in the story.

Here's another example of a nontraditional lead. When police made an arrest in a case involving a missing child, the Associated Press led the story this way:

RIVIERA BEACH (AP)—In one hand Pauline Zile clutched a stuffed animal. With the other, she wiped the tears streaming from her red, swollen eyes.

Looking into the TV camera, she made a near-hysterical plea for the return of her 7-year-old daughter, claiming Christina Holt had been abducted from a rest-room at a flea market.

One problem: The woman kept referring to her daughter in past tense.

Days later, police announced that Pauline Zile had concocted the abduction tale to cover up her daughter's beating death more than a month earlier at the hands of the girl's stepfather.

Pauline Zile's grammatical slip was just one of the inconsistencies investigators uncovered in the death of the second-grader, whose body was found Friday in a shallow grave behind a convenience store.

For other stories, reporters use anecdotal leads to show readers the feelings of the people they're writing about. *The Courier-Journal* in Louisville wanted its readers to understand what it's like to grow up in poverty. Here's the lead to one story in its package:

Mary Rose White sits on a kitchen chair, its foam seat cushion chewed away, holding a generic cigarette and rubbing her bare feet on a buckling plank floor.

Dozens of roaches skitter around the kitchen. Some explore a stack of junk mail on a table while others nibble on a box of instant mashed potatoes in one of a dozen milk crates used as shelves.

Inside this shotgun house in Louisville's Germantown neighborhood—its foundation slightly shifted, its busted kitchen-door window covered with plywood, its secondhand furniture and rust-colored living room carpet well worn—Mary Rose smiles.

"It's one of the best houses we've lived in," she says as she takes a drag on her cigarette.

(@ 1993 The *Courier-Journal*. Reprinted with permission.)

The reporter's clear description of the house sets up the irony of the quotation that follows, giving the story great impact.

Anecdotal leads also can help readers understand less dramatic news. Here's an example from the *San Francisco Examiner:*

When a friendly young man offered to patch and seal the roof of Robert Manseau's home, the retiree couldn't believe the price.

"For $1,800, he offered to do the whole thing," said Manseau, 68, who lives near St. Francis Wood.

Now Manseau is $1,800 poorer and his roof still hasn't been fixed.

DEVELOPING THE STORY AFTER DELAYED LEADS

Stories with delayed leads don't usually follow the inverted pyramid. Instead, writers tell the story much as they would in conversation. They write vivid descriptions of the news events and present the people in their stories as real people rather than the two-dimensional newsmakers in traditional stories.

To achieve these effects, reporters use colorful words, contractions, and even some slang. They also organize their stories in more relaxed ways. Look at the way a *St. Petersburg (Fla.) Times* reporter covered what would commonly be considered a hard-news event: a small plane having to make an emergency landing on a busy freeway.

Ed Fullerton was giving flying lessons 1,000 feet above Fort De Soto Park on Thursday when his engine choked off, the propeller stalled and the airplane went into a fast glide.

Fullerton, 46, radioed for help, then searched frantically for a place to land.

Then he saw it. Miles of smooth asphalt that stretched as far as the eye could see. It was the highway approach to the Sunshine Skyway bridge.

Maneuvering past stunned motorists, Fullerton executed a safe landing on Interstate 275 in the northbound lanes, north of the bridge. Neither he nor his passenger was injured, and the plane showed no outward signs of damage.

"All you could see was cars, cars, cars," said Juanita Johnson, 57, a student pilot from St. Petersburg. "I was just hoping the traffic would slow down so we could land."

Their ordeal began about 10 a.m., 30 minutes after the pair took off on a training flight from Albert Whitted Municipal Airport, Fullerton said.

The engine cut off once, restarted, then cut off again. Fullerton knew he was in trouble.

"My first thought was, 'I need some new shorts,'" Fullerton said while smoking a cigarette moments after the emergency landing. "I had a dead stick and a dead prop (propeller)."

Fullerton had started back for Albert Whitted but realized the Aeronca Champ two-seater wouldn't make it.

"I radioed to Albert Whitted for help, but then I told the tower I was too busy to talk and I'd call them later," Fullerton said.

Meanwhile, airport officials told Coast Guard crews to look for a plane in trouble near the Skyway.

"The Sunshine Skyway was the perfect runway," said Fullerton, who said he has been flying airplanes since he was 16. "We got out in front of one car, and he stopped traffic for a moment until we had stopped. I am very grateful to him, whoever he is, for having done that."

The plane traveled about 100 yards on 1-275 about 10 miles north of the bridge before stopping, Fullerton said.

Federal Aviation Administration officials investigating the landing said contaminated fuel probably caused the engine to fail.

"If the airplane sits up (idle) for a month at a time, say, it can cause condensation, which builds up in the tanks," said FAA spokesman Ernest Wilson. "It could be water or a little rust in the tank that gets into the carburetor and then restricts the flow of fuel."

Wilson said no punitive action would be taken against the pilot because he was properly certified.

The plane is registered to V. R. Harris of Largo, according to FAA records. A man at the scene who identified himself as the plane's owner refused to discuss the incident.

Meanwhile, Mrs. Johnson, who has been taking lessons since October to learn how to fly her husband's plane, got the lesson of her life.

"It's something you hope you never have to do," she said. "But Ed is an experienced pilot, and I knew he knew what he was doing."

Mrs. Johnson plans to continue her flying lessons.

"Next time, though, I'm going in my own plane," she said. "You couldn't get me up in this one again if you paid me."

(Used by permission, *St. Petersburg Times.*)

The lead for this story differs from a more traditional summary lead, which would read something like, "Engine failure Tuesday forced a private plane to make an emergency landing on the Sunshine Skyway bridge." Instead, the St. Petersburg reporter used an anecdotal lead. It describes the event so vividly that readers can share the emotions of the people in the plane. In this story, the lead makes up the first four paragraphs.

Let's look at what follows this lead. The reporter divided the story into four blocks. The first block is the anecdotal lead, which ends with the plane landing safely on the bridge. A quotation from the student pilot in the fifth paragraph serves as a transition to the second block, where the reporter tells the story of the flight chronologically ("Their ordeal began about 10 a.m. . . . ")

This block runs eight paragraphs. The reporter maintains the conversational tone, which makes reading the story like reading a novel—or listening to a good storyteller.

The next block, which begins "Federal Aviation Administration officials investigating," explains what may have caused the problem and is four paragraphs long. With the transitional word "meanwhile," the reporter concludes the story with a block that describes the student pilot's reactions.

Although our example is a short, breaking-news story, reporters frequently use this organizational pattern on longer stories that explain complicated issues. Their delayed leads may describe the plight of one person or family or business so that readers can see the issue in flesh-and-blood terms, not just in quotations from authorities.

The lead is usually followed by a *nut graf*, which tells the reader exactly what the story is about (*graf* is what journalists often call a paragraph). For example, after an anecdotal lead describes the financial problems of the Jones family, a nut graf might say, "The Joneses are just one of 452 Centerville families who have lost their homes because they did not read the fine print when they applied for loans from Crafty Credit Corporation."

A variation of the nut graf is the *more-and-more graf*, which might read: "More and more Centerville families are losing their homes because they did not read the fine print when they applied for loans from Crafty Credit Corporation."

Even a budding copy editor will suspect that the "just one of" and "more and more" approaches to nut grafs are hackneyed. With a little bit of thought, reporters—or copy editors, if need be—can present the nut graf without resorting to these clichés.

Let's see how the nut graf works in an example. Here's the lead to a *Pittsburgh Post-Gazette* story:

> Before he walks into a job interview, Collin McRoberts slips off the medical alert bracelet he wears around his wrist. The simple band has one word stamped on its underside: epilepsy.
>
> "I'm not going to walk into somebody's office and say, 'Hey, I have epilepsy, let's get on with the interview,'" says McRoberts, 27, of Pittsburgh. "I'm going to wait until after they've made an offer—maybe."

After another paragraph about McRoberts' background, the fourth and fifth paragraphs serve as the nut graf, stating the focus of the story:

> McRoberts' plight underscores the uneasy relationship between people with disabilities and employers, who are now legally required to at least consider them for jobs.
>
> But more interviews don't necessarily translate into more jobs.

The organization of stories after the nut graf is often much like the organization of the story about the emergency plane landing, with reporters unfolding the story in a series of blocks rather than presenting the facts in order of importance. The blocks will vary in length, but they average four or five paragraphs.

EDITING THE ANECDOTAL LEAD

In some ways, anecdotal leads place more demands on copy editors. First, the editor has to make sure that the anecdotal lead illustrates the story fairly. Writers sometimes select the most dramatic cases possible to use as their anecdotes. But the anecdote needs to be a fair representation of the problem. Suppose that you were coaching the reporter who wrote this story:

Billy Jones knew he was in trouble in American History 101. He had taken two tests and flunked each of them badly.

Even though he thought he had studied hard, he had guessed wrong about what Professor Janet Smith would put on her tests. He knew another F would mean academic probation and delay his graduation by a semester.

He was literally crying in his beer one night when a Gamma Delta Iota fraternity brother led him into another brother's room.

There, in a rusty metal file cabinet, Jones found his salvation.

Jones pulled out a dog-eared folder and found copies of tests Smith had given the past two years, tests that were nearly identical.

"I memorized every word on those tests and every answer," he said. "You can't believe how I felt when she handed me the test and I saw she hadn't changed a word on it."

More and more college students are taking the easy way out and cheating their way through school. Some experts estimate that as many as 80 percent of today's students nationwide will cheat at least once before they graduate.

Most of the cheating involves plagiarism, according to experts. Students either buy term papers or get them from friends and then submit them as if they had done the work.

"The days of the fraternity files packed with ready-made term papers are history on most college campuses," Charles White, a sociologist who has studied cheating, said. "Today's student cheaters are more high tech. They can find all kinds of A-quality work in computer databases and on the Internet. It's theirs for the downloading."

When you first read this anecdotal lead, it seems to work well. It would probably get readers' attention and it gives some insight into why some college students cheat. But editors wouldn't let it fly. After they read the quotation from Charles White, they would recognize the anecdote in the lead doesn't illustrate the point of the story. A good assignment editor would suggest that the writer do more reporting and write an anecdotal lead about cheating using the Internet.

Content editors face an even more basic question with anecdotal leads: When should a story have a hard-news lead and when will a delayed lead work better? There's no pat answer. Some newspapers, such as the *St. Petersburg Times*, use delayed leads commonly. Other papers reserve them for special stories.

A common practice is to use delayed leads to personify a larger problem. Most readers can relate to the farm problem more readily by reading about the plight of a farmer than by being bombarded with statistics. After readers gain a basic understanding of the problem, the facts and figures may make more sense.

PRESERVING THE WRITER'S VOICE

Many newspapers are moving away from the strict editing that made all newspaper stories read much the same. They want writers to show some of their own personalities, to put some of their own voice in their stories. Editors are emphasizing the use of voice throughout all their sections, but nowhere is voice so important or widely used as in feature stories—the lifestyle pieces and profiles that run in sections with names like "Living," "Style," "Leisure," or "Today's Life."

What do we mean by "voice"? We'll give you a definition in a moment. But first, let's look at a rather extreme example that appeared in the *Orlando Sentinel*:

OK, kids, it's time to tawk amongst yuhselves.

Suggested topic: Ex-New Yoorkuhs can live happily ever aftuh in Orlando.

Discuss.

"Orlando is a very conservative community, and that's one of the things I don't like about it," says Annette Gluskin, 42, an unrepentant Manhattanite with a "Northeast, liberal, educated sensibility."

Fellow Manhattan native Ron Habin begs to diffuh.

"Orlando is probably what you want it to be," says Habin, 44, an anthropology instructor at Valencia Community College in Orlando. "It's magic; it's a new city; it's emerging."

Despite their differing views of life in The City Beautiful, these former New Yorkers are drawn to each other—and to other ex-Big Apple residents—like lunatics to the New York subway.

"There's just a certain language, sensibility, outlook" among New York City natives, explains Gluskin, who works at Winter Park Hospital.

"No matter where you live, if you're from New York, you have a certain attitude"—an attitude that's, oh, about 180 degrees from the typical Orlando attitude, she says.

If your knee-jerk instinct was to correct the spelling from "tawk" to "talk," "yuhselves" to "yourselves" and "Yoorkuhs" to "Yorkers," you need to be more sensitive to the use of voice. If you realized that the writer was conversing with readers in a New York City accent, you recognize voice when you see it. Essentially, voice is personality injected into a story as a writing device. It may be the writer's personality or an assumed one, as in the New Yorkers story. A caveat: Voice can provoke strong reactions in some readers. The *Orlando Sentinel* reporter who wrote this piece received several angry calls from New Yorkers.

Let's look at some less extreme, but no less effective, uses of voice in other *Sentinel* stories, such as this one about a new book:

Sure signs that you're not a sophisticate:

A Timex and a Patek Phillippe look pretty much the same to you.

Your Ford Festiva sports a tree-shaped deodorizer drooping from the rearview mirror.

You figure Gianni Versace is some new spaghetti-type thing.

Well, darlings, despite your lack of *savoir-faire*, there is hope for you.

It's a book called *Simply Sophisticated* (The Summit Group, $12.95).

In it, author Suzanne Munshower has thoughtfully outlined everything one needs to know to pass oneself off as a cultured, knowledgeable citizen of the world. Topics include shopping, sipping (wines and international beers), speaking (how and when to drop Latin and French phrases), eating, investing, arts appreciating, driving and traveling.

To tell this story about a book aimed at would-be sophisticates, the writer has adopted the persona of a sophisticate, addressing the readers as "darlings" and using the third-person singular ("everything one needs to know to pass oneself off") traditionally associated with the upper crust. The writer maintains this tone throughout the story, meanwhile imparting information from both the book and experts on the value of appearing sophisticated in the workplace. Here's a passage from later in the story:

Beware, however, of becoming a pseudosophisticate.

"In their effort to be sophisticated, sometimes people do things that actually hurt them," warns Mimi Hull, a licensed psychologist in Maitland.

"They use language that's more sophisticated than the situation requires. They'll say, for example, 'the precipitation is descending with amazing rapidity' instead of 'it's really pouring outside.'"

Or pronounce *crudités* KREWdites instead of krew-dee-TAY.

Which just SCREAMS g-a-u-c-h-e.

(Oh, all right, if you really don't know: *crudités* are those darling little raw veggies served with dip as hors d'oeuvres. Surely you've heard of hors d'oeuvres.)

Notice the effect of capitalizing "screams." You can just picture a stylish if annoying sophisticate, pinkie finger extended while sipping tea and proclaiming in high-pitched tones a disgust with gaucheness.

The wise copy editor recognizes when bending style rules serves readers by enhancing the voice in a story. Indeed, the copy editor on this particular story got into the spirit of things with a headline and drop head that mimic the voice adopted by the writer:

Sophisticated aspirations but gauche inclinations?

Do pardon our frankness. But being wise in the way of the couth, as detailed in a new book, is *de rigueur* for getting ahead.

Writers use voice in more ways than just mimicking accents and affectations. They can also use voice to tell very serious news in conversational prose that's easy, perhaps even fun, to read. The *Pittsburgh Post-Gazette* opened a long front-page story with this lead:

In the heart of coal country, where movie theaters might be 40 minutes away and recreational facilities are scarce, there's often nothing to do but stay home and eat.

Or go to someone else's home and eat. Or go to a fast-food restaurant and eat. Or go to a place like the Coal Miner's Kitchen—where the menu includes corn dogs and hot dogs and fried cauliflower—and eat.

For proof, check the scales. Nearly 40 percent of the adults in this rural county are obese, more than anywhere else in West Virginia.

Notice the conversational tone the reporter takes. You can almost hear the reporter's voice as you read it. The repetition of the words "and eat" gives the lead attitude. It also helps drive home the cause of a very serious health problem.

Reporters can also add their own voice by letting their clever, even cynical senses of humor slip into their copy. Here's an example from the *Houston Chronicle*:

When the tornado and rain played out and the sun revealed the ugly truth, it was apparent Tuesday that Lancaster's Town Square was no longer historic.

It was just plain history.

The *Chronicle*'s lead works well. The wordplay on "historic" and "history" is clever. And the short second paragraph is set up nicely by the longer, more descriptive opening paragraph.

PRESERVING COLOR

Another component of good feature writing that copy editors should strive to preserve is color.

Reporters may use description to set the scene the way a stage designer creates a set for a theatrical production. Or they may weave in carefully chosen details about dress or behavior that help readers form an impression of the subject. These examples of "color" in writing are a way to help readers connect with stories. This fine example was written by Margo Harakas of the *South Florida Sun-Sentinel*:

Karen Halperin, motionless on her pedestal, could see the female cop on the sidelines waiting for a break in the crowd. It was obvious the officer was going to shoo away the human canvas.

As the officer approached, Halperin silently extended a brush. The officer extended handcuffs. They mimed back and forth, the officer finally picked up a brush, painted on Halperin, laughed and walked away.

Another disarming performance by the 22-year-old anthropology graduate from Weston who conceived her gig as "Canvas the Clown" on the faulty premise that "people in an urban setting are not willing to make contact with each other." "I was wrong," she says. Her laundry and paint bills attest to just how wrong she was.

With face painted white and dressed in white canvas overalls, white shirt, white gloves, white hat, white shoes and white stockings, Halperin stations herself on a street or, as she did on Saturday, near the fountain at Riverfront in Fort Lauderdale, silently and subtly beckoning passers-by to participate in her performance.

Paint is flying now. Great gobs are being slathered on shoes, arms, legs. "Yuck, that must feel so gross," observes one onlooker.

A pack of teenage boys arrives. One steps forward, picks up a brush and traces a circle on Halperin's breast, and then a line down the inside of her thigh. Giggling, he moseys off with his pals.

"I wanna do it again, I wanna do it again, Mommy," pleads 4-year-old Julia Van de Bogart, who paints a rainbow on Halperin's leg.

It doesn't take long for Halperin to be colorized. On her hat, a blue flower blossoms. Stars and initials stream down her arms.

Canvas the Clown is actualizing, losing her whiteness to splotches and dribbles.

Hours later, before washing and bleaching her $22 overalls, Halperin will examine the finished canvas and marvel once again at the human craving for contact and creativity.

Harakas' careful presentation of the interaction between the officer and the artist; her detailed depiction of the white "canvas" Halperin makes of herself; and her word choices in describing the scene (for instance, "great gobs" of paint being "slathered") all contribute to her portrait of this performance artist. They are not wasted words but integral parts of the picture she is painting of Halperin.

NARRATIVE STORYTELLING

Narrative storytelling is a relatively recent arrival to the world of newspaper feature writing. It is a more literary, magazinelike approach to feature and enterprise stories. Narrative storytelling has gained favor with publications such as the *Orlando Sentinel*, the *Sun* in Baltimore, and the *Oregonian* in Portland.

In narrative, the reporter combines any or all of the components already discussed—delayed and anecdotal leads, voice, conversational quality and color—and may add a few other devices, such as dialogue, internal monologue, and metaphor. The intent is to, quite literally, tell a story—as opposed to just reporting the facts of a story.

A narrative requires the writer not only to get the facts right but also to offer insight and interpretation, whether from the reporter's own observations or from well-chosen quotes.

The journalist assumes the literary mode style of the third-person omniscient—the observer who knows all and is leading the reader by the hand.

Narrative encourages the writer, and thus the reader, to get inside someone else's skin, to experience what the subject has experienced. Typically, the reporter must recreate events from the subject's past. Thus, the writer must be a skilled interviewer, adept at asking questions that elicit memories of thoughts and emotions as well as events.

Because the writer gets inside the head of the subject, he or she can be tempted to go overboard. For instance, writers may inadvertently slip in a descriptive detail that came from their own imagination rather than from the actual scene, or they may ascribe thoughts to a subject that they imagine would have gone through the subject's mind.

That's why it's crucial for both assignment editors and copy editors to keep in the back of their mind one question while editing narratives: How do we know this? If the writer painstakingly reconstructed a scene based on eyewitness accounts, we're on solid ground; if subjects told the writer what they were thinking as events unfolded, we're in safe territory. If, on the other hand, the writer can't verify those details or thoughts, the writer needs to recast those parts of the story.

In skilled hands, narrative storytelling is a very effective way to touch readers where they live. This strong narrative was written by Darryl Owens of the *Orlando Sentinel*:

Cassie Lehman sits backward on a folding chair, fumbling with the stapled papers in her hands, folding them. After a time, she lays the papers on a vacant seat inside the John and Rita Lowndes Shakespeare Center and stares at patches of type streaked in yellow ink.

Her lines.

She knows the words. A snap compared with the lyrics she had to deliver a week before in the Celebration School's revival of *The Sound of Music*. As one of the chorus nuns, the maturing mezzo-soprano sang "Dixit Dominus" in Latin.

She knows the entire script—stage directions too. Still, she runs through the words in yellow, and repeats her ritual pep talk in her head.

I can do this. This is my home.

Again. And again.

She wants to anchor the lines, so the words don't shake free when her eyes twitch and her shoulders tremble.

She's embarrassed by attention, and her need to blend in has been compromised twice. The first time was when an unexpected clatter left her incapable of saying her lines; the second time was when she so violently whipped her neck that as Maude in *The Music Man* she had to wear a neck brace concealed under the costume.

In this story about an aspiring actress who suffers from Tourette's syndrome, Darryl Owens uses scene setting and internal monologue—Cassie's words to herself, "I can do this. This is my home"—to introduce us to this determined 13-year-old.

In the following story, Owens uses the metaphor of dance as a thread to weave all the story's elements together. The story is about Robyn, who has cystic fibrosis and is deciding whether to have a baby.

Sunlight sneaks past the half-drawn slats, casting shadows on a rail-thin woman on a sofa and several contraptions propped against it.

Robyn DeKeyser reaches down and cranks up one of the machines. Minutes earlier, she had walked into the kitchen and raided the cabinet that has become her pharmacy.

She ran her hands over the rows of amber bottles and transparent tubes bearing her name on white labels and gathered what she needed: antibiotics, and Pulmozyme and albuterol sulfate—the powerful drugs that help her breathe. Drugs that carry comfort, but no cure.

She reaches down again and collects what looks like a life vest. Flotation is not its purpose. Once strapped on, vacuum hoses extending from it will cause the vest to inflate, pulse and pound against her back and chest, shaking free the thick mucus coating her lungs, the signature of cystic fibrosis.

This has always been her life: Two hours, several times a day, spent inhaling medicinal mist, clearing sputum. Once her life possessed an air of fabulousness. She brought audiences to their feet as a ballerina with the Southern Ballet Theatre and Joffrey Ballet; later, she helped bring criminals to their knees as a manager with the U.S. Attorney's Office.

The disease has snatched that all away.

She empties the contents of the bottles and the vial into cups. She pinches her nostrils shut with what looks like a plastic clothespin, parts her lips and guides the nebulizer pipe into her mouth. Wisps of vapor envelop her.

Through the haze, she now clearly sees her options. Pass on motherhood and prolong her life—at 30, she has already quadrupled the life span pediatricians forecast—or have a child, shorten her life.

As she does, her husband wants children. If adoption promises her more time, he'd rather do that, he says.

But the decision is hers.

Just like the others.

She cups her hand against her lips to quiet her coughing, but it still comes in repeated bursts.

One. Two . . .

She remembers her pointe shoes now thick with dust.

Three. Four . . .

The disease mocks her greatest dream yet.

No.

She vents a cumulous cloud.

No. She will not bow this time.

She sinks deep into the sofa. Her lungs are clear, her decision clearer.

Morgan for a girl, Madison for a boy.

Nancy Osborne meets Bill Simmons in a communications class at Brevard Community College in 1964. She is 18; he is 13 years older. It isn't long before he asks her out for pie and coffee.

After a time, she relents. Instead of pie and coffee, Simmons, an ex-Air Force pilot, takes her flying in a Piper Cub. They marry two years later.

In 1968, she learns she is pregnant. To stay fit, she swims and dives. She doesn't gain much weight, maybe 20 pounds. The pregnancy is uneventful. So when doctors show her the tiny child, Nancy is not alarmed. The girl weighs barely 5 pounds; at birth, so did she.

They name her Robyn Rene.

But doctors express concern. The infant needs to weigh more before she can go home. They place her in an isolette in intensive care. She sheds 5 ounces. Something is wrong.

The doctors have their suspicions. They run tests on her lipid levels and draw blood. They feed her pancreatic enzymes to see if that halts the weight loss.

It does. Still they dodge. After all, the child is too young to perform an accurate sweat test, which measures high salt levels in perspiration, a more definitive test that would shore up their wobbly suspicion.

The young mother presses for answers.

It looks like cystic fibrosis, they finally say, 21 days after her birth.

It's as if the doctors are speaking Martian.

The parents need more information.

The doctors offer precious little. It causes severe lung damage and digestive problems, they say.

Nancy is concerned but does not know enough about the malady to be scared. Days later, a specialist gives her cause.

Cystic fibrosis is a children's disease that causes mucus to thicken and clog tubes, ducts, and passageways in the body. The baby will have trouble gaining weight. She will battle frequent respiratory infections. She will taste like salt. Her lungs will fail.

Why?

They don't know. Only later were tests developed that identified the defective gene that causes CF inherited by the child from both parents.

The prognosis, the specialist tells them, is gloomy.

The Simmonses stare, stunned.

How long?

Maybe seven years.

Only God knows why their daughter was born this way. They are parents now. Whatever happens they have to be strong. Whatever time God gives them with their daughter they will cherish. Whatever it takes, they will make her life as normal as they can.

They bring her home to Merritt Island the day they learn the diagnosis.

At 2 months old, Robyn is sleeping in a misting tent that Bill framed with scrap metal and covered with plastic sheeting stretched over two-thirds of her crib, fastened to the rails.

Every day, to reduce the risk of infection, they sterilize the nebulizer and wash the plastic with acid. Every chance she gets, Nancy nuzzles her baby. She likes to feel her child's breath on her cheek, and marvel at this . . . this perfect child.

Sometimes she wonders whether the doctors are wrong.

Robyn feels normal, soft and cuddly in her arms. She looks normal: At 6 months, she favors the Gerber baby. Her brown hair rises in a Kewpie peak. Her eyes are brown saucers. Her nose an adorable pink dollop. She smells normal.

Sometimes, swept up in the waves of her enormous love, Nancy presses her lips against her daughter's chubby cheeks.

And then she knows the doctors are right.

Salt.

Her baby tastes like salt.

Robyn swims, snorkels, jumps on the trampoline, and does cartwheels. As a reward for breaking her habit of biting her nails to the quick, she persuades her parents to buy her a minibike. But mostly, she dances.

Although she worries about exposing Robyn to sniffles and germy hands, Nancy enrolls her 3-year-old in the Village School of Dance in Cocoa.

She shines.

Five years later, in her first recital, "A Chance to Dance for You," the 8-year-old wears a pink tutu, matching crown, and a smile that even absent a missing tooth shimmers like a string of pearls.

In 1980, she joins the School of Southern Ballet Theatre. Commitment takes on a new meaning.

Mornings, she endures nebulizer treatments. Then she eats a hearty breakfast, sometimes four centercut pork chops. CF patients risk becoming malnourished

because thick secretions block the pancreas, preventing enzymes that digest fats and proteins from reaching the intestines. She chases the chops with pills to maintain and promote weight gain.

Then it's off to school. Afterward, she climbs in her mother's car, eats, and does her homework during the 90-minute drive to Orlando. They get home around 11 p.m. and engage in a session of postural drainage, which involves Nancy drumming on Robyn's back to loosen the mucus from her lungs.

Though the routine is rigorous, Robyn doesn't mind. For her, she will say years later, dance "is like a tickle inside your stomach that develops into a whirlwind, and the wind moves you with the music."

It moves her far from the nebulizer. Far from the pills. Far from school days lost to raging fevers and strep throat.

When she dances, it's as though she's nestled in her dad's arms.

She feels safe.

She feels special.

She feels normal.

Each birthday brings parties with bunches of friends, buckets of chicken, hunks of watermelon, and rounds of hugs. And each birthday carries with it a threat: This could be the year.

Nancy can't push the fear from her mind. But, it never leaks out. As Robyn butts against each deadline, age 7, age 8, age 10, the CF experts keep moving the barrier.

And the hope grows.

After a summer with the San Francisco Ballet in 1983, Robyn expresses an interest in performing with the Joffrey Ballet to Russell Sultzbach, a ballet master with Southern Ballet, who performed with the Joffrey for seven years in the 1970s.

Sultzbach puts in a good word with Robert Joffrey, the noted dancer/choreographer.

When Joffrey sees her, he is surprised at her size.

Joffrey—maybe 5-foot-2 in platform shoes—tells Robyn she is too small. Despite sometimes consuming 6,000 calories a day—triple what the average person eats—the 14-year-old would not look out of place on Romper Room.

She is barely 4 feet tall and weighs 70 pounds immediately after a pork chop breakfast. She has a slightly distended abdomen, noticeable enough that her chief adjustment in ballet class has always been suck in your rib cage or tuck in your tummy.

A year later, Robyn is maturer, sturdier for the demanding Joffrey. She dances with the company during summer appearances in San Antonio from 1984–86. She performs a duet in "Ramonda," a solo in "Don Quixote."

By 1988, she is ready to move to New York and dance with the developing Joffrey 2 troupe. Joffrey dies that year.

Shaken, she hangs up her pointe shoes.

Her hiatus lasts six months. She shakes off the rust and grief during a summer at the North Carolina School of Performing Arts.

Later, she enrolls at the University of South Florida. She is cast in solos in two productions. In addition to her course load, each day, she practices up to six hours.

That Christmas, her body betrays her. She is in the grip of bronchitis. The only thing that keeps her from a hospital bed is her weight: at 5-foot-4, 114 pounds, she's the heaviest she's ever been.

Classes missed because of colds and respiratory infections start to pile up, as do practices for the spring performance. She dances the spring show, then visits her parents. And suddenly, she falls sick with her first major CF infection.

Doctors prescribe powerful antibiotics. Her weight dips to 98 pounds. Her lungs are ravaged by scar tissue; they fall to 60 percent efficiency.

After she recovers, she sees her doctor. The news is bad.

Your lungs will never fully recover, the doctor tells her. The right lower lobe is almost completely useless. With each infection, things will worsen.

The words aren't sticking.

Your body, he tells her, can't take the beating.

Confusion crosses her face. Until now, dancing has been a boon, helping loosen mucus in the airways, strengthening her heart and lungs. Now, the disease is casting a longer shadow over her life. Dancing was not what she did, but who she was.

Her soul aches at the words she knows come next.

"Do you want to live, or do you want to dance and die?"

"I felt like, 'There goes my dream. Now what do I do?' The only thing I've done all my life is dance. That's been my title—ballerina—with my family, friends, my colleagues. It's been my success in life. I felt sad, and I felt like a big disappointment."

She chooses life.

In a way, it is a relief. No more long hours. No more staying up late. No more coughing up blood after practice.

She can relax. Slow down. Embrace the disease that is choreographing her life. Come to terms with who Robyn Simmons was.

She had never intended to pursue college. But now college looks attractive. Because she likes to write, she decides to follow that path.

That changes when she lands an internship at the U.S. Attorney's Office in Tampa. There, she meets Steven DeKeyser, a lanky, ex-college basketball player turned budget analyst. He shares her passion for rollerblading and doesn't bolt the next time she's knocked flat by a lung infection.

They marry in March 1997 and settle in Lutz, near Tampa. A year later, she graduates with honors with a degree in marketing and management. She wraps up an MBA in 13 months.

But her body is crashing. She is hospitalized for the first time in 1998 with her first bout of Pseudomonas aeruginosa, the most common infection for CF patients, a bacterium that can cause increased inflammation of the respiratory tract. Antibiotics can reduce the attacks but never completely evict pseudomonas from the lungs. Robyn, now an administrative manager, collapses twice at work. She is missing days.

And she is missing something else. A baby. Unlike some career women, she doesn't want to wait for later.

Later may never come.

Still, she knows having a baby may take a miracle. For many CF women, conception is no easy thing.

But she wants to try, she tells Steven. If there is a chance.

If you want to have this baby, I'm right there, he tells her. If not, we'll adopt.

To explore the prospect, she pays Dr. Mark Rolfe, a CF expert, a visit.

"All I want to know is," she says—pleads really—"is it even possible?"

Rolfe hedges.

"Yes, it is definitely possible," he tells her. "But . . . He looks into her hazel eyes, serious. "Is it reasonable for you to have children?"

Reasonable.

Reasonable?

When has this disease ever been reasonable? CF has been a dark moon progressively eclipsing the light in her life. And now, it is threatening this, something so basic, so natural, so . . . normal. Is it reasonable to live always in its shadow?

She has her answer. She combs through her blond-streaked brown hair with her fingers, her face brightening at the possibilities.

She chooses life.

"I knew I had to try to have this baby. This was something I needed to complete for my husband and myself. I had said, even if I did pass away at birth, or in a few years, at least I felt that I gave my husband a son, my mom and dad a grandchild. I had something to carry on."

Eight months into her pregnancy, Robyn can barely move. Her breathing is labored. Her chest is heavy, as if a boulder rests on her ribs. And her mind is troubled.

What if the baby has CF?

Easy. Her parents provided her the gift of normalcy, a can-do attitude. She'll do the same.

What if she never has the chance to see her child venture its first steps or hear it mew "Mama"?

Not so easy. Steven promises he'll tell their child his mother loved him more than words can say.

Her water breaks around 2 a.m. Sept. 24. Steven drives her to Tampa General Hospital. In the delivery room, Robyn is told not to push. Doctors fear during such exertion she may rupture a lung. The doctor positions himself at her feet, and with every contraction, tugs on the baby.

Soon, a robust shriek rings out and grows into a hearty cry. Robyn cranes her neck and sees her child on a scale. She examines the longish beet-red child, an impressive 7 pounds, 8 ounces.

Doctors and nurses count his fingers and toes, swab him down. He is handed to his mother. Robyn examines the child, her son. Perfect. She feels his tiny heartbeat drum against her chest and looks up at Steven and her mother, beaming.

And she tells her son his name.

Madison.

And suddenly she feels something, a familiar tickle rising in her tummy.

Her soul is dancing.

EDITING VOICE AND COLOR

William Blundell, author of *The Art and Craft of Feature Writing* (New American Library, 1986), which was based on a guide he developed for reporters at *The Wall Street Journal,* says a conversational quality makes readers feel that the writer is talking informally and directly to them.

"The building of reader-writer intimacy begins with the writer's attitude," Blundell writes. When a writer strives for a one-on-one conversation, the resulting story is free of stuffiness and formality. A conversational writer "tests whatever he thinks of writing with one question: *Would this be the way I'd tell it over drinks with an interested, intelligent friend?*"

Good copy editors are aware of the various techniques—such as posing questions, using colloquialisms and even slang, and writing in sentence fragments—that writers use to provide an informal tone. Writers striving for such a tone also have been known to invent words. The attentive copy editor knows when these techniques are being used for effect, as opposed to being used inadvertently because of sloppy writing. The following example includes several of these approaches:

> Bernie Richmond is a most happy fella.
>
> He's the kind of guy who, when the weather's drizzly and your hair is frizzy and you're soaking wet and just want somebody to empathize, will say: "The sun is out—it's just on the other side of those clouds!"
>
> Grrrrrrrr.
>
> What is it about perpetually perky people anyway? How can they be so relentlessly upbeat? And why do so many of us find it annoying?
>
> Happy folks "have a radically different philosophy than the average person," says Albert Ellis, a New York psychologist and author of *How to Stubbornly Refuse to Make Yourself Miserable.*

Blundell reminds us that "when people talk they sometimes use exclamations, ejaculations, one- or two-word sentence fragments and other forms avoided by many writers." To writers, he suggests, "Don't be afraid to try those." To copy editors, we suggest, Don't be afraid to let writers use those. If they're effective as storytelling tools, don't feel compelled to edit them out. You run the risk not only of offending the writer and assignment editor but also of producing a stylistically correct, but stultifyingly bland, story.

None of this is to say that all stories with a strong voice or conversational tone are off-limits to good copy editing. Profanity, obscenity and ethnic or racial parodies are always inappropriate, for example. Also, writers sometimes get carried away. The voice in the story may be inappropriate for the story's subject matter—too lighthearted, too flip, too sarcastic. The conversational techniques may be done to excess.

"Too many question marks, exclamations, fragments divert the reader from the substance of the tale to the performance of its author," Blundell points out, "and no one buys the paper to watch writers tap-dance through it."

Typically, though, the assignment editor will recognize and correct problems with the voice in a story long before the story makes it to the copy desk. Nonetheless, copy editors sometimes do have to make judgment calls regarding overdone punctuation and excessive use of conversational techniques. They must make their decisions in accordance with common sense and their newspapers' style guide. And, as editors continue to blur the line between hard-news writing and feature writing to make stories more appealing, copy editors will be making more of these calls.

Discretion and judgment are the best guidelines we can offer to copy editors working on feature stories. Or, to put it another way: Apply the rules of good copy editing—but know when to back off.

TRIMMING FEATURES

Now we come to the problem of what to do when the story runs longer than the space set aside for it. In the last chapter we asked you to think of trimming the hard-news story as performing a surgical procedure. The kinds of stories we have discussed in this chapter require even more surgical care. Editors can ruin a story if they fail to understand what the reporter is doing. Because stories are often told chronologically or the facts are arranged in blocks, cutting from the bottom is out of the question.

Then there's the temptation to shorten the story by eliminating some of the colorful descriptions and details in anecdotes. This sin has become even less forgivable as newspapers strive to improve the quality of their writing. Reporters are being encouraged to spend time creating clever leads and flowing narratives. Yet all too often, after an insensitive copy editor is finished with a story, the color is gone, as well as the transitions that made the copy flow elegantly. All that's left is a lifeless collection of words.

Don't misunderstand us. We're not advising copy editors to leave unneeded, flowery passages in stories just to satisfy the ego of reporters who fancy themselves budding literary geniuses. We're saying that everyone in journalism should be sensitive to the need to make newspaper copy more readable. If an anecdote or colorful writing helps achieve that goal, good editors will try to find other passages to cut. But if the story is clear and doesn't need linguistic flourishes to be interesting, editors should take them out and leave as many facts as possible.

EDITING COPY FROM THE WIRE SERVICES 8

Organizations such as the Associated Press are called wire services because they used to use telegraph wires to send their stories. Of course, they no longer do. These days, their material gets to news outlets via satellites rather than over land. However, the term "wire service" has been used for more than a century, and old terminology dies hard, so you'll still hear it. Increasingly, though, you'll also hear the term "news services."

If you've had a media history class, you know the story of how the wire services came about. Throughout the 19th century, several newspapers made efforts to share news with papers in other cities. Most of these press associations sputtered or died. The AP came into existence in the mid-1800s and provided news to one—and only one—newspaper in each city. Papers that weren't lucky enough to be chosen members of the AP had to scramble to get national and international news. So, two newspaper chains, Scripps-Howard and Hearst, started their own services to rival the AP and began to sell news to any newspaper willing to pay for it. In 1958 these services combined to form United Press International. However, when UPI started having financial problems in the 1970s, it began to cut its newsgathering operations. Its future as a major news supplier looked dim in the mid-1990s.

But that doesn't leave the AP with a monopoly. Several years ago, major newspapers and newspaper chains began to market their stories to other papers. They formed their own news services, independent of AP, to sell their stories to papers throughout the nation. If you glance at the bylines in your hometown paper, you may see stories written by reporters at the *Washington Post*, *Miami Herald*, the *New York Times* and other papers. You also may find stories from the London-based Reuters news service.

When a newspaper subscribes to a service, stories from that service are fed directly into the newspaper's computer. Editors call them up on their screens much as they do locally written stories. In theory, copy editors should handle wire stories as they do local material. In reality, they don't.

Perhaps the major difference between local and wire stories is that the latter often need to be cut more drastically. News services write their stories for newspapers all over the country, so they cover stories in detail and assume that local papers will use what they need. Larger papers will have the space to run their stories at length, whereas smaller papers will trim 1,000-word stories down to two paragraphs in the world news roundup. The result is that the AP or *Washington*

Post story in your local paper may be only a small part of the original story.

A second key difference between editing wire copy and editing local copy is that wire editors often need to combine stories. On papers that receive news from more than one news service, wire editors will get two or more stories about major events. They may find some good information in the AP version of the event and some important details in the *Washington Post* or *New York Times* version. The wire editor may write a story that includes facts from each story. These stories usually get bylines that say something like "From the wire services." If the bulk of the story is the AP version, the story may have the AP byline, but a note at the end of the story will credit the *Post* or *Times*.

Cutting and rewriting wire stories takes time. That brings us to another fact of life. At some small papers, editors are pressed for time, so they "railroad" wire stories, meaning that they run them in the paper without having edited them. We hope you never have to do that.

In this chapter we concentrate on cutting wire stories down to size and combining stories from two wire services to make one story that will better serve your readers.

CUTTING WIRE COPY

In the previous two chapters, we discuss trimming stories—making minor cuts to get them to fit the space. In this chapter we're talking about making major cuts, slashing stories so that they're only half or even a third as long as the originals. Wire editors make cuts that size every day. (On occasion, locally written copy must be cut. You should be even more careful in these cases. You're dealing with the copy of a colleague—a colleague who could make your life difficult if you go overboard.) Here are some goals to keep in mind when you're making major cuts to a wire story:

1. Good editors preserve as much information as possible. They get rid of needless duplication and windy digressions before they start removing facts from stories. But they avoid taking out all the color and vivid descriptions that give a story life.

2. Good editors keep as much of the reporter's writing style as possible and maintain the story's tone. If the writer has shown a deft touch in writing a lighthearted story, editors shouldn't turn it into a snoozer.

3. Good editors follow the doctor's credo: First, do no harm. Trimming for space is never a good excuse for introducing error into a story. When editors make dramatic cuts in a story, they have many opportunities for error. They may misstate complicated issues while trying to reduce several paragraphs of explanation to a few sentences. Or they may present information out of

context when they start trimming the background. Or, as we mention in Chapter 6, they may chop out a whole block in a story and create an unsupported lead.

4. Good editors watch out for *headless snakes*. These errors crawl into copy when editors delete a paragraph or sentence with a person's first name and identification. Then, a few paragraphs later, the person is quoted again—but referred to by last name only.

5. Good editors make cuts judiciously. The days of mindless hacking from the bottoms of stories have passed. Good editors can explain why they make their cuts.

Try trimming a story from the AP. It's not a bad story. It probably appeared in many newspapers without much editing. However, space in our paper is tight, so you have to cut the story to fit the space set aside for it. After you've edited the story, you'll have the opportunity to compare your editing with that of an experienced copy editor.

The following AP story just exceeds 325 words. Cut it by about 70 words to fit the space available.

JACKSON, Miss. (AP)—A former college president facing trial next month on embezzlement charges was captured in California hours after he became a fugitive by skipping a hearing in his case.

Lewis Nobles Jr., ousted in 1993 after 25 years as president of Mississippi College, was arrested at a San Francisco hotel about midnight Thursday, said Laura Henry, a spokeswoman for the FBI's Jackson office.

Nobles, who apparently flew to San Francisco from Memphis, will be returned to Mississippi as soon as possible, Henry said.

Nobles, 69, is charged with mail fraud, money laundering, tax evasion, and transporting women across state lines for sex. His trial is due to begin Feb. 7.

The FBI claims Nobles, who was named president of the school in 1968, began siphoning off donations in 1978 and embezzled more than $3 million that he spent on prostitutes, gifts and investments. The statute of limitations permits authorities to go back only five years for prosecution.

Thursday's hearing in U.S. District Court was to be on defense attempts to keep most of the material found in Lewis' office on Aug. 3, 1993, the day he resigned, from being used at the trial. U.S. District Judge William Barbour issued an arrest warrant when Nobles did not show.

Authorities say they found receipts for $2 million in donations the school business office says it never received; $27,844 in cash; books on how to hide money overseas; and a bottle of deadly strychnine.

Nobles has said the money went to needy students at Mississippi College, a Baptist-affiliated school that is the oldest private college in the state.

Nobles' wife and other family members said they last saw him Tuesday. They were fully cooperating with the FBI, said David W. Johnson Jr., special agent in charge of the FBI for Mississippi.

The FBI found Nobles' 1992 Oldsmobile in a Memphis airport Thursday night, Henry said. Authorities received permission from Nobles' family to search the vehicle before it was returned to his wife.

Now look below at the reasoning the experienced editor went through as she read the story. We hope you caught all the problems she did. (For instance, she found two inconsistencies.) If you didn't cut the story the same way she did, don't be overly concerned. Compare your reasoning with hers. You may find places where your thinking is better.

JACKSON, Miss. (AP)—A former college president facing trial next month on embezzlement charges was captured in California hours after he became a fugitive by skipping a hearing in his case.

EDITOR: *Lead is a tad wordy. We don't need to say when his trial is in the first graf of the story. His capture is what's newsworthy. We can save the information about how he became a fugitive for the second graf.*

Lewis Nobles Jr., ousted in 1993 after 25 years as president of Mississippi College, was arrested at a San Francisco hotel about midnight Thursday, said Laura Henry, a spokeswoman for the FBI's Jackson office.

EDITOR: *The fact that Henry is with the Jackson FBI office is unimportant.*

Nobles, who apparently flew to San Francisco from Memphis, will be returned to Mississippi as soon as possible, Henry said.

EDITOR: *"As soon as possible" can go. The only reason to mention when he'll be returned is if there was going to be a delay.*

Nobles, 69, is charged with mail fraud, money laundering, tax evasion, and transporting women across state lines for sex. His trial is due to begin Feb. 7.

EDITOR: We can recast this sentence so that we don't end up starting with "Nobles" again. We should also drop the "due to begin" as excess verbiage. The trial either begins on the 7th or it doesn't. If it doesn't we haven't committed a mortal sin—the best information available right now is that it's set to begin Feb. 7.

The FBI claims Nobles, who was named president of the school in 1968, began siphoning off donations in 1978 and embezzled more than $3 million that he spent on prostitutes, gifts and investments. The statute of limitations permits authorities to go back only five years for prosecution.

EDITOR: "Claims" is a loaded word, implying that we don't believe the FBI. Also, we said in the lead that he spent 25 years as president of the school, so we don't need to repeat that here by giving the year he started.

Thursday's hearing in U.S. District Court was to be on defense attempts to keep most of the material found in Lewis' office on Aug. 3, 1993, the day he resigned, from being used at the trial. U.S. District Judge William Barbour issued an arrest warrant when Nobles did not show.

EDITOR: AP swapped the guy's first and last names here, referring to Lewis's office rather than Nobles' office. We need to call to verify that it's "Lewis Nobles" not "Nobles Lewis." Also, the sentence about the statute of limitations belongs in this graf. Defense is clearly trying to get around the statute by barring evidence found within the last five years. Another question for AP: The lead says he was ousted; here it says he resigned. Did he get canned? Or was he pressured into quitting?

Authorities say they found receipts for $2 million in donations the school business office says it never received; $27,844 in cash; books on how to hide money overseas; and a bottle of deadly strychnine.

EDITOR: This graf is fine.

Nobles has said the money went to needy students at Mississippi College, a Baptist-affiliated school that is the oldest private college in the state.

EDITOR: His defense is pretty interesting. I'll try to keep that.

Nobles' wife and other family members said they last saw him Tuesday. They were fully cooperating with the FBI, said David W. Johnson Jr., special agent in charge of the FBI for Mississippi.

EDITOR: The fact that his family is cooperating isn't especially newsworthy.

The FBI found Nobles' 1992 Oldsmobile in a Memphis airport Thursday night, Henry said. Authorities received permission from Nobles' family to search the vehicle before it was returned to his wife.

EDITOR: The last sentence doesn't add important information.

When our editor was finished, almost 70 words were gone from the story and its writing had been improved. Here's her final version:

JACKSON, Miss. (AP)—A former college president facing trial on embezzlement charges was captured in California just hours after becoming a fugitive. Lewis Nobles Jr., ousted in 1993 after 25 years as president of Mississippi College, failed to show for a pretrial hearing Thursday, said FBI spokeswoman Laura Henry. U.S. District Judge William Barbour issued an arrest warrant.

Nobles, 69, apparently flew to San Francisco from Memphis, Henry said. He was arrested in a San Francisco hotel about midnight and will be returned to Mississippi, she said.

On Feb. 7, Nobles stands trial on charges of mail fraud, money laundering, tax evasion, and transporting women across state lines for sex.

The FBI says Nobles began siphoning off donations in 1978 and embezzled more the $3 million that he spent on prostitutes, gifts and investments.

The statute of limitations permits authorities to go back only five years for prosecution. Thursday's hearing in U.S. District Court was to be on the defense attempts to keep most of the material found in Nobles office on the day he left—Aug. 3, 1991—from being used at the trial.

Authorities say they found receipts for $2 million in donations the school business office says it never received; $27,844 in cash; books on how to hide money overseas; and a bottle of deadly strychnine.

Nobles has said the money went to needy students at Mississippi College, a Baptist school that is the oldest private college in the state.

Nobles' wife and other family members said they last saw him Tuesday. The FBI found Nobles' 1992 Oldsmobile in a Memphis airport Thursday night, Henry said.

COMBINING STORIES

Most larger newspapers subscribe to more than one news service. Often, each news service includes details in its stories that the others don't have, complicating life for wire editors. Not only must they cut stories to fit, they also must combine stories so that readers will have the best information available. Typically, wire editors will take a few paragraphs from various news services' stories and arrange them all into a new story. Doing that is not as easy as it sounds. In addition to the challenges editors face whenever they edit and cut the stories, they have two new problems:

- *Context.* When you're rearranging paragraphs, misplacing one of them is easy. For example, suppose that you're combining two wire service stories—one about flooding in Texas and the other about flooding in Georgia. If you pull a great quote out of the Georgia story and inadvertently stick it after a paragraph about the Texas flood, the reader will assume that the quote came from a Texan.

- *Transitions and smoothness.* When you combine stories, you must make sure that the new story reads seamlessly. Keep in mind that all wire-service stories are not written the same way. One service's account of an event may be written in a very matter-of-fact tone. Another may have more of the writer's individual voice. Your combined story shouldn't sound as though a committee threw it together. Good transitions can help achieve the right effect.

Let's look at an example. Editors at the *Orlando Sentinel* decided to run a short story about some letter bombings in Austria. Jon, a wire editor, is assigned the task of preparing a four-inch story for the paper's A section, the front section where most of the international news appears. On his computer, Jon calls up the AP budget and finds a story slugged "BC-Austria-Letterbombs." Let's take a little time to talk about wire-service protocol. The wire services prepare different versions of their stories for morning and afternoon papers. They do this partly because of the differences in writing styles and partly so that morning and afternoon papers in the same market won't have exactly the same stories. Stories for morning papers are slugged AM, those for afternoon papers are slugged PM, and stories that can be used by either afternoon or evening papers are slugged BC (for "both cycles"). This story was slugged BC-Austria-Letterbombs; Jon knows he can use it but will have to be careful that its style follows that of the *Sentinel*.

Jon can call up the AP version on the *Sentinel*'s computer system and view it side-by-side with the Reuters version of the same story. That way, he can easily see the differences between the two wire stories as he reads them.

The AP version:

1. VIENNA, Austria (AP)—The government issued a nationwide alert today after three letter bombs apparently sent by extreme right-wingers were discovered and defused by police.

2. A surge in attacks the past 10 months against people with links to foreign workers has been blamed on neo-Nazis.

3. Two of the bombs were sent Tuesday, one to a publishing house that prints Slovene books in the southern city of Klagenfurt and the other to an agency that assists Turkish workers in the western town of Dornbirn.

4. The third, discovered and defused early today, was sent to a paper manufacturer in Hallein, south of Salzburg. An accompanying letter accused the employers of hiring foreign workers over Austrians.

5. Vienna Mayor Helmut Zilk, a strong advocate of minority rights, lost part of his left hand in December when a letter he was opening exploded. Three other people with links to foreigners were also injured in separate letter bombings the same month.

6. A police bomb expert lost both arms, and two other officers were injured Aug. 24 when a pipe bomb exploded after being removed from a school that teaches bilingual classes to Austria's Slovene minority in Klagenfurt.

7. Two suspected neo-Nazis are in investigative custody for possible complicity in the earlier attacks. Two of the most recent letters had the same return address as those last December, news reports said.

8. Interior Minister Franz Loeschnak told Austrian radio the latest bombs were similar in construction to the ones sent in December.

9. The Interior Ministry issued a warning today urging care in opening any envelopes with unfamiliar return addresses that bulge suspiciously at the bottom.

The Reuter's version:

1. VIENNA, Austria (Reuters)—Austria was on nationwide alert for letter bombs Wednesday after a judge presiding over a neo-Nazi trial in Vienna warned that a new campaign could be under way in the campaign before general elections Sunday.

2. Interior Minister Franz Loeschnak said investigation of three letter bombs intercepted and defused in the past 24 hours indicated neo-Nazis may be responsible.

3. "From notes enclosed with the bombs, it is clear that this action is motivated by hatred of foreigners and that it is more likely to come from right-wing extremists," he told Austrian state television.

4. Loeschnak said police had no hot leads.

5. Austrian radio quoted Judge Klothilde Eckbrecht as saying there were indications at least 10 such devices had been mailed. Three were intercepted Tuesday and Wednesday and defused.

6. Their targets were a publisher of Slovenian books in the southern city of Klagenfurt, a foreigners' advice centre and a paper factory employing a large number of foreign workers.

7. "There are indications that there may be altogether 10 letter bombs on their way. This is according to Judge Klothilde Eckbrecht, who is currently conducting the trial of neo-Nazi Gottfried Kuessel," the radio said.

8. The Interior Ministry, under fire for failing to inform provincial authorities, declined to comment.

Jon recognizes that there's more information in these two stories than he can fit into four column-inches. He's got room for only the basics. He figures his readers will want these questions answered: Who were the victims and who were the culprits, why did they do it, and just how big a deal is this, anyway?

Jon believes Reuters stories are often more lively reading than AP stories. But on this story, the Reuters lead is awkwardly worded; the bit about "the campaign under way in the campaign before general elections" is confusing. Also, although the lead brings up a connection between the letter bombs and the elections, the story never explains what the connection might be—in fact, the elections do not appear again in the story.

Jon likes the AP lead better. It tells what happened and, by introducing the idea of a "nationwide alert," it gives a sense of how important officials consider these bombings. Because he doesn't have time to do a complete rewrite of the story, Jon decides to use the AP lead, making only one change. He substitutes "Wednesday" for "today" because the *Sentinel* is a morning paper. (Afternoon newspapers often refer to "today," "yesterday," and "tomorrow"; morning papers usually refer to the day of the week.)

Jon is satisfied with this lead:

> VIENNA, Austria—The government issued a nationwide alert Wednesday after three letter bombs apparently sent by extreme right-wingers were discovered and defused by police.

Now he wants to explain who planted the bombs. The AP story is vague. It takes too long (six paragraphs) to tie the neo-Nazis to the bombings and doesn't say who's accusing the neo-Nazis of the crimes. The Reuters story explains both points in its second paragraph, so Jon uses that one:

> Interior Minister Franz Loeschnak said investigation of three letter bombs intercepted and defused in the past 24 hours indicated neo-Nazis may be responsible.

Jon needs to answer the two "why" questions: Why was a "nationwide alert" sounded? Why were the bombs planted? He thinks the reason for the national alert is explained quickly and clearly in the fifth paragraph of the Reuters story:

Austrian radio quoted Judge Klothilde Eckbrecht as saying there were indications at least 10 such devices had been mailed. Three were intercepted Tuesday and Wednesday and defused.

That works. They've issued a nationwide alert because seven bombs haven't been found. But why would a judge know so much about these bombings? Jon needs to explain the judge's role in all this. So, after Judge Klothilde Eckbrecht's name, Jon adds the clause, "who is presiding over the trial of a neo-Nazi in Vienna."

The story's shaping up. Jon likes the judge's quote from Reuters about the letter bombs being linked to a "hatred of foreigners," but there isn't room. He still needs to tell where the bombs went off. The Reuters version answers this question in fewer words. Also, Reuters emphasizes that the targets were associated with foreign workers, thus hinting at the "hatred of foreigners" angle. So Jon uses the sixth paragraph in the Reuters story, changing the British spelling "centre" to "center":

Their targets were a publisher of Slovenian books in the southern city of Klagenfurt, a foreigners' advice center and a paper factory employing a large number of foreign workers.

Jon now edits his creation. He notices that Reuters spelled "letter-bomb" as one word in the lead and used the word "Slovenian" to refer to the people, but the AP spelled "letter bomb" as two words and used the adjective "Slovene." Jon checks with *Webster's New World Dictionary*, which the *Sentinel* uses to settle such disputes. It prefers "letter bomb" and "Slovenian." After he's satisfied that his copy is clean, he sends the story to the copy desk, where another editor will check his work and write the headline. At smaller newspapers, wire editors write their own heads and often are responsible for laying out pages that contain only wire stories. Here's the final story:

COMPILED FROM WIRE REPORTS

VIENNA, Austria—The government issued a nationwide alert Wednesday after three letter bombs apparently sent by extreme right-wingers were discovered and defused by police.

Interior Minister Franz Loeschnak said investigation of three letter bombs intercepted and defused in the past 24 hours indicated neo-Nazis may be responsible.

Austrian radio quoted Judge Klothilde Eckbrecht, who is presiding over the trial of a neo-Nazi in Vienna, as saying there were indications at least 10 such devices had been mailed. Three were intercepted Tuesday and Wednesday and defused.

Their targets were a publisher of Slovenian books in the southern city of Klagenfurt, a foreigners' advice center and a paper factory employing a large number of foreign workers.

From an original AP story of more than 250 words and a Reuters story of just over 200, Jon has created a story of only 112 words that covers most of the important facts.

WIRE EDITING AND NEWS JUDGMENT

Wire editors not only edit wire stories but also monitor the news services. As good wire editors read through the news services' offerings, they are alert not only for stories that ought to be in the paper but also that might be of interest to other staff members. For example, say that Congress has decided to cut millions in defense spending. If any companies in the area have contracts with the defense department, wire editors will check these stories carefully for local angles. Even if they find none, they'll forward the stories to an assignment editor or to reporters who normally cover local businesses.

At other times, wire editors forward stories to reporters to help them on their beats. Suppose that the Federal Communications Commission changes the way it licenses low-power television stations. The wire editor may send that story to a reporter who covers the communications industry. It may not spark a story today, but the reporter will appreciate having the information.

MATH AND THE JOURNALIST 9

People become journalists because they're no good at math. We've all heard that saying. There may be some truth to it. Even prestigious papers such as *The New York Times* have had to run corrections because reporters and editors messed up the numbers.

DOING BASIC MATH

This chapter is about numbers. We start with some basic mathematics and then we take a brief look at the statistics of opinion polling.

AVERAGES

Calculating an average may seem simple. You take a list of numbers, add them up, and divide by the number in the list. But sometimes this "average" may be misleading. Suppose that the following is the salary structure at a small TV station:

Anchor	$100,000
Reporter	$18,000
Reporter	$15,000
Reporter	$15,000
Reporter	$12,000

The company could correctly advertise that the average salary of its news staff is $32,000. That's the average you get by adding the five salaries and dividing by five. Yet when journalism graduates apply for jobs there, they will be disappointed when the station offers them a salary of $15,000 and tells them that's higher than some reporters get. These graduates assumed that "the average salary" would be representative of salaries at the station. In this case, they might feel as though they had been duped.

As with the job applicant, mathematicians want "averages" that reflect the real world. They have three ways of figuring averages, and then they pick the "average" that seems to fit the situation best.

- The *mean* is what most of us think of as the "average." The mean salary at the TV station is $32,000.

- Another way to figure the average is the *median*. When you call someone an "average" student, you are probably using this understanding of average. You mean that some students do better and some do worse. An average student performs in the middle. Mathematicians call this kind of average the *median*. It is the middle number in a list. Because the list of salaries at the TV station has five numbers, the median salary is the third one, $15,000.

- A third average is the *mode*. The mode is the most common number in the list. At the TV station, the most common salary, the mode, is $15,000.

Which is the correct "average"? All three are mathematically correct. Editors and reporters must make sure that they are using the most appropriate one. Be particularly careful when politicians or press releases use the term "average." It may be the one that best suits their spin on the story. Journalists, in particular copy editors, need to check the numbers themselves.

PERCENTAGES OF CHANGE

News stories frequently report change, such as: "Unemployment is up 10 percent"; "Senate wants to cut taxes 5 percent"; "SAT scores are down 6 percent"; "Stock market takes a 32 percent plunge." These figures are called "percentage of change." They probably present more problems for journalists than any other math procedure.

Say that an education writer doing a story about school growth comes across these enrollment figures:

	Last year	This year
Lincoln Elementary	400	500
Jefferson Elementary	300	400

One way to report the change is to say that each school grew by 100 students. That would be factual but not very meaningful. A better way to report the change is to use the percentage of change at each school. To figure the percentage of change, the reporter would follow these three steps:

1. Figure the amount of change by subtracting the smaller number from the larger number. The numbers for Lincoln Elementary would be 500 minus 400. The amount of change is 100.

2. Last year, 400 students attended Lincoln. Divide the amount of change (100) by last year's number (400): 100 divided by 400 equals .25.

3. Change the decimal into a percentage by multiplying by 100: .25 times 100 equals 25. The percentage of change is 25 percent. Because Lincoln has increased from 400 to 500, the reporter could write that 25 percent more students go to Lincoln this year than last year.

After figuring the percentage of change at Lincoln, the reporter could calculate the percentage of change at Jefferson. The story could then compare the percentages of change: Jefferson's enrollment grew 33 percent and Lincoln's grew 25 percent. In most instances, reporting the percentages of change adds more meaning to the story than just reporting the changes in the number of students.

Imagine that the reporter is working in a school district that is losing population. The numbers may look like this:

	Last year	This year
Lincoln Elementary	500	400
Jefferson Elementary	400	300

To calculate the percentage of change, we would follow the same steps:

1. Calculate the amount of change: 500 minus 400 equals 100.

2. Divide the amount of change by last year's total; last year's total was 500: 100 divided by 500 equals .20.

3. Multiple by 100 to get a percentage: 100 times .20 equals 20 or 20 percent.

The reporter could write that enrollment at Lincoln Elementary has declined 20 percent. Test your understanding by answering this question: By what percent has enrollment at Jefferson Elementary declined? The answer is at the end of the chapter.

PERCENTAGE POINTS AND PERCENTAGES

Reporting changes in tax rates presents a different problem for journalists. Suppose that the state sales tax is going up from 4 percent to 6 percent. Many journalists would be tempted to write that the sales tax will go up 2 percent. And they would be wrong. They need to apply the same mathematics to tax rates that we used in the school enrollment story.

Just as in the enrollment example, we subtract the numbers to find the amount of change. Subtract the old tax rate (4) from the new tax rate (6). Now here's the part that confuses many journalists. The reporter could report that the sales tax has gone up 2 percentage points. Think of it this way: When we subtracted 500 students from 600 students, we got 100 students, not 100 percent. When we subtract 4 percentage points from 6 percentage points, we get 2 percentage points.

Reporting that the sales tax is going up 2 percentage points may or may not satisfy our needs. Just as with the school enrollment story, we may want to figure the percentage of change. You do that by following the same steps we used earlier.

1. Figure the amount of change by subtracting the smaller number from the larger: 6 minus 4 equals 2.

2. Divide the amount of change (2) by the older number (4): 2 divided by 4 equals .50.

3. Multiply by 100 to get the percentage: 100 times .50 equals 50 percent.

Journalists could correctly report this information in two ways. They could write, "The state sales tax is going up 2 percentage points." Or they could write, "The state sales tax is going up 50 percent." The journalists will have to pick the one that best suits the story.

REPORTING RATES

The police reporter comes across these numbers: 500 people were murdered in Rosewood and 80 were murdered in Athens. Those numbers have little meaning unless they are related to the size of the city. A common way to do this is to report the rate per same number of citizens. Here are the data and the steps to follow to figure rates.

	Murders	Population
Athens	80	20,000
Rosewood	500	100,000

1. Divide the number of murders in a city by its population. For Athens, divide 80 by 20,000. The answer is .004. Do the same math with Rosewood and you get .005. That means there are .004 murders per person in Athens and .005 murders per person in Rosewood.

2. To most people, it seems both silly and confusing to report four-thousandths of a murder.

3. If you wanted to report those figures per 1,000 residents, multiply each of them by 1,000. For Athens, the answer is 4. For Rosewood, it's 5. Athens has 4 murders per 1,000 residents and Rosewood has 5 murders per 1,000. Those numbers are easier to understand.

4. If you wanted to report those figures per 10,000 residents, multiply by 10,000: .004 times 10,000 equals 40 and .005 times

10,000 equals 50. You could report that Athens has 40 murders per 10,000 residents and Rosewood has 50 murders per 10,000 people.

Another example: A reporter is doing a story about the most dangerous intersections in town. He discovers that Main Street and Union Avenue seems to be the city's most dangerous intersection because more accidents happen there. But he knows the information would be more accurate if it was presented as a rate based on the number of cars that pass through the intersection. Here's the information:

Intersection	Number of accidents	Number of cars
First and Grand	98	164,000
Main and Union	104	305,000
Second and Wilson	45	102,000

How many accidents per 10,000 cars did each intersection have? Do the math and check your answers with the ones at the end of the chapter.

Related to the reporting of rates is the reporting of odds. Reporters sometimes make careless mistakes. A paper recently reported that the chances of winning the state lottery were 77 million to one. Knowing that, a smart reporter would have bought a lottery ticket and quit the news business. In reality, the chances of winning the lottery were one in 77 million.

REPORTING POLLS

Opinion polls are a major part of political coverage and lifestyles pieces. Serious political polling began early in the 20th century. A magazine called *Literary Digest* did some of the most famous early polling in presidential races. In one edition of the magazine, editors printed a facsimile ballot and asked readers to vote for their favorite candidate and mail the ballot back to the magazine. Thousands did. The edition of the magazine that predicted the winner sold lots of copies. And when the magazine's prediction proved correct, editors knew they were on to something. For the next presidential election, editors found ways to increase the size of the sample. Again, the edition with the prediction was a big seller. And again, the magazine successfully predicted the winner.

Editors were enthusiastic. In 1936 they conducted the most elaborate—and most expensive—poll ever attempted. The magazine searched phonebooks and lists of car registrations for names and address. They mailed hundreds of thousands of postcards to homes and asked the residents to vote and mail them back. After tabulating all the votes, the magazine confidently predicted Alf Landon would be our next president.

Meanwhile, a young researcher named George Gallup was doing his own poll. He had a much, much smaller sample, but he predicted the election of Franklin Roosevelt.

The magazine learned a painful lesson. The size of the sample alone does not ensure success. In the 1930s the nation was in the midst of the Great Depression. Cars and phones were expensive. By surveying people who had cars and phones, the magazine had missed many of the factory workers, farmers and the unemployed who supported Roosevelt. The botched poll may be one reason you won't find the *Literary Digest* at any newsstands. Gallup used a more scientific way of drawing his sample, and today his name is synonymous with polls.

RANDOM SAMPLES AND MARGINS OF ERROR

Valid polls use random samples. The word random has a very specific meaning. In a random sample, every person has an equal chance of being polled. Serious pollsters make every effort to live up to that goal. In telephone polls, they select the phone numbers at random. If no one answers, they don't substitute another phone number. They keep calling that number. When someone answers the phone, poll takers select whom they will interview, perhaps asking for the oldest male or youngest adult. Even with all that effort, a true random sample is nearly impossible. Recluses, the homeless and the very busy are unlikely to be tracked down.

Critics of polls doubt that a sample of 2,000 people can truly reflect the entire population of the United States. Oddly enough, pollsters would agree.

Suppose that a coin is perfectly balanced. The odds of flipping it and getting heads are 50-50. If we flip the coin 10 times, we should get heads five times. However, we know that won't happen every time. Sometimes our 10 flips will yield six heads or six tails.

Statisticians would say that we have been taking samples of coin flips. We know that in the entire world, half the flips will be heads and half will be tails. However, we're not surprised that the results of our very small samples will differ slightly from what we know of the whole population.

In much the same way, pollsters know that when they sample people, their samples will not perfectly reflect the population every time. They call this *sampling error*. They use probability theory and other mathematical concepts to determine how close the match is likely to be. They may say that the *margin of error* may be plus or minus 3 percentage points.

A poll might say that Johnson is favored by 40 percent of the voters. If the poll were taken again, it is likely that the second poll may find that 39 percent back Johnson. A third poll may find that 42 percent support him. Mathematicians would say that all three polls are within the margin of error.

Here's where too many journalists get confused. They assume that the margin of error takes into account real errors made by the pollsters—things such as poorly worded questions or respondents who lie. But margin of error has nothing to do with these kinds of problems. Margin of error concerns only the mathematical likelihood that the sample is not perfectly representative of the general population.

When statisticians report the margin of error, they also report another statistic: the confidence level.

Think again about flipping coins. Could you flip a coin 10 times and get 10 heads? It won't happen often, but it is possible. Pollsters also know that occasionally their samples will miss the mark completely. It's possible that they might draw a random sample that has considerably more Democrats than Republicans. Pollsters again use math and statistical theories to calculate how often this is likely to happen. They call this statistic *confidence level*. If they may say the confidence level of a poll is 5 percent, they mean there is a 5 percent chance (or one chance in 20) that their sample won't be within the margin of error. There's one chance in 20 that the poll is completely wrong. It may say that candidate Johnson has 40 percent of the vote whereas in reality he has considerably more support or less support.

WRITING ABOUT POLLS

Sometimes journalists and the public overlook the importance of sampling error. A poll might say that Candidate Johnson is favored by 40 percent of the respondents and Candidate Brown by 38 percent of them. The sampling error is plus or minus 3 points. Many reporters might be tempted to write a story stating flatly that Jones is ahead of Brown by 2 percentage points. A more accurate story would point out that the difference is within the margin of error and that the race is too close to call.

Similar problems develop when polls find that a candidate has gained or lost support. Suppose that a poll on June 10 finds that Candidate Wilson is favored by 40 percent of the respondents. On June 11, a story breaks that Wilson was once convicted of drunken driving. A poll on June 12 finds that Wilson is now favored by 38 percent of respondents. The temptation is to report that the conviction has cost Wilson votes. In reality, the second poll is within the margin of error. Wilson may have lost votes, but that assumption can't be supported with these numbers.

Journalists also need to be aware of other problems in polls. People sometimes lie to pollsters. Or they give politically correct answers on questions about sensitive social issues. Or they misunderstand the questions. Or they refuse to answer the questions and hang up. Clearly, each of these actions is going to affect the accuracy of the poll. (And remember that these actions are not included in the margin of error.)

The wording of questions can also affect poll results. National polling companies such as Gallup try to ask questions that are as neutrally worded as possible. But some groups ask slanted questions to make their positions seem stronger politically. A group opposed to a tax increase might ask, "Do you favor Proposition 32, which would make our county taxes the highest in the state?" A group in favor of the tax might ask, "Do you favor Proposition 32, which would improve the quality of our schools?" Even if these two sets of polls were conducted the same night on the same people, they are likely to get different answers.

Because of all the possible reasons a poll might be off, journalists need to do a better job of understanding and reporting the pollsters used. They should report poll findings only after they are satisfied that the poll was properly done. The National Council on Public Polls lists twenty questions that journalists should ask before reporting polls. Among them are these:

- Who paid for the poll? The council says polls conducted by the staff of a political campaign are suspect. "These polls are conducted solely to help the candidate win—and for no other reason."

- When, how, and where was the poll done?

- Was it a dial-in poll, a mail-in poll or a subscriber-coupon poll? Newspapers, TV shows, and Web sites often invite readers to call or e-mail their opinions. Those polls are popular and fun. But the results of those polls are not trustworthy. The samples are not random, and advocates of one side of the argument can flood the switchboards or servers with scores of votes.

- What was the exact wording of the question? If the issue is complex, the story should report the question. At the very least, the reporter should judge whether the question is a neutral one.

- What was the margin of error?

- How many people were surveyed? Also, how many people did not respond to the survey? This last question is important. If a mail survey is sent to 4,000 people and only 1,000 return it, the validity of the results is questionable.

Answers:
Jefferson Elementary enrollment has declined 25 percent.
First and Grand has nearly 6 accidents per 100,000 cars; Main and Union, 3.4; Second and Wilson, 4.4.

WRITING HEADLINES **10**

Writing headlines is something of an art. The headline "artist" must create a picture of an entire story in just a few words—and make it appealing to readers. A good headline not only tells the story but also sells the story. Much of the time, the headline is the key factor in a reader's decision to read a story or skip it. Hours of work by the reporter and assignment editor will be wasted if the headline writer doesn't come up with the right eight or ten words.

As newspapers begin to offer their stories online, headlines take on even greater importance. Some research suggests that unlike print readers, online readers see the headlines before they see the pictures.

We're not suggesting that you write headlines to hype stories or trick people into starting to read stories. We're encouraging you to present the news as interestingly as you can.

SIX STEPS FOR BEGINNERS

Knocking out heads is second nature to the pros—something they don't even think about, like swimming or riding a bike. But headline writing involves some definite steps. If you're a beginner, you'll have an easier time if you follow suggestions made by the late Martin Gibson, a journalism professor at the University of Texas:

1. Read and understand the story before you start to write the headline.
2. Write a rough headline, experimenting with word combinations that will form one or more lines of the headline.
3. Choose specific, precise words.
4. Make each word count.
5. Use action verbs—and some creativity.
6. Start over if you're stuck.

Sounds easy enough, right? Maybe; maybe not. Some of these steps are easier said than done. Let's look at them more closely.

Step 1. *Read and understand the story.* If you don't know what the reporter is saying, you can't explain it in 10 words or fewer. If you write an inaccurate headline, you not only fail to serve the reader but also hurt the credibility of the newspaper.

Of course, understanding a story means more than just mastering the facts. Copy editors also look at how a story is organized and at the tone the writer is using. If the story is serious, they don't put a lighthearted

139

headline on it. However, if they recognize that the reporter has worked hard to achieve a lighter tone, they write a head that's equally clever.

Copy editors also pay attention to whether the reporter has used attribution and qualification. If a reporter's story says the governor proposes a tax cut, the headline shouldn't say taxes are going down. Rather, it should hedge or "qualify" the information. For example: "Governor calls for lower taxes." If a story reports that a consumer group says a fast-food chain buys week-old meat, the head shouldn't find the chain guilty of that unsavory practice.

Step 2. *Write a headline-like sentence.* Experiment with various word combinations and story angles in your search for the perfect fit. As you'll learn in this chapter, you'll probably make some compromises in the quality of the head to get it to fit the space. But if your original idea for a headline isn't very good, by the time you've made all the compromises, you'll have something *really* awful.

In an article for Poynter.org, Jim Barger, sports editor of the *Pittsburgh Post-Gazette,* says good headlines should sound as much like conversation as possible. Barger says no one has ever said to a friend, "Woodley, defense propel Dolphins past NY." Admittedly, because of space concerns, headlines have to be written in truncated English. But they should sound as much like normal speech as possible.

Step 3. *Choose specific, precise words.* A one-word description of a head that's too general: boring. And a boring headline achieves none of the goals of good headline writing. You must examine every story to see what the key elements are and what makes this story different from others. Write heads that allow readers to visualize what happened. Look at this lead:

> A dump truck loaded with dirt slammed into a car, killing a family of four on State Road 58 Tuesday night.

Now read this headline:

Accident kills 4 people

There's nothing wrong with this headline factually. Four people did die in the accident. But it doesn't give readers a *picture* of what happened. How about:

Truck rams car; 4 die

In the following pairs of examples, notice how the second one is more precise, either helping the reader picture something more vividly or giving more specific information:

Study of journalism grades released
70% of journalism students get all A's

FBI chief wants stiffer punishment for criminals
FBI chief urges death penalty for all drug dealers

Mayor disagrees with Council on need for more police
Mayor calls Council's plan to hire more police 'crazy'

Child nearly drowns in river
Passer-by pulls baby from river

Always ask yourself: Is there a more specific way to say what I want to say? If so, use it. Is there a way I can work two angles into the headline instead of just one? If so, do it.

Step 4. Make each word count. Filling up headline space with unnecessary words—padding—may make a head fit but doesn't serve readers or the reporter who labored to produce the story. Say you're working on the copy desk of the student newspaper at Northern State University, where the football coach is named Jenson. Look at this headline:

NSU president raises Coach Jenson's salary

This head is packed with useless words. You don't need to say the "NSU president" is giving Jenson a raise—who else would be in a position to do that? You don't need to say both "coach" and "Jenson." Jenson's name is likely to be recognized on campus. If he's not well-known, you can refer to him simply as "coach." By taking these wasted words out, you give yourself room in the headline for a better angle. Some alternatives:

Jenson signs 3-year deal, gets $9,000 raise

Jenson gets raise despite losing record

Jenson rehired over faculty objections

Jenson rewarded after undefeated season

Size of Jenson's raise shocks faculty

Sometimes the padding in a headline can be subtle, as in this one:

Mayor testifies at bribery trial

When readers see the word "testifies," they will assume that the story is about a trial or some kind of legal hearing. You don't need to use both "trial" and "testifies" to get across the idea. Instead, you might try to work on another angle. What did the mayor say during this testimony?

'I took no bribes,' mayor testifies

Another padded headline:

FAA plans to investigate radar at airport here

You can delete "plans." Using an infinitive such as *to investigate* suggests that an investigation is planned to happen in the future. You rarely need the word "here." The only time you might use "here" in some heads is when the location is unexpected. A western Ohio paper might say "Major studio to make movie here" because movies aren't usually made in western Ohio. (Even then, a more specific head such as "Greenville to star in new movie" would be better.) With the space left by getting rid of "plans" and "here," you can dig another angle out of the story. Perhaps one of these:

FAA to investigate airport's faulty radar

FAA to investigate airport's costly radar

Step 5. *Use action verbs—and some creativity.* Consider this a commandment: Thou shalt forsake bland verbs. If a headline is bland, readers are likely to skip the story. You can improve your headlines (and most of your other writing) by second-guessing your choice of verbs. Colorful, active verbs give you a head start on bagging a reader. Check out these lively headlines:

Power outage enrages hospital patients

Court dashes hopes of anti-porn group

Council slashes funds to day-care center

Jones blasts prosecutor for 'witch hunt'

Study doubts vitamins fight cancer

Step 6. *Start over if you're stuck.* Agonizing to make a particular angle work just wastes time, a precious commodity on the copy desk. If an idea isn't working, abandon it. Look for a fresh angle and fresh word combinations.

MAKING HEADLINES LIVELY

Newspaper headlines are getting livelier. Although word plays, puns, and even rhymes have long been popular in sports sections, they now are spilling onto the front page. Also, many papers now have centerpiece packages on most open pages. These centerpieces have led to the development of art headlines, which resemble magazine headlines more than they do traditional newspaper headlines.

These headlines tax the cleverness of copy editors. Occasionally, you'll have a moment of inspiration and the perfect head will spring automatically onto your screen. Often, though, you will have to work to come up with something effective.

One strategy is to create a word play by relating the verb to the story, almost like a pun. But make sure that your pun actually helps tell the story rather than just shows off how clever you are. Here are some effective heads with word plays:

Zoning law flattens pancake house

Sea World deep-sixes undersea ride

Fort Pierce flags down stop on high-speed train

You'll come across lists of colorful heads in journalism publications such as *American Journalism Review* and newsletters put out by the Associated Press Managing Editors organization. You may not like some of the heads you'll see. After all, cleverness is in the eye of the beholder. In fact, you may run into copy desk chiefs who will reject headlines that other people would put on their lists of winners. Here are some heads that have been praised:

Nudists invite public to see how they live
(The Orlando Sentinel)

What to chew and eschew
(USA Today, on healthier eating)

Give your heart a break
(Newsday, on healthier living)

Suitcase bomb proves to be bag of duds
(The Oregonian [Portland])

Massage parlor rubs them the wrong way
(The Times-Picayune [New Orleans])

A hint for those times when you're in a creative funk, verbwise: Try the thesaurus. You'll be amazed at how often the perfect verb choice is there for the looking. Go on—try it. Select some verbs from recent headlines you've composed (or from writing you've done for other classes). Look up the verbs in a thesaurus; you'll probably find other verbs you'll wish you had used instead.

Another hint: If a story obviously calls for some clever turn of phrase but your clever juices have dried up, consult your dictionary. Dictionaries show how words are used by citing adages or common sayings we've all heard at one time or another. Sometimes these adages can provide the kernel for a great headline. In addition, dictionaries typically list colloquialisms that can spark a headline idea. For example, after listing several definitions of the word *high*, *Webster's New World Dictionary* offers definitions of *high and dry* and *high and mighty*. One of those might be turned into a play on words that would work well in a headline.

Jim Heinrich, a copy editor at the *Pittsburgh Post-Gazette*, described for the Poynter Institute (www.poynter.org) some rather unusual places he looks for inspiration. "My best tools for writing headlines are my rhyming dictionary, my dictionary, my thesaurus and www.imdb.com (the extraordinary Internet Movie Data Base)," he wrote.

He cautions that he isn't trying to write headlines that rhyme. "Instead, I look up words that rhyme with or sound like a key word, phrase, name or concept in the story." Seeing the list of words often sparks the idea for a word play. He uses imdb.com as a word-association tool. He uses the site's search engine to find how the word has been used in the movies. "Just type in the relevant words and get immediate inspiration," he says.

Heinrich adds, "Many good headlines come from thinking of words that *sound* like key words you're writing about." Some art headlines and hammer headlines that Heinrich likes:

Carnival knowledge

Bra, humbug

Paradise lofts

Show me the monkey

Believe in ferries

One of his favor tactics is "to take common quotes and phrases and give them a twist:"

America discovers Columbus

All things come to those who waitress

Woolf in sheep's clothing

Let's hear it for sushi—raw, raw, raw

We know other successful headline writers who are constantly on the search for word plays and potential headline ideas. When they think of one, they write it down and file it away. When they can't think of a clever headline, they go through the file in hopes of something that might revive their creativity.

CAN HEADS BE TOO CLEVER?

Now here's the hard part. Although we're encouraging you to be as creative as the story allows, we also want to warn you against getting carried away with your own wit. No story deserves a boring headline, but the headline must match the tone of the story and the personality of the newspaper. Playful stories call for playful heads with puns and snappy verbs, but a cutesy head on a serious story can be an embarrassment. Even well-meaning copy editors occasionally lose their judgment and write a head they regret the next morning. Fortunately, good copy desk chiefs review headlines before they go in the paper. We know one who killed a headline on a story about a fatal shooting at a McDonald's restaurant that referred to it as a "McTragedy."

Nevertheless, tasteless headlines occasionally do make their way onto America's breakfast tables. A few years ago, one Midwestern newspaper was embarrassed when a hurried copy editor slapped this headline on a story about a child who was killed on his way to elementary school: "Tot flattened by school bus."

How colorful should headlines be? Like many things in journalism, the answer varies from one newspaper to another. Big-city tabloids often pay bonuses for headlines that would get copy editors fired at other papers. The *New York Post* once filled its front page with this head: "Headless man in topless bar." For a story about police questioning O.J. Simpson about the murder of his ex-wife, the *Post* said, "Cops squeeze the Juice." And when President Gerald Ford refused federal aid to help bail out New York City, the *New York Daily News* headline read "Ford to City: Drop Dead." None of these heads would pass the taste test at *The New York Times* or at most hometown newspapers.

If you suspect you've stepped over the line, ask a few other copy editors to second-guess your headline. The head you think is exceptionally colorful may have them groaning.

HEADS ON ANECDOTAL LEADS AND SECOND-DAY STORIES

Hard-news stories often have traditional leads and follow the inverted pyramid. Headlines for these stories are almost always based on the first and second paragraphs. But there's more to newswriting these days than the traditional story format, and headline writers have to make sure that their headlines tell the story. Here are the top few paragraphs from an investigative story in the *South Florida Sun-Sentinel*:

> Kathleen Mallon-Stone's apartment was brimming with bottles of prescription drugs. She used them to fight unrelenting pain from a congenital back deformity and the surgeries she endured to try to cure it. When the drugs weren't enough, she often curled into a ball to ease the

pressure on her spine. She died on the floor of her Fort Lauderdale condo at age 41, kneeling with her forehead touching the floor. An autopsy found that a combination of painkillers and muscle relaxants, prescribed by several area doctors, killed her.

Richard Oetinger, 44, a Palm Beach County Sheriff's Office detective on disability leave, lived with an excruciating bone disease that had required dozens of surgeries. When he went to the hospital, police said, Oetinger carried with him a case full of painkillers. He died in a hospital bathroom, his body loaded with prescription narcotics.

June Stoops, a 46-year-old homemaker in West Palm Beach, depended on drugs for two decades to treat severe arthritis. She died from an accidental overdose of a combination of five different prescription painkillers while her husband was away on a business trip.

None of these three people—Mallon-Stone, Oetinger or Stoops—had a life-threatening illness, yet they, and hundreds of others, are dead from overdoses of drugs prescribed by their doctors.

A *Sun-Sentinel* investigation documented 393 prescription drug-related deaths over the past two years in the seven-county area stretching from Okeechobee to Miami-Dade County.

Because no agency tracks such deaths, the newspaper's study confirms what medical examiners, prosecutors and police in South Florida suspect: Powerful legal narcotics are killing the very people they are supposed to help.

A thoughtless headline writer might read the lead and be tempted to write:

Woman dies after taking prescription painkillers

Reporters Fred Schulte and Nancy McVicar have written a much better story than that. They have used a delayed lead to show examples of people dying from prescription drugs. The fourth and fifth paragraphs serve as the "nut graf" and explain what the lengthy story is really about: the problems with powerful painkillers. The headline ought to be about this topic. Here's the headline the *Sun-Sentinel* used:

Rx for Death:
Patients in pain overdosing in alarming numbers

Many stories are news for days and days. Copy editors want to make sure that their headlines reflect the new developments. Look at the first two paragraphs of this story, also from the *Sun-Sentinel*:

> The defense attorney for a Broward County teen charged with killing an autistic 5-year-old boy wants to try to subpoena pro wrestler The Rock for the trial despite a recent ill-fated attempt to do the same thing in another Broward case.
>
> Gorman Roberts, 17, is charged as an adult with the manslaughter of Billy Walker, who drowned in a Pompano Beach canal last year. A 10-year-old boy who was also there is facing a juvenile charge of culpable negligence.

A bad headline would be:

Teen kills autistic 5-year-old

Or

Teen drowns 5-year-old in canal

Or

Teen charged with manslaughter

That's the old news. The murder happened months ago. The new news is that the attorney wants a professional wrestler to testify at the trial. The headline should tell that story:

Lawyer wants pro wrestler to testify
Lawyer wants The Rock to testify

The temptation, of course, is to write a headline with a really bad play on the wrestler's name.

SOME RULES AND TRADITIONS

Over the years, copy editors have created a set of customs that they follow when writing headlines. Some of these rules and traditions result in better headlines, but to be honest, some only make the job harder. Many copy desks are moving away from the split rules, but many religiously adhere to them. We look first at the rules about avoiding bad splits and then at the problems of repeating words and using attribution and qualification correctly.

OBEY THE SPLIT RULES

Of all the traditions that copy desks follow, the split rules are probably the most demanding. And, if these rules don't make much sense to you, join the crowd. Lots of copy editors will agree with you. Yet that's not a good reason to skip this section. If you become a copy editor, you'll need to know them. Most desks want their headlines to comply with one or two of the split rules, and a few desks diligently enforce all three.

Here are the most common split rules:

Rule 1. *Put modifiers and words modified on same line.*

These headlines wouldn't be allowed at most papers:

Board approves special
education program

Council passes new
water restrictions

The modifiers "special" and "new" are on one line and the nouns they modify—"program" and "restrictions"—are on the next, violating our first split rule.

Rule 2. *Don't split the verb parts.*

The following heads would be rejected because the verbs "to close" and "have found" aren't on the same line.

University to
close library

Hawks have
found center

Some students go overboard with this rule and think they can't separate subjects from their verbs or verbs from their objects. You can. These heads would be fine:

University
to close
library

Hawks
sign
center

Rule 3. *Don't split prepositions from their objects.*
These heads would be turned down because the prepositions "in"
and "between" are separated from their objects, "vat" and "guards,
inmates":

Woman drowns in
vat of chocolate

Fighting breaks out between
guards, inmates after game

Curiously, tradition allows headline writers to violate all three split
rules between the second and third lines of three-line heads (and the
third and fourth lines of four-line heads). Therefore, the following
heads would be accepted even though the preposition "on" is split
from its object "icy highway" and the adjective "language" is split
from the noun it modifies, "requirement":

4 die as truck
rams car on
icy highway

NSU lowers
language
requirement

DON'T REPEAT WORDS

The second traditional rule makes more sense. Unless you're trying for
some special effect, you shouldn't repeat words or use similar words in
a head. Look at this one:

GM plans to buy 10 acres for planned plant expansion

This copy editor could stand to add a few words to the old vocabulary to avoid relying on "plan" as both a verb and an adjective.

As we discuss later, many headlines have a main line and then a smaller line called a *deck*. You shouldn't repeat words in decks, unless you're going for some effect.

Zoo fined for mistreating animals
Animals kept in filthy cages, fed spoiled meat

Copy desk chiefs would reject that head because the word "animal" is repeated in the deck below the main headline. Substituting more specific words can improve the headline:

Zoo fined for mistreating rare tigers
Animals kept in filthy cages, fed spoiled meat

A related rule has to do with repeating words—particularly colorful verbs—on the same page. At larger papers, where several editors write the heads for a page, the copy desk chief ought to check all the heads for repetition. At smaller papers, where one copy editor writes all the heads for a page, that editor should eliminate any repetition.

Also, your headline shouldn't repeat the lead sentence verbatim or even echo its wording. This headline seems pretty good:

Dump truck rams car; 4 die

But it's a lousy headline if the lead to the story says:

> A dump truck loaded with dirt rammed a car on State Road 58 Tuesday night, killing four people.

USE ATTRIBUTION AND QUALIFICATION

The last of our traditional rules is the most important. The information in some stories can make people look bad: Accusations are flying, suspects are being charged, and claims are being made. Reporters will attribute all of these statements to the people who made them so that it's clear the newspaper is not saying these things. Or they will qualify the statements with words such as "may" or "could." Here are some examples:

President called 'liar'

Smith charged with murder

Tuition may double

Lawyer accused of misusing funds

In the first example, the verb "called" means that somebody called the president a liar; readers can assume that the story will elaborate on who's doing the calling. The attribution is implied. The use of the word "charged" in the second headline also implies that an official action has been taken. The third headline uses a classic fudge word, *may*. The use of *may* suggests that something is being considered, presumably by the appropriate body, but doesn't say emphatically that it will happen. In a tight headline count, "may" comes in handy. The fourth headline implies that someone or some group has made the accusation.

Some headlines use direct attribution that spells out the source of the information:

Vitamin C prevents colds, study says

Client says lawyer misused funds

NSU president: Tuition will double

Jenson predicts Blasters will win title

Make sure that you don't find people guilty in headlines if they have only been charged with a crime. Suppose that you have this story:

> The former principal of Freelander Heights Elementary stole cash and took home hundreds of dollars worth of electronic equipment, according to accusations in a school district investigation report.

You do not want to write a headline like this:

Principal steals equipment from school

The principal may be wrongly accused. Or he may hire a good attorney and get off. You need to qualify the headline:

Principal accused of stealing from school

Or

Report: Principal stole school's equipment

FINE POINTS OF HEADLINE WRITING

Now we can move from the traditional rules to more straightforward concerns: the tense, punctuation, capitalization and grammar of headlines.

VERB TENSE

Most headlines are written in the present tense, which lends an air of urgency and freshness to the news: "Ship hits iceberg." Past tense headlines are used when you're writing about events that aren't current: "Titanic missed iceberg, new study finds." Future tense in headlines is handled in three ways:

Student senate will debate tuition increase

Student senate to debate tuition increase

Student senate debates tuition increase Monday

The infinitive form (to debate) is probably the most common. "Will" might be best if there's been some question about whether an event will actually happen. The third option is used when you want to specify when the action will take place.

PUNCTUATION PROBLEMS

Punctuation rules change a bit when we get to headlines. Here are the most common departures:

1. You don't put periods at the ends of headlines.

2. Commas can be used to replace the word "and." Here are some examples:

Mississippi, Alabama increase school funding

GM closes plant, lays off 2,000

UAW to strike Ford, Chrysler

Dodgers sign Jones, trade Smith to Angels

3. Most newspapers, but not all, use semicolons rather than commas to separate clauses in headlines:

GM closes plant; 2,000 lose jobs

Dodgers sign Jones;Smith sent to Angels

4. Single quotation marks are used instead of double quotation marks because the single marks take up less space. So we get heads like:

'We cannot lose,' Democrats say

5. Dashes and colons can replace "said." A common pattern is to use a dash when the speaker's name comes at the end of the head and a colon when the name is first in the head:

Mayor: 'I took no bribes'

'I took no bribes'—mayor

6. Dashes also can be used for emphasis:

Neighborhood's unwanted guests—thousands of frogs

Disney raises entrance fees—again

7. Colons sometimes can replace verbs:

Sumo wrestling: survival of the fattest

(Some newspapers will capitalize the s in *survival*; others won't.)

CAPITALIZATION

At one time it was common for newspapers to capitalize the first letter of every word in a headline. The approach was called *upstyle*. Many papers switched to *modified upstyle* and capitalized all words except short prepositions. Upstyle and modified upstyle are still popular at many papers. But about 30 years ago, a few adventurous papers decided to capitalize only the first word of a headline and, of course, any proper nouns. They called it *downstyle*. Today, downstyle is the most common headline style in American newspapers. The styles look like this:

Papers Used
To Use Only
Upstyle Heads

Modified Upstyle
Began to Replace
Upstyle in Heads

Downstyle now
reigns supreme
at most papers

ABBREVIATIONS

Because space in headlines is tight, newspapers allow headline writers some leeway in using abbreviations. For example, it's common for the Republican party to be called GOP in heads (with no periods). But make sure that readers will recognize the abbreviations. It's tempting to fill a short line with heads such as:

CPC OKs TDC development despite AS objections

In English, what happened was that the county planning commission approved Thompson Development Corporation's development despite objections from the Audubon Society. Don't yield to temptation. Most papers include in their stylebooks which local organizations can be abbreviated and which are to be spelled out.

Some papers allow copy editors to abbreviate state names in headlines; some don't. Make sure that the abbreviations are clear. Most copy desks would reject these heads:

Robbery suspects found in Ark.

Ind. lottery winner gets $50 million

Miss Pa. wins title

N.D. firm to open factory

(Although many newspapers are beginning to use the two-letter abbreviations concocted by the U.S. Postal Service, most still use the traditional ones: Ark. for Arkansas; Ind. for Indiana; Mich. for Michigan; and so on. These abbreviations are listed in your *AP Stylebook*.)

A related rule: Use figures in headlines rather than words. This is another example of how headline writers bend rules to create more space in their headlines. As you know, newspapers spell out "five" in the body of the story, but they use the figure in the headline:

5 die in car crash

GETTING THE HEADLINE TO FIT

Quick! Tell us about your summer vacation in a sentence with exactly 22 letters. Yes, letters! Stymied? Anyone would be. Yet that's how many beginners try to write headlines. Right away, they start worrying about how to get a headline to fit exactly.

Let's rephrase our request: Tell us about your summer vacation in eight or 10 words. Easier? That's why you're better off starting a headline without too much concern for exact fit.

Professional copy editors have two advantages over you. They know from experience about how many words they can use in a headline, and they use computer systems specially designed to make fitting headlines easy. They type a headline, and the computer indicates how many letters too long or too short the headline is. Or they type the word directly on the page and can see how long or short it is.

If you follow this approach to writing headlines that fit, you'll be on an even footing with the best of the pros:

Step 1. Read the story carefully, looking for strong angles and colorful verbs. Follow the rules we suggested previously.

Step 2. If your computer has a cumbersome way of fitting headlines, type some nonsense words to get an idea of how many words you can have in your headline. (If you don't have access to computers, you need to count your headlines yourself. See Appendix 2 to learn how that's done.)

Step 3. Concentrate on writing the best possible headline. Try to come close to using the number of words you estimated in step 2. Don't go on to step 4 until you have a first-rate headline.

Step 4. If your head is short, look through the story for more angles you can work into it. If your head is long, you may need to try another approach. If your headline is just a few letters long or short, go on to step 5.

Step 5. Try substituting shorter (or longer) words. Suppose that you have this head:

Truck slams into car

If it's a little long, you might try:

Truck rams car

If this makes your head too short, you may look for another angle and get a head like:

Truck rams car; 4 die

Dump truck rams car

As you change words, beware of the problems discussed previously: lame words, lead repetitions and padding. You'll be tempted to settle for weak words just because they make the head fit. You don't want to end up with:

Truck, car have accident

Step 6. Bump the size of your head a little; that is, use type that is just a little smaller or larger than the copy desk chief ordered. But do this only if your copy desk chief allows it. We go into more detail about type sizes later in this book, but for now, bear with us. If the copy chief has asked you to write a head in 36-point type, many desks will allow you to bump the head up or down a couple of points. If it just doesn't quite fit in 36-point type, you might try 35-point type.

However, don't think you can solve all your problems by changing the type size. Most desks will limit how much you can bump heads, typically restricting you to only 2 points. That might allow you to squeeze in a couple of extra letters or maybe a short word.

But that's all. The difference between a headline that's 36 points tall and one that's 35 points is only $\frac{1}{72}$ inch.

A few newspapers may let you change the scaling and tracking of your headline a little. (Tracking and scaling are discussed in Chapter 12.) If you're allowed to change the scaling, you can sometimes fit an extra letter in. Keep in mind that changing the tracking also changes the way the type looks. That's why most papers won't let copy editors tinker with tracking and scaling.

Step 7. If the head still doesn't fit, it's time to look for a new angle. It's painful, we know. But sometimes great ideas just don't work.

THE LOOK OF HEADS

So far we've shown you one-line headlines:

Con men take elderly man's life savings

and two- and three-line heads:

Con men take man's savings

Con men take elderly man's life savings

Editors have a variety of headline styles that allow them to add other story angles to their headlines. We show you some of those styles in this section.

KICKERS, DECKS AND OTHERS

One way to add information is to add a *kicker*, such as:

'Bank examiners' steal $500,000

Con men take elderly man's life savings

In this head, the kicker ('Bank examiners' steal $500,000) allows the headline writer to tell the nature of the scam. Kickers are often italicized, underlined, or centered.

A variation of kicker headlines is the *reverse kicker. (*You'll also hear it called a *hammer head.)* In this head, the top line (A textbook con) is the hammer. It's in big type and only a couple of words long, leaving plenty of white space. The second line explains the story. Usually the type is about half the size of the hammer.

In Figure 10.1, the front page of Cleveland's *The Plain Dealer* has several types of decked headlines. The lead story has a hammer head. The extra white space around the top line of the hammer head sets the headline apart from other heads on the page and helps draw attention to the story.

Similar to hammer heads are *drop heads*. *The Plain Dealer*'s front page also has a drop head. The top line reads "Ohio's intelligent-design crusader." As in a hammer head, the top line is in larger type; however, it fills the line. The bottom line explains the story:

Ohio's intelligent-design crusader
Devout Hudson chemist tirelessly touts bringing a generic creator into curriculum

When copy editors write hammer heads and drop heads, they often begin with the top line They want that line to say something provocative or interesting. Often these headlines do not tell the story directly. Instead, they offer an impression of what the story is about. Unlike most headlines, these top lines often do not have verbs. For that reason, many copy desks call them *label heads*. For a story on a complicated court case involving the custody of a young child, one headline read:

A case for King Solomon

Figure 10.1. Front page of *The Plain Dealer* has several styles of headlines.

A daughter's gift
When Elise died, doctors knew it was a chance to save her mother's life

HELEN O'NEILL
Associated Press

MOTHER'S DAY

SHE KNOWS BEST: Readers share their moms' wit and wisdom. **L1**

MOTHERS AND DAUGHTERS: Piecing together an American life. **Sunday magazine**

AN INDELIBLE MARK: Maybe all of us are waiting for one more perfect meeting with our mother. **H3**

CHICAGO — Before the child transformed her life, Michele Garibay felt doomed in love and cursed by bad health.

Her sisters were pretty and petite. She was chunky and tall.

Her sisters had boyfriends and jobs. She was sick, always struggling with another collapse, another fever, another round of delirious nights in the hospital.

There were times when she didn't care whether she lived or died.

And then along came an angel, a child who taught her love and strength and laughter, who wrapped her in happiness, who assured her with every hug and every smile and every cry of "Mommy! Mommy!" that she was the most special person in the world.

Michele knew it was a miracle — and she knew it was too precious to last.

And so, when the doctor broke the news, she accepted his words with a strength that seemed unimaginable.

She didn't cry when her 3-year-old daughter was declared brain dead.

She didn't hesitate when asked about donating her daughter's organs.

For years, Michele had been on a waiting list for a kidney transplant; she understood her child could save other lives.

But what the doctor suggested next seemed so unbearable, she almost fainted in horror.

SEE GIFT | **A15**

Here's another example of hammer or label head that might provoke interest:

One more casualty of war

Editors can then add a second line that explains the story. The
decked head might read:

One more casualty of war
Defense spending ends hopes for balanced budget

The second line of these heads is often called the drop head. But you
will also hear them called *drop lines, underlines* or even *subheads*.

The *St. Louis Post-Dispatch* modified the drop head for a story
about scores on the state's multiple-choice drivers test. Copy editors
turned the headline about into a multiple-choice quiz. The top line
asked the question in larger type. The second line suggested answers in
smaller type:

What percentage of exams result in failing grades?
A. 8 percent B. 28 percent C. 53 percent

The main headline ran above a picture. A drop head below the picture said, "If you answered C, you're right."

Another way of working more information into headlines is to use
an even longer deck. Often these decks are complete sentences set in
type not much larger than regular body type. Just as editors haven't
made up their minds what to call drop heads, they've had problems
naming these additional decks. Among the names in use are *summary
heads, talking heads, blurbs* or even *superblurbs*. A few papers call
them *nut grafs*, but we'd rather reserve that term for discussions of
leads and story organization. Figure 10.2 shows what they look like.

We need to mention one other kind of headline. For years, editors
have tried to break up long stories with small headlines that are usually
called *subheads*. Many papers use subheads to break up longer stories,
reduce grayness and prod readers to continue. Figure 10.3 shows a few
contemporary versions of the venerable subhead.

ART HEADLINES

Many newspapers now use magazine-style headlines in special packages. Some designers refer to them as "art heads." Other names include

Figure 10.2.
Summary heads, kickers, sigs and bylines.

tactics, as troops went house to house, breaking down doors and even walls to avoid exposing themselves to fire from the street as they moved between apartments.

Days of planning ← Subheads → What to Avoid

The Israeli army said it had been planning the operation for several days.

"There was a feeling that in camps like Balata, the army couldn't operate," said Israeli Col. Aviv Kohavi, the paratroop commander who led the operation and surveyed it Thursday night from atop nearby Mount Gerazim. "Ob-

summer doldrums is a fine time to go shopping for stocks. Call it a midyear portfolio tuneup.

The trick, of course, is to figure out where to shift your dollars so that they might best work for you.

Some pros think you should avoid the big, traditional growth names that helped power the market in the 1990s. Instead, consider the smaller, lesser-known companies—the so-called midcap and small-cap stocks.

John Rogers, chief executive officer at Ariel Mutual Funds in Chicago, says he continues to think the Standard & Poor's 500-stock in-

Figure 10.3.
Two versions of subheads.

"labels," "titles" and "hammers." These heads are much like traditional hammer heads. They usually have only a few words and try to provoke reader interest. They differ in that they are often given special treatment. Different typefaces are used, or the type is arranged much differently from the rest of the headlines on the page.

The Free Press used a label head *Eating health away* for a centerpiece on the problem of obesity. The decks fill in two key pieces of information: They tell the reader the series is about obesity, and they suggest the magnitude of the problem. To see the full page, look ahead to Figure 12.7 in Chapter 12.

You can see more examples of art heads in Chapter 12.

Eating health away

➤ **U.S.:** Obesity is No. 2 death risk behind smoking
➤ **MICHIGAN:** State is especially prone to epidemic

PUTTING IT ALL TOGETHER

Let's go through the process of writing a headline. This story by Vicki Agnew is from the *South Florida Sun-Sentinel*:

DAVIE—Richard Chin-Loy has probably had better days. According to the FBI, he spent Tuesday robbing a Davie bank, fleeing from bikers intent on punching him out, swimming with alligators and winding up in a set of handcuffs.

A suspect in at least three other bank robberies in Broward County, Chin-Loy, 40, an unemployed landscaper, ran out of luck and breath in a canal near the Wachovia Bank at 4491 S. State Road 7, police said. He was charged with one count of armed robbery.

The ordeal began about 12:30 p.m. when Chin-Loy walked into the bank and passed a note to a teller demanding $50 and $100 bills, FBI Special Agent Paul Russell said.

The teller wasn't going along. She set off a silent alarm and began arguing.

"I don't have any hundreds, and I'm not giving it up," she reportedly said.

But she put some cash in a bag and tried to hold onto it until Chin-Loy ripped it from her grip, Russell said.

The suspect fled the bank and headed toward a strip shopping center where he had parked a truck. But a witness to the robbery began chasing him.

With the man on his heels, Chin-Loy ran into Moose's Used H.D. Parts and tore through the shop where mechanics Bones Alberigi and Eric Bray were working on motorcycles, police said.

"He ran right by me and someone yelled that he was a bank robber, so I just took off after him," Alberigi said.

Alberigi gave chase for about 50 yards, closed in on the suspect and was about to punch him when the man told him he, too, was chasing the bank robber and continued running.

"The guy could have had a gun and shot me dead," Alberigi added.

By then, Bray and a store customer, Shawn Henderson, picked up the chase and followed the suspect across Southwest 47th Avenue and Orange Grove Road to a canal.

"He ran out of one shoe, kicked the other one off and jumped into the canal," Bray said.

Bray, dressed in steel-toed boots, a leather vest and black jeans, jumped in after him, along with Henderson.

"He's lucky we did because he was starting to go under," Bray said.

Bray and Henderson hauled the man onto the canal bank and held him for Davie police.

Then came the final surprise.

"After they handcuffed him, we turned around and saw [two] gators about 20 feet away," Bray said.

The FBI said Chin-Loy matches the description of a man who robbed banks recently in Hollywood and Hallandale Beach, as well as an April 15 robbery at the same Wachovia Bank robbed on Tuesday.

The money stolen Tuesday has not been found.

Our design editor wants a two-line headline with a two-line drop head.

Reading the story, we realize that this is an amusing piece. The robber is reminiscent of a Carl Hiaasen character—and, because nobody was killed or seriously hurt, our initial instinct to write a lighthearted headline is okay.

We can't call this guy a robber, though, because he's been charged, not convicted. He remains a suspect, which is how we'll describe him.

Let's see:

"Ran out of luck and breath"—these words in the well-written lead leap out. But we don't want to repeat the lead in the headline.

How could we sum up this story in one line?

Simple: A robbery suspect had a really bad day.

So let's put together all the bad stuff that happened to him and see whether we have an alliterative sequence—perhaps "something, something and gators."

He tangled with a defiant teller; bike mechanics so tenacious they chased him into a canal then pulled him out; and gators that almost ate him for dinner. Nope, nothing alliterative and pithy comes to mind.

Okay, what are some obvious word plays related to this crime?

"Bank on it"; "aid and abet."

Hmmm . . .

Bank on it: Robbery suspect's day went from very bad to much worse

Robbery suspect didn't bank on pursuers, canal plunge or gators

Gators ready to aid and abet man suspected in three robberies

These hold some promise.

Okay, let's try some word combinations that succinctly describe what happened to him: "Suspect tangles with defiant teller, bike mechanics, almost drowns, almost becomes gator bait." We can boil these down to:

"Hot pursuit, not much loot and gators to boot."

Or:

"His day went downhill fast"—ha! He wound up in a canal: "Robbery suspect's day goes downhill—and downstream." And it happened in Davie! Now there's some alliterative punch:

main head:

Robbery suspect's day goes downhill—and downstream—in Davie

drop head:

Man chased into canal nearly drowns, narrowly escapes becoming gator bait

Or:

Robbery suspect's day goes downhill—and downstream—in Davie

He leaps into canal to flee pursuers, nearly drowns—20 feet from gators

As you can see, headline writing can be tough, but the challenge also can be fun.

EDITORS, LAW AND ETHICS 11

So far, we've talked about editors as coaches who help guide reporters as they gather the news and as wordsmiths who improve the writing of stories. But that's not all editors are good for. It also falls to editors to keep their newspapers out of libel suits, and they play a role in making sure that all people involved in stories—newsmakers, sources and readers—are treated with fairness and respect.

Journalism majors are usually required to take courses in media law and journalism ethics. Don't think that taking a couple of courses or reading a few books will turn you into an expert on law or answer all your questions about journalism ethics. As a matter of fact, many people have landed in trouble because they thought they did understand media law. This chapter skims the highlights of media law and ethics, mainly to alert you to some of the issues.

LIBEL

We live in an age in which people are willing to sue at the drop of a coffee cup—which actually happened when a woman spilled coffee in her lap and then sued McDonald's (and won), claiming the coffee was too hot. In litigious times such as these, journalists, who often write unpleasant things about people, have become frequent targets for lawsuits. Increasingly, jurors are awarding big settlements to people who claim the media have done them wrong. When the media lose, the average award is about $9 million, although these amounts are often reduced on appeal and sometimes the case is thrown out altogether.

The legal definition of libel will vary from state to state. A simple version might say only that libel is any published defamation of a person. Defamation is any representation that holds a person up to hatred, contempt or ridicule; that causes the person to be shunned or lose respect; or that harms that person in an occupation or profession.

The definition says material must be published. Obviously, that covers everything in a newspaper. If a published letter to the editor libels someone, your newspaper could be sued. If someone says something libelous and you quote that person correctly, you could still end up in court: In many circumstances, the courts will decide that your newspaper is responsible for all the information in the story, including the quoted material. Newspapers have been sued over headlines, cartoons, photos, advertisements, features, graphics and, of course, news stories. A few reporters have even lost libel suits after they wrote letters to authorities—letters that did not appear in the paper but that raised questions about the actions of other people in the community.

The final key word in the definition of libel is *person*. From a legal standpoint, *person* includes organized groups, associations and even corporations. You can also libel groups and classes of people, although it's fairly difficult for members of large groups to collect.

Keep in mind that you can identify people without using their names. Using fake names will not necessarily avoid a libel suit. And using references like "a professor in the history department" may not provide protection, either. The issue that the court will decide is whether people are likely to figure out who was being written about. If the history department is small (and most are), a court may conclude that readers might guess who your anonymous professor is.

Parodies can present other problems. You may think you have written a very clever column about the decisions your university president might make if he had been smoking marijuana. If he sues, a court will decide whether readers are likely to understand that you have written a parody—or whether readers might think the president smokes pot. Courts may not share your sense of humor. A columnist in Texas wrote that a first-grader was going to be tried as an adult because she gave a book report on a book that contained violence. A judge and prosecutor who had recently tried a young teen as an adult were named. They were not amused and sued. A court let the suit proceed.

It is fairly easy for people to sue over anything. For a libel suit, they have to show publication, identification and defamation—and it's "see you in court." The First Amendment's guarantee of press freedom makes winning a libel suit difficult. Still, defending a libel suit can cost a newspaper thousands of dollars in legal fees.

TRUTH AS A DEFENSE

The first question your lawyers will ask when you've been named in a libel suit is this: "Is your story true? Did the people identified in the story do what you said they did?" You'll hear a sigh of relief if the answer is yes. In most states, truth, or truth with justification, is a complete defense. But be aware that the lawyer isn't asking you whether you're sure the story was right, whether you're positive your quotes are accurate, or whether you know in your heart you're right. To a lawyer, truth means something that can be proved in a court of law.

Generally, it is not enough to say that someone told you the information was true. Attribution alone is not a defense. Suppose you quote someone as saying he saw Johnson commit crime. If Johnson sues, it may not be enough to show that you quoted your source accurately. You may need to prove that Johnson really did what you said he did.

Some beginners think they can solve their libel problems by inserting "allegedly" throughout their copy. "Allegedly" is a perfectly fine word when used correctly: to remind readers that the information you are reporting is part of an allegation that may or may not be true. But it's not a magical cure to your libel problems. Generally speaking, inserting an "allegedly" doesn't make your copy libelproof.

PRIVILEGE AS A DEFENSE

Our laws normally protect major governmental figures from being sued for libel in the official performance of their duties. The rationale is that we want our political leaders to be able to voice their opinions freely and without fear of being sued. Therefore, prosecutors at trials can argue that the accused is guilty without fear of being sued if the jury decides the person is innocent. Also, members of Congress speaking on the floor of the House or Senate cannot be sued for libel, even if their comments are wrong and defamatory. This protection is called *absolute privilege*.

In a democratic society, the public needs to know what elected officials are saying and what's going on in the courts. That's why reporters are given qualified privilege. *Qualified privilege* means that a journalist can report speeches on the floor of Congress, testimony in trials, and other official actions and not be sued for libel as long as the report is fair. What a sheriff tells you while on duty is usually privileged and thus reportable. However, a thin line exists between official statements and unofficial elaborations made in conversations with reporters. Those unofficial comments may not be privileged. Also, the statutes vary from state to state, and certain documents that might be privileged in one place might not be in another.

Here are two sentences. Which one would be easy to defend in a libel suit?

> Police arrested two brothers just minutes after they held up a liquor store on South Orange Avenue.

> Police charged two brothers with armed robbery just minutes after a liquor store on South Orange Avenue was robbed.

The second sentence would be easier to defend. All it says is that the brothers were charged with a crime. The information is privileged. To prove the truth of that statement, you would need only a copy of the legal paperwork. The first sentence is entirely different. It says "they held up a liquor store." Your burden of proof is much tougher.

THE NEW YORK TIMES DEFENSE

In 1964 the U.S. Supreme Court made a dramatic change in the way libel suits involving public figures are handled. The case involved an advertisement in *The New York Times*. (Newspapers are responsible for the entire content of the paper including ads, letters to the editor, personal notices, and everything else.) The advertisement charged that police were abusing civil-rights protesters in Montgomery, Ala. L.B. Sullivan, a member of the City Commission; three other commissioners; and the governor of Alabama each sued the paper. The *Times* couldn't use truth as a defense: The paper acknowledged during the trial that the ad contained factual errors and exaggerations. Alabama courts awarded Sullivan and another commissioner $500,000 each, which was big money back then. Hoping to cash in, other commissioners also sued.

The Supreme Court agreed to hear the *Times'* appeal. The court held that erroneous statements are "inevitable in free debate" and must be protected. The court reasoned that fear of large libel suits might have a "chilling effect" on debate. The news media might be afraid to discuss controversial issues involving political leaders if they knew a reporter's error might cost millions of dollars. The court said that for public officials to win libel suits, they must show that the media acted with "actual malice," which the court defined as (1) knowing the story was wrong but printing it anyway or (2) showing "reckless disregard" for the truth when gathering information.

Here's a *Times v. Sullivan* example: Your reporter is told that the mayor accepted a vacation paid for by a construction company that wants to build a new city hall. After the story runs, the mayor produces receipts proving she paid her own way. She sues. If you use *Times v. Sullivan* as your defense, the trial will not be about whether your story was true. Instead, your abilities as a reporter will be questioned. If the official can convince the jury that your paper knew the information was false or that you were reckless in the way you gathered it, your employer will pay—quite a bit, we suspect—for your mistake. On the other hand, if you can convince the jury that you didn't know the information was wrong and that you had followed good practices in tracking down the information, you won't have to pay the official a dime even though your story was wrong. (Your lawyer, of course, will demand payment, and good lawyers don't come cheap.)

If you've concluded that *Times v. Sullivan* is an easy ruling to apply, you're wrong. Later court rulings have had to deal with two major problems. One concerns proving actual malice. How do you separate honest mistakes by reporters and editors from "reckless disregard for the truth"? How do you prove that reporters suspected the story was wrong before it was printed? Another problem in applying *Times v. Sullivan* is deciding who's a public figure. Traditionally, public officials were elected officials: members of Congress, legislators and mayors. But in our society, lots of other people also play public roles: leaders of protest groups, actors, high-profile lawyers. For *Times v. Sullivan* purposes, the courts usually define public figures as elected officials, people who have decided to get involved in public affairs and people who are extremely well-known.

Many journalists have mixed feelings about *Times v. Sullivan*. They appreciate the ruling's contribution to debate. They know that many papers would be hesitant to do investigative stories if a factual error might cost them millions of dollars. But these journalists worry that some reporters use *Times v. Sullivan* to cover up sloppy reporting.

FAIR COMMENT AND CRITICISM

Another major protection against a libel suit is called *fair comment and criticism*. It has two conditions: The statement must be fair, and it must consist of comment or opinion (as distinguished from fact).

Although each state has its own rules governing fair comment, the general idea is that we all have the right to offer opinions about many people (or their products). In a democratic society, citizens must be able to criticize their political leaders without fear of lawsuits. In a developed society such as the United States, people can also express their opinions about governmental agencies, artists, speakers, writers, athletes and entertainers. By extension, newspapers can and do say bad things about the talent of actors or the performance of athletes, and these comments are usually not libelous under the provisions of fair comment and criticism.

Don't confuse opinions with statements of fact. If you write "Jones is a thief," you're making a statement of fact, not expressing an opinion. Either he stole something or he didn't. Adding a phrase like "in my opinion" won't help your case. If you write, "In my opinion, Jones is a thief," the courts may consider that a statement of fact. You will have to present evidence that proves Jones stole something. However, if you write "Jones is a terrible writer," you're asserting an opinion. What you think is terrible, someone else might think is clever, creative or brilliant.

COPYRIGHT

Not long ago, copyright law was simple for most journalists: They weren't supposed to copy other writers' stories or reprint photographers' pictures without permission. But modern technology has changed all that. Today, anyone with a little computer training can violate copyright laws easily and often without realizing it.

Copyright laws protect people from having their property stolen. Curiously, people who would never steal a TV set or even shoplift a candy bar are not as troubled when they "borrow" words, graphics and pictures produced by someone else. They fail to recognize that intellectual property belongs to the person who created it. Chances are, that person is trying to earn a living off his intellectual property just as the store owner is trying to make money by selling candy bars.

The law tries to protect creative people. Everything people create is copyrighted at the moment of creation. You do not have to apply for copyright. You do not have to put a copyright symbol on your creation. You have copyright protection automatically. However, using the symbol, the date and the name of the copyright holder will probably be helpful if you have to go to court to defend your property.

Daryl Moen, a journalism professor at the University of Missouri, put together a guide to copyright law for *Design* (Summer, 1994), the magazine of the Society of Newspaper Design. Here's some of the advice he offered about copyright issues regarding art and design:

- The legal test of whether copyright infringement has occurred is whether an ordinary person can see similarities when comparing the original and reproduction.

- Use of copyrighted material in a collage is an infringement if the original can be recognized, even in part.

- The copyright laws don't ban all uses of copyrighted materials. Under the fair-use provision, a newspaper can use examples without permission to illustrate a story about artists or photographers, and can quote excerpts of a book in news stories and reviews.

- Design elements such as typography, spacing and the arrangement of text are generally not eligible for copyright. However, if you have copied the original so closely that the public might confuse your version with the original, you may be in trouble. (Recently some type companies have filed successfully for patent protection for their typefaces. Also, changes in international copyright law may give type companies more opportunities to protect the typefaces they create.)

Applying these standards can be tricky. Let's look at a couple of examples. Suppose that a major forest fire occurs in the southern part of your state. You want a map to illustrate the extent of the fire. So, you take your trusty Rand McNally atlas and scan into your computer the atlas' map of the southern part of the state. Using another computer program, you eliminate all the roads and towns that clutter the original version. In a few minutes, you have a map that may get praise from your editor, but it also may get you into trouble for violating Rand McNally's copyright. To be legally and ethically correct, editors and graphic artists would need to get permission from the copyright holder to copy the maps. Or they can use material that their papers have already received permission to use, such as maps and graphics from news and graphics services (such as the Associated Press or Gannett Graphics Network). Or they can draw their own, basing them on reference material.

Here's another example. You regularly design the front page of your paper's features section. When you're on vacation, you buy a paper and are impressed with its layout on a feature about fall fashions. You like the way the editors arranged the elements on the page and their choice of type. When you get back home, you discover that your paper is doing a fall fashion spread and decide to "borrow" the design you saw on vacation. Then your conscience—and your fear of being sued—begin to haunt you. You think you may have violated the other paper's copyright. Chances are, you can rest easy. Design isn't usually eligible for copyright. For the editors of the other paper to win a copyright suit against you, they'd probably have to prove that readers mistakenly bought your paper thinking it was their paper. But you could run into trouble with your boss, who might not appreciate having the staff lift ideas from other papers so blatantly.

The Internet has made stealing pictures and text—copying a picture off a Web site and pasting it onto yours, for example—easy. It's also against copyright law. Just putting a credit line on the picture ("Photo by Joe Johnson") does not solve the problem. Johnson may be trying to earn a living by shooting pictures. He deserves money if you are going to use his work.

Generally, placing a link to another Web site on your pages is not considered a violation of copyright. However, some kinds of framing (where the page appears to be on your Web site) may cause copyright problems. To be safe, having the linked document open in its own window is best.

FAIRNESS

All too often when journalists discuss libel, their conversations center on what they can do without being sued. That makes sense. They know that losing a million-dollar judgment will not endear them to their bosses. But avoiding libel suits shouldn't be your only concern when editing copy. It's even more important to make sure that the story is fair. As an editor, you'll run into copy that doesn't violate anyone's understanding of libel, but you'll decide to have the story revised or even killed because it's potentially unfair.

Even beginning reporters know the importance of getting the other side of a story. If a conservation group claims that a factory is polluting a lake, reporters know they need to call factory officials and get their response. They know the conservation group might be wrong or might have misunderstood the evidence. Reporters aren't required by law to do this, but it's the fair thing to do, and readers want to believe their newspaper is playing fair.

But there's more to fairness than allowing the accused to make rebuttals.

Editors make sure that stories include the points of view of as many participants as possible. Suppose that county officials prefer one location for a new highway whereas city officials want another. Obviously, the story should quote both city and county officials. However, an editor might suggest to the reporter that other voices need to be heard also—for example, businesses and residents in those areas where the highway might be built. It's only fair to allow all people who have a major stake in a news event to speak their minds—including those who don't have easy access to the media spotlight.

Editors also should make sure that people in the news are treated with an appropriate degree of respect. Cheap shots sometimes liven up a dull personality profile, but they usually can't be justified. Likewise, people under stress may blurt out things that make great quotations but don't accurately represent how they feel or may embarrass them later. Some editors and reporters won't use such quotations, particularly if the person involved is not used to dealing with reporters.

Often when we discuss fairness and journalistic ethics, we think only of sensational cases. But journalists run into more mundane tests of their fairness every day. For example, when heavy winds and rain hit a community, an editor told his photographers to shoot some pictures that showed the force of the storm. One photographer took a vivid picture of a heavy-set woman battling the storm with her umbrella. He got the woman's name and told her he had taken her picture and it might be in tomorrow's paper. She had no objections. After the picture was processed, both the photographer and his editor agreed it was a great picture. But the editor had reservations about using it. The woman was drenched. Her wet clothes were clinging to her body, her hair was hanging limp and her makeup was running down her face. She looked like an extra from the movie "Night of the Living Dead." The editor figured that when the woman saw the picture in the paper the next morning, she'd be embarrassed. He reasoned that he wouldn't run the picture if it were of his wife or mother, so he rejected it out of respect for the woman involved. The paper used its second-best photo to illustrate the storm.

SEXISM AND RACISM

If you look at newspapers from 30 or 40 years ago, you'll be stunned by the way many of the stories were written. Stories about successful women often carried a "gee whiz" tone. Leads would say something like: "Joan Doe may look like a fashion model, but she's really the new vice president of the Acme Accounting Agency. That pretty little head of hers is a real noggin for numbers." Stop gagging. You get the idea.

African-Americans rarely appeared in the news. Someone once said that if Martians depended on the front pages of that era's newspapers to learn about American life, they would think we were an all-white society.

Things are better now. But copy editors still must police stories to rid them of racism and sexism. One way to combat sexism is to use gender-neutral words. Members of the police force are "police officers," people who combat fires are "firefighters," and people who deliver the mail are "letter carriers" or "mail carriers." However, most newspapers balk at the practice of inventing new titles. For instance, such papers haven't accepted the practice of substituting the word "person" in formerly male-sounding titles. They don't use the contrived word "spokesperson." Instead, they use "spokesman" for men, "spokeswoman" for women, or "representative." Similarly, many papers prefer "chair," "chairman" and "chairwoman" for the heads of corporations and academic departments unless the organization has officially adopted the title "chairperson."

The quest for gender neutrality isn't limited to the use of neutral titles and identifiers. Most papers abide by a style that calls for men and women to be treated the same in news columns and for occupational stereotypes to be eliminated. We no longer describe someone as a "male nurse," as if nurses are supposed to be women, nor do we note with surprise that a doctor or truck driver is female.

Copy editors have devised a simple but effective rule for ridding prose of sexist descriptions. Ask yourself: Would I use this passage if the story were about a man? If the answer is no, don't use it in a story about a woman. You wouldn't describe a man running for mayor as "the perky, 56-year-old grandfather of two," so you shouldn't use similar words for a female candidate. You can often use the same technique to decide whether a story needs racial identification. Unless the context demands it, you don't need to point out the race or ethnicity of people in your stories.

The key thing to remember is that the sex and race of people in the news should be mentioned only if their sex or race plays a direct role in why they're in the news or if the people are breaking through a long-standing social or occupational barrier. For instance, when the first woman, Hispanic or African-American is elected president, you can bet that election-night stories will mention the candidate's gender or ethnicity.

Copy editors should be sensitive to other kinds of bias that can creep into newspaper copy. They can check the diversity of sources the reporter has contacted. For instance, a copy editor was reading a feature about off-the-wall wedding ceremonies at local churches. He noticed that the only churches named were large and Protestant, with white congregations. He reasoned correctly that the feature would be improved if a wider spectrum of the city's religious and ethnic groups were included.

Editors also should be alert to stereotyping sources. An African-American banker recently complained that the only time his local paper quoted him was in stories about race or race relations. When reporters needed information about banking, they called his white colleagues.

It's not enough for copy editors to improve the quality of writing in their papers. They should make sure that the paper is serving all its readers well and treating all people fairly.

III. USING PICTURES, GRAPHICS AND DESIGN

Learning the Lingo

Terms vary from newspaper to newspaper. These are common.

Nameplate or flag

Promo boxes or teases

Sig or logo (a headline or graphic that indicates a series or standard feature)

Art head. Also called display head or label.

Initial cap or drop cap (a large cap at the start of a story)

Centerpiece or package (the grouping of stories, grahics, pictures to give the topic prominence)

Infographic, graphic, chart or table

Creditlines give credit to the graphics reporter or photographer

Byline gives credit to reporter

Standing heads are used for features that run frequently (here it says Weather)

Cutout picture (picture with background removed)

Headline

Deck (a smaller head under the main head)

Box (lines--called rules--that surround a package)

Cutoff rule (a line separates stories vertically)

Picture (also called cuts and art)

Cutlines or captions

Gutters (the space between columns)

Gutter rule (a vertical line in a gutter)

Jumplines say "See Page 5"

Orlando Sentinel

SUNDAY

The books of summer

Celtics win Game 3 vs. Nets

Florida's Water Crisis | A SPECIAL REPORT

PAVING
IT OVER

By DEBBIE SALAMONE

Two big towers soar above the booming south Lake County community of Clermont.

The shorter of the two landmarks holds the city's water. The taller tower advertises itself as a beacon for growth.

GROWTH SHIFTS OUR WAY

The barrier

Burnham children cope in Kansas

By ROGER PÉREZ

One year after the missionaries were kidnapped in the Philippines, their kids miss them but try to tell people their own lives are normal.

Young Burnhams

DCF fails to visit each child in its care

A report showed caseworkers didn't reach the goal for May.

By DAVID A. KAHEDA, SHANA CERWON, SALLY KESTIN and ROBB SANDERS

FORT LAUDERDALE — A report released Saturday shows that caseworkers for the Department of Children & Families have fallen short of their goal of visiting once a month the foster care children in their charge.

Out of school, into jobs

Summer jobs hot at theme parks — but not elsewhere

By SARAH HALE and ROY M. JACKSON

WEATHER 87 INDEX HOLIDAY PAPER DELIVERY

TYPOGRAPHY 12

We've looked at how to write headlines that will entice readers. But there's more to headlines than just their wording. The typography—the shape and size of the type and sometimes the shape and size of the overall headline—can play a key role in getting readers interested in the news. Headlines achieve this in three ways:

- The size and weight of type helps readers judge the importance of the news.

- Type can take on dramatic shapes and appearances that provoke readers to look at the story.

- Type plays a crucial role in the appearance of the paper and in establishing the paper's personality.

In the past, newspaper designers did not have as much freedom as their magazine counterparts in selecting typefaces and designing headlines. But that is changing. The front pages of entertainment, travel, lifestyles and food sections often involve very creative uses of type. Even on the front pages, designers are experimenting with typography. "Art headlines," as some newspapers call them, are frequently used to set centerpiece packages apart on Page 1 and throughout the paper.

MEASURING TYPE

Copy editors don't use inches or centimeters for most of their measurements. Instead, they use units called picas and points, a system created in 1737 by Pierre Simon Fournier, a French printer. Here are three important facts to remember:

- 72 points equal 1 inch

- 6 picas equal 1 inch

- 12 points equal 1 pica

When typographers talk about the size of type, they mean one thing: the height of the letters from the tops of the ascenders (the tall letters, such as *H* and *T*) to the bottoms of the descenders (the letters that hang below the baseline, such as *p* and *y*). See Figure 12.1. When

177

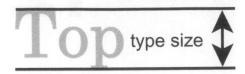

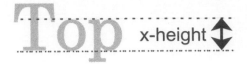

Figure 12.1.
Measuring the type size.

Figure 12.2.
Measuring the x-height.

an editor says a headline is in 24-point type, that means the type is 24 points tall.

However, typefaces of the same point size do not always look the same size on the page. Sometimes designers do not use all the space they have available and will make their letters a bit smaller. Also, the x-height of a typeface can make it seem larger or smaller on the page. *X-height* is the size of the letters, not counting the ascenders and descenders. Larger x-heights tend to make letters look bigger. Each of the "wimps" that follow is set in 24-point type. Yet the letters in some typefaces look larger or smaller than the same letters in another typeface.

Wimps Wimps **Wimps** Wimps **Wimps** Wimps Wimps **Wimps**

Points are also used to measure the width of vertical and horizontal lines on a page. Newspaper designers usually call smaller lines *rules* and heavier lines *bars*. Vertical lines in the gutters (the spaces between the columns of type) are often called *gutter rules*. Horizontal lines that separate stories are often called *cutoff rules*. When a designer puts lines on all four sides of a story, it's called *boxing the story*.

Half point
_____
1 point
_____
2 points
_____
3 points
_____
6 points
_____
12 points

WORKING WITH LEADING

The size of type is often given with two measurements. Editors might say their newspaper uses body type that is 9 on 10. That means the letters themselves are 9 points tall and the type will be placed in a space that is 10 points tall. The difference between these two numbers determines how much space will be between lines. Software programs often call this *leading*, pronounced *ledding*. The term comes from the days of hot-metal composing, when printers put small pieces of lead between the lines.

Newspaper body type is usually 9 points, 9.5 points or 10 points tall. The amount of leading needed varies. Some typefaces can be set 10 on 10, whereas letters in other faces might appear to overlap when set this close. Generally, newspapers use a half point or a point of leading with body type.

This is 10-point type with the leading set at 10 points. Some papers set their leading and type the same. Many make the leading a half point larger.

This is 10-point type with the leading set at 12 points. This is more leading than most papers would use. The default setting on some software programs is about this size.

This is 10-point type with the leading set at 15 points. Newspapers would rarely use this much leading unless they were reversing the type or wanted to create a special effect.

Headlines get similar treatment. Some designers want the headlines to seem more compact on the page, so they use only a little leading. Many set the leading at one point more than the size of the head. And some like more leading.

Most of the time, you will not want to use the "automatic leading" settings in QuarkXpress, In Design or PageMaker. These settings place more space between the lines than most newspaper designers would want. You will need to set the leading manually—or create styles to change the leading.

18-point type on 18 points of leading

18-point type on 19 points of leading

18-point type on 22 points of leading

SCALING

Just as you can decide how much space to have between lines, you can decide how much space to have between letters.

24-point headline scaled very tightly
24-point headline with tight scaling
24-point headline without any scaling
24-point headline with loose scaling
24-point head scaled very loosely

Scaling is used primarily in three ways. Many designers are beginning to scale headlines more tightly. That's becoming more important as the width of newspaper columns becomes smaller. By having all the headlines scaled more tightly, copy editors can fit more words in headlines and make them more interesting.

Scaling is sometimes used in art headlines to create special effects. (We discuss art heads later in this chapter.) One designer wanted to make the letters seem more like a wall; the other used scaling to achieve a strong visual effect.

MEMORIAL DAY MEANS WORK

She's on the case to get repeat DUIs off roads

Scaling can be used as part of the everyday appearance of the page. The *Orlando Sentinel* and other newspapers use scaling to give a special identity to *labels* or *kickers*. The words "Memorial Day Means Work" are loosely scaled in the following headline:

One way that scaling is not used at respectable publications is to get a headline to fit the space. Copy editors who have written a headline that is just a little bit too long may be allowed to make the headline a point or two smaller, but they cannot change the scaling.

KERNING

Although people frequently confuse these terms with one another, *scaling* and *kerning* do not mean the same thing. Scaling refers to changing the spacing between all the characters. Kerning involves changing the space with certain pairs of letters. The word "Toe" on the left has no kerning. The space between the "T" and the "o" looks larger than the space between the "o" and the "e." It's an illusion created by the space made by the T. When the "T" and the "o" are kerned, they move closer. To the eye, it seems as though the spacing is now consistent.

Toe Toe

QuarkXpress, In Design and PageMaker allow you to control the amount of kerning. As with scaling, kerning is not done to shorten long headlines. It is part of the overall design of the page.

MEASURING WIDTHS

Pictures, headlines, columns and just about everything else in a publication are measured using a combination of points and picas. A picture may be 25p4 wide and a graphic 11p wide. 25p4 means that the picture is 25 picas and 4 points wide. If that sounds confusing, think about how we use feet and inches. If someone is 5-foot-6, she is 5 feet and 6 inches tall. The relationship between inches and feet is much the same as the one between points and picas:

12 points equal 1 pica

To make it easier for national advertisers, most newspapers use standardized sizes for their columns. Until the late 1990s, the standard newspaper column was 12 picas and 2 points wide. Gutters (the white space between columns) were 1 pica wide. With these standardized sizes, a one-column picture, headline or graphic was 12p2 wide. A two-column headline, ad or picture was 25p4. Why 25p4 and not 24p4? Don't forget the gutter. It's 1 pica wide.

In the late 1990s, many newspapers slimmed down. Instead of pages being 13 inches wide, they shrank to 11.625 inches wide. The smaller size achieves two goals. Publishers have to buy less paper, thereby reducing costs. And many readers find the smaller size more convenient. However, the smaller page size has often meant less space for news on the page. The result has been that many papers now have fewer and shorter stories. Many editors and designers have been very critical of this movement to the 50-inch web (referring to the 50-inch-wide ribbons of paper that run through the presses).

Because the size of the paper is getting smaller, the column widths are also being reduced. As this is being written, no one is sure what the next standard column width will be. Many expect publishers to set standards that will fix column widths at about 11 picas. Gutters will probably be either 9 points or 12 points (a pica) wide. So a one-column picture, headline or graphic will be 11 picas wide. A two-column ad, headline or picture will be 22p9 or 23p. You can see the differences:

Story set in standard 12p2 columns

Thieves break into 3 cars

Three parked cars were broken into early Friday on the parking lot near the Administration Annex.

Campus police said radios and

books were stolen.

The cars had been left on the lot by members of the Financial Aid staff.

←————→ **12 picas and 2 points**   ↑   ←————→ **12 picas and 2 points**

1-pica gutter

Story set in 11p columns

Thieves break into 3 cars

Three parked cars were broken into early Friday on the parking lot near the Administration Annex.

Campus police said radios and books were stolen.

The cars had been left on the lot by members of the Financial

←————→ **11 picas**   ↑   ←————→ **11 picas**

9-point gutter

Many editors have redesigned their pages to suit the smaller page sizes. Because the narrower pages tend to encourage more vertical pictures and graphics, one result is that newspapers are beginning to look more like newspapers from an earlier era. Some call it the retro look. Newspapers have also adopted new typefaces to be legible in the skinny columns. Because smaller pages usually mean a smaller news hole (the space in a paper for news), some editors have reconsidered how their papers use graphics. Graphics are still important news-telling devices, but editors make sure they serve a purpose other than dressing up a page.

Most people expect that the size of newspapers will continue to shrink. Some suggest that many papers will shift from the *broadsheet* format, the standard size now, to the *tabloid* size. Pages in tabloid papers are usually half the size of a broadsheet page. (*Tabloid* in this sense refers to the page size. Because many tabloids emphasize sensational news, the word is often used to refer to that brand of journalism.)

RECOGNIZING TYPEFACES

Printers have been studying typography for hundreds of years and, as you might expect, have developed a lot of jargon. They classify type into a few large groupings, often called *races*. These races are divided into *families*, families are split into *typefaces*, and typefaces are sepa-

This is an example of serif type
This is an example of sans serif type

rated into *fonts*. Font originally meant all the letters of one size in one typeface. Unfortunately, not all typographers use the same names for some of the races, and some classify them differently. Some want to retain the distinction between *typeface* and *font*; others use them interchangeably. In this chapter, we avoid these arguments and stick to the distinctions that matter to copy editors and page designers.

The first distinction is whether the type has serifs. Serifs are finishing flourishes on the ends of some letters. Type with serifs is called *serif* type; type without serifs is called *sans serif* type (*sans* is French for *without*).

Although the most obvious difference between these two type styles is the serifs, they differ in another way. Imagine that you're drawing these letters with a pen. Each mark you make on the page is a *stroke*. The strokes in most sans serif faces are all of the same thickness:

Sans serif has uniform strokes

Serif type has both fat and skinny strokes. The tops and bottoms of the letter o, for example, are skinny whereas the downstrokes are heavy:

Serif has fat and skinny strokes

These seemingly small differences can make a big difference in how people react to a page.

THE SERIF FACES

Typographers have been designing serif typefaces for hundreds of years. They have modified the shapes of the serifs and the weight of the strokes and have produced at least four classifications of serif type:

Oldstyle which looks like this Garamond
Modern like this Bodoni
Transitional like this Baskerville
Another transitional is Californian
Slab or square serifs like Rockwell

"Oldstyle" faces weren't necessarily designed by monks in the sixteenth century, and "modern" doesn't mean that the typeface was created during your lifetime. Some Modern faces are older than many of the Oldstyle faces.

Why are the names so misleading? Until about 30 years ago, type was usually made out of metal. In the early days of printing, the metal wasn't very strong. The pressure of the printing presses would wear out the type quickly. Some letters would even break. So, type designers had to design type that would hold up well. They avoided using really skinny strokes because the type would be more likely to bend. Instead, they made the strokes fairly uniform, and they put little arches on the serifs to increase their strength. (See Figure 12.3.) Here are two ways to identify Oldstyle type:

Figure 12.3.
An Oldstyle face (we used Cheltenham).

Hold

- The letters have fairly uniform strokes

- The serifs have supporting arches called *brackets*.

In the 18th century, stronger metals were developed. These metals could take a beating from the presses and still produce legible type. These stronger metals gave type designers more freedom. They could design type with extremely fat and extremely skinny strokes. And they could stop using brackets. These new typefaces were called *modern* faces. (See Figure 12.4.) Modern faces have:

Figure 12.4.
A modern face (we used Bodoni poster).

Hold

- Strokes that vary greatly in weight; some fat, some skinny.

- Serifs that do not have brackets.

Probably the most popular Modern serif type is Bodoni, named after Giambattista Bodoni, who designed it in the 1700s. During the 1960s and 1970s, Bodoni was the most common serif headline typeface used by American newspapers.

More recent typographers have blended the characteristics of Oldstyle and Modern into new typefaces, which are lumped together under the label *transitional serif* type. You can find similarities to both

Hold

Oldstyle and Modern faces. Baskerville has brackets much like an Old-style, and fat and skinny strokes like a Modern face. (See Figure 12.5.)

Many of the newer typefaces are difficult to place in the traditional categories. Some typographers have created a new grouping called Synthesis. Herman Zapf is considered the founder of these designs. His Berkeley, based on Frederic Goudy's Californian, has become popular, as have his Palatino and Zapf Renaissance.

Typefaces with slab serifs, sometimes called square serifs, are becoming more popular and have been used in several newspaper redesigns. As the name suggests, the serifs are square. Another characteristic is that the strokes tend to be more uniform in weight than other serif faces. (See Figure 12.6.)

Figure 12.5.
A transitional face (we used Baskerville).

Hold

Figure 12.6.
Slab-serif face (we used Rockwell).

THE SANS SERIF FACES

Sans scrif typefaces were not widely used until the early 1900s. Helvetica, the most common of the sans serif faces, appeared in 1951. (Microsoft has a very similar face called Arial.)

Helvetica type looks like this

A few years ago, a typographer argued that Helvetica was in use—in some capacity—at nearly every American newspaper. He probably was not exaggerating. Helvetica was the standard choice as an accent face, used in infographics, bylines and cutlines. This extreme popularity has led some designers to think Helvetica has become trite and boring. Many designers prefer to use other sans serif faces, including:

Futura is popular
Franklin Gothic is common
Avant garde has its fans
Gill Sans looks like this
Optima looks like this
Myriad looks like this

TYPEFACES HAVE COMPLETE FAMILIES

Type designers usually provide a variety of typefaces within a type style. Some faces have as many as 30 different variations. Here are six members of the Franklin Gothic family. The type size for each of them is 18 points.

Franklin Gothic Book
Franklin Gothic Medium
Franklin Gothic Heavy
Franklin Gothic Bold
Franklin Gothic Bold Condensed
Franklin Gothic Bold Extra Condensed

Most type families also have italic and roman versions of the letters. Don't confuse these specially drawn letters with those produced by word-processors such as Microsoft Word. Computer-generated italics are okay in many uses, but they tend to lack the clarity and personality of true italics. Newspapers and professional designers prefer the real thing.

DIFFERENT TYPE FOR DIFFERENT USES

Most newspapers use three or four typefaces on a daily basis:

- Body type (also called text type) is the typeface for the words in stories.

- Display type is the typeface used for most headlines.

- Secondary display type is a second font used for headlines.

- Accent type is used in refer boxes, infoboxes, index items, bylines and so on.

DISPLAY AND ACCENT TYPE

In the past few years, many newspapers have changed the type fonts they use for display and accent type. The movement to smaller page sizes is one reason. These editors needed a type that was more condensed so that it would better suit the skinnier columns. Other editors want to keep pace with contemporary styles. They want their papers to appeal to young adult readers.

Changing typefaces is not a decision made hastily. Editors, designers and typographers work together to find display and accent fonts that are both easy to read and that reflect the personality of the paper. In addition to selecting the main display font, editors choose an accent typeface. They want typefaces that are compatible, yet capable of providing contrast. Some papers, such as *The Arizona Republic,* have focus groups of readers give their opinions.

The last 40 years have seen major changes in the headline typefaces. In the 1960s and 1970s, Modern faces such as Bodoni were the most popular. Although sometimes criticized for looking too mechanical, these faces project a formal and authoritative tone that many papers want.

When the *Detroit Free Press* was redesigned in 1999, editors replaced its old Bodoni with a new version designed specially for the *Free Press*. The headlines for the centerpiece and one of the headlines have been enlarged in Figure 12.7. The "Eating health away" headline is in Detroit Bodoni, as is the top deck of the "Detroiter" head. The paper uses a lighter version of the Bodoni for decks.

To complement the Bodoni, the *Free Press* uses a slab-serif face, Rockwell, as its accent type. The accent type is used in all caps in "U.S.," "Michigan" and "Special Series." These two typefaces work well in the page's centerpiece. The bold Rockwell and the lighter Detroit Bodoni create contrast, which helps draw attention to the centerpiece. You can see the contrast in the enlarged portion.

Designers have used other typographic devices to make the centerpiece seem special. To add additional contrast, the words "Special Series" are centered and colored red. The story begins with a drop-cap. Because it's the only drop-cap on the page, it both signals that the story is something special and helps readers find where the story starts.

In the late 1970s and 1980s, many papers began to use sans serif typefaces for their headlines. Designers thought the sans serifs seemed less stuffy than Modern serifs such as Bodoni. Sans serifs are still the choice for many papers. *The Tampa Tribune* started using an unusual sans serif face, Agenda, in 2001. (Look back in Chapter 1 at Figure 1.1.) The widely acclaimed *St. Petersburg Times* uses sans serif display type.

The front page from the *Star Tribune* (Figure 12.8) has most of its headlines in a bold sans serif, Franklin Gothic. Much as the *Free Press* did, the *Star Tribune* uses a much different typeface as its accent font. In the enlarged part of the page, you can see how the sans serif Franklin Gothic contrasts with Walbaum, a Modern serif typeface.

The movement to the smaller page size has caused many papers to change typefaces. Often they adopt one of the Transitional serif faces

Figure 12.7.
Detroit Free Press makes effective use of Bodoni with Rockwell as an accent face.

Figure 12.8.
The *Star Tribune* of Minneapolis uses sans serif type for its headlines.

for most of their headlines. The *Orlando Sentinel* (Figure 12.10) and *South Florida Sun-Sentinel* use Myriad, a Transitional face that is heavily influenced by Oldstyle serif faces.

BODY TYPE AND SERIF FACES

Nearly every American newspaper uses serif type for the words in the stories. Serif faces are considered easy to read in large blocks. Perhaps the most famous body type is Times Roman. Some call it "generic serif" because it is so commonly used and because it is available on every home computer. Times Roman is based on a typeface designed for *The Times* of London in the early 20th century. In America, competing companies created faces called Times Roman and Times New Roman. Today, Adobe and Apple call their versions Times Roman, whereas Microsoft labels its version Times New Roman.

As popular as it is, Times Roman is no longer the dominant face for body type. A key reason for its decline is that Times Roman was designed to handle the demands of older printing technologies when type was made of lead. Today type is produced by computers and printed on modern offset or flexo presses, and other designs produce more legible text. Also as newspapers become narrower with less space for news, designers are looking for body type that allows for more words per line—yet that is still easy to read.

Editors at the *South Florida Sun-Sentinel* tested four typefaces before they decided. They produced facsimile pages in their newsroom and then printed them on the paper's presses. Doing that allowed them to know exactly how the faces would look in the paper.

USING TYPE IN ART HEADLINES

Art headlines are one way that designers use typography to help tell the news. Copy editors come up with a few emphatic words that they think will arouse interest in the story. Designers then apply common typographic techniques to the words. Often the results are exciting headlines for centerpieces.

For example, a designer at the *Savannah Morning News* created the effective art head in Figure 12.9. Editors liked the phrase "The fast and the infuriating." They thought it summed up a story about the problems young race-car drivers have been causing on race tracks. The designer stayed with the *News'* standard headline font, Century, a clean-looking Transitional typeface. But he combined two type sizes and put words in both roman and italics. The headline was then wrapped around the front of the race cars.

A copy editor for the *Orlando Sentinel* wrote the headline "Wither the springs" for a centerpiece about how

Figure 12.9.
An art headline in the *Savannah Morning News.*

Figure 12.10.
Art head draws attention to the centerpiece in the *Orlando Sentinel.*

Florida's springs were drying up. The designer used the *Sentinel*'s standard headline face, Myriad. However, to achieve impact, the designer used wildly different sizes of type. The word "Springs" is in gigantic type and is all caps. The "Wither the" is in smaller type that seems even smaller sitting on top of "Springs" with white space to its right. Additional contrast is created by the sans serif type used in "Florida's Water Crisis." Finally, the sig (a standing head used in series or columns), "A special report," is scaled tightly and is in capital letters. This art headline, shown in Figure 12.10, has three characteristics that make it work:

- The typography draws attention to the centerpiece.

- The type remains consistent with the rest of the page.

Figure 12.11.
C's are modified in this art head
from the *Orlando Sentinel*.

Figure 12.12.
Art head in *The Daily Breeze* in
Torrance, Calif. Courtesy of *The Daily
Breeze*.

• The words of the headline "Wither the springs" are just unusual enough to draw readers' curiosity.

Occasionally, *Sentinel* designers modify the typeface in art heads. For a feature page on a local coffeehouse that rents videos of foreign and arty films, they enlarged the C's in "Cup of Cinema Culture." They added color and drop shadows. (See Figure 12.11.)

For a story on the declining number of police recruits, editors at *The Daily Breeze* in Torrance, Calif., also manipulated type in several ways to create the art headline in Figure 12.12.

To emphasize "thinning," designer Margaret Magee used a light sans serif face for the top line. She set the tracking very loose so that the additional spaces between the letters made "The thinning" seem even thinner. She wanted a different effect for "Blue line." She used a bold sans serif face and set the tracking tight. By bringing the bold letters closer together, she made the words seem more like a line. To play on the "blue" idea, Magee tried using blue type for "BLUE LINE." She thought it looked tacky, however, so she gave the words a blue drop shadow.

Editors at *The Jacksonville Courier-Journal* in Illinois had a good story recommending that readers take a day trip to a classic-car dealership in nearby East St. Louis. (See Figure 12.13.) But they did not have good pictures or graphics to use for the centerpiece. So, designer Guido Strotheide used type much the way he would have used a picture. The headline gives focus to the page and creates interest in the story.

Strotheide set the tracking of the letters in "Rte." and "incarnate" very tight. The "66" consists of two 6's that overlap. Two drop shadows, one blue and one gray, keep the numbers distinct. The 6's are set in gigantic 417-point type. "Rte" is smaller, but still it's huge by newspaper standards (about 300 points). Finally, Strotheide used italics to drive home the pun in "incarnate." The headline and the deck are in the *Courier-Journal*'s standard typeface, Industrial.

Running type over pictures was at one time considered a no-no in most newsrooms. However, many papers are using the effect to their advantage, as did some of the front pages of the *San Jose Mercury News* in Chapter 14.

When art heads work well, they give page designers an opportunity to tell the news and draw readers to the story. However, noted newspaper designer Ron Reason cautions designers that there is also a downside to art heads, particularly when they are overdone.

"I've seen an outrageous variety of headline displays that do nothing but stroke the ego of the designer and put his fingerprints on the page," Reason says. "Shadowed type, unusual color combinations, fonts that seem to have dropped out of outer space—all are a plague on the nation's feature pages and all are symptoms of an inconsistent, unprofessional approach to design."

Reason believes that the choices for fonts and colors should be in keeping with the rest of the newspaper. He also worries that too often, art heads don't tell the story as well as more conventional heads would.

Figure 12.13.
The Jacksonville Courier-Journal used typography as the visual element in this package.

EDITING PHOTOGRAPHS AND GRAPHICS 13

In the 1860s, editors at *Frank Leslie's Illustrated Weekly* made a major breakthrough in newspaper journalism. They discovered that they could tell stories better with graphics and that readers liked to see the news. When the quality of picture reproduction improved, the emphasis on photos and graphics increased to the point that the *New York Daily News* billed itself as the "picture newspaper." To this day, a highly stylized drawing of a camera appears in the paper's nameplate.

Research done at the Poynter Institute shows that most people, including loyal newspaper readers, are more likely to read and remember stories that are accompanied by pictures. That makes sense. Visual images can report the news in a way that draws on the emotions. Photography can *show* poignancy—a child's tears, an athlete's accomplishment, the destruction caused by a disaster—more forcefully and immediately than words can *tell* about it. Information graphics can explain complicated issues quickly and accurately. For example, a reporter can write about changes in this year's county budget. A few bar charts can instantly show readers that spending for schools is going down while the budget for law enforcement is going up. Reporters can then use their stories to explain why political leaders have made their decisions and why a lot of people are angry at them.

Copy editors play an important role in the creation of visual images. In this chapter, we look at that role.

TELLING THE NEWS WITH PICTURES

Compare pictures from two front pages. Both are good pictures; the photographers have produced arresting images.

The picture of the dejected man on the front page of *The News & Observer* of Raleigh, N.C., surely will catch the reader's interest. The picture is played huge so that readers can sense the anguish of the fisherman. (See Figure 13.1.)

The picture from a Florida paper in Figure 13.2 has many visually interesting images. The composition of the photograph is excellent. Look at how the webbing of the deck chairs creates dark parallel bars that are echoed by the vertical stripes in the background. Even the woman's swimsuit has vertical lines.

Both are fine pictures. Yet we argue that editors used one picture well and the other poorly.

The story in *The News & Observer* shows the dejection of a man who is experiencing "fishing funk," as the headline calls it. The headlines, the graphic and the picture all tell the reader that North

193

Figure 13.1.

Large picture of fisherman helps tell the story on Page 1 of *The News & Observer.*

Carolina's commercial seafood industry is facing hard times.

Now let's look at the other picture. The story is about the onset of spring break when college students from the cold North make their annual pilgrimage to the sunny beaches of Florida. The story's lead reports that other parts of the nation were having a particularly bad winter, so bad that it was causing college students "from across the nation" to flock to Florida. But is that story being told by showing rows of empty deck chairs and one woman sitting alone with only a book for companionship? The picture, even though it is technically great, doesn't help tell the news. It doesn't belong on this page. Had the story been about a blizzard that had kept most students home, we would have a great picture.

REMOVING THE UNNEEDED

Much as a copy editor working with a story removes words that are not needed, editors working with pictures remove the sections of the image that do not help tell the story.

(Some terminology is needed here: Many editors refer to the process of selecting, editing and sizing pictures as *cropping*. Others use the word *cropping* only when they are selecting and editing images. They call the process of making those images fit the space limitations of the page *sizing* or *scaling*. In this text, we think of cropping and sizing as two distinct processes.)

Look at the images in Figures 13.3 and 13.4. They show two ways that a photo editor might crop the same picture. One shows a long view of the area; the other is a close-up of the kids on the slide. Which is the better crop?

The answer depends on what story the picture is supposed to tell. Assume that the story is about a new green space in an urban area. It has a playground for neighborhood children. A picture showing the trees and general pleasantness of the park is needed. The nature of the playground equipment is important to the image. The crop shown in Figure 13.3 is the best choice.

Now suppose that the story is about single fathers raising their children, or about stay-at-home dads. The trees, grass and space draw readers' attention away from the image the story needs. The picture needs to be cropped to show the happy faces of the father and the three kids. The crop in Figure 13.4 is better for this story.

CLOSER DOESN'T ALWAYS MEAN BETTER

Although you do not want to leave wasted space in the picture, remember that some space is necessary. For example, moving objects tend to seem less static if they have a little space to move into. Sometimes the surroundings add impact or help tell the story. Also, you want to be careful when cropping people. A general rule is not to crop them at their joints.

If the pictures in Figures 13.5 through 13.7 are about the successful landing of the shuttle at Kennedy Space Center in Florida, the one in Figure 13.6 probably tells that story better. The swamp in the foreground and the shuttle's proximity to the runway are key pieces of information. Also, by having space in front of the shuttle, the picture in Figure 13.6 gives a sense of motion to the shuttle.

Figure 13.2.
Lonely woman on spring break.

DON'T SHOEHORN PICTURES

Beginning designers sometimes feel pressured. They want their pages to have dramatic images. They have to fit all the pictures and stories into neat rectangles (modules) on the page. They want variety on the page. They decide that the perfect solution would be a strongly vertical picture. The problem is that none of the available art is vertical. Unfortunately, they decide to see whether they can't use Photoshop to get a picture to fit their preconceived notions.

One way to do this is a terrible crop like the one in Figure 13.7. The picture doesn't give the shuttle anywhere to go. With so little sky above the shuttle and so much air below it, the reader's mind decides the craft must be dropping straight down—not a healthful maneuver. To create a sense that the shuttle is moving forward, you have to leave space in front of the shuttle.

No one would intentionally crop a picture in this way. Yet a combination of a great idea for a page design and fast-approaching deadline can cause designers to convince themselves that the crop "really isn't all that bad." It is.

Before you begin laying out a page, look at the pictures and graphics that are available. Determine the basic shape of the picture and the

Figure 13.3.
Long view shows park and greenery.

Figure 13.4.
Close-up emphasizes relationship between people in the picture.

size it will need to be to tell the story. Then figure out how you can use those pictures and graphics to best tell the story. Don't design the "perfect" page and then hope you can shoehorn the pictures into the sizes you want them to be.

Designers know that computers can manipulate images in fantastic ways. But they also can distort images. Beginners sometimes try to get pictures to fit by using Photoshop to squeeze or stretch them. The results are often distorted images like those in funhouse mirrors. The picture in Figure 13.8 is the original image. In Figure 13.9, Photoshop has been used to stretch the image to fill space.

If the original picture does not fill the space vertically, it's tempting to try to make a picture more vertical by stretching it with Photoshop. The point guard in Figure 13.10 becomes a really tall player with arms that are amazingly short compared with the rest of her body in Figure 13.11. Sports fans—and the player—will recognize that the image is not honest.

Many editors are concerned that the people in their pictures should look into the story, not away from it. Occasionally, that's a legitimate concern. However, most pictures do not lead the readers' eyes strongly enough to worry about it.

The temptation is to flip the image to make the person seem to be looking into the story. There are three problems with doing this. The

Figure 13.5.
Shuttle cropped very
closely.

Figure 13.6.
The shuttle now has a
space to move forward
and the reader can see
that the shuttle is landing.

Figure 13.7.
Shuttle has nowhere to
go in this crop—unless
it's straight down.

Figure 13.8.
Original picture.

Figure 13.9.
Picture stretched horizontally to make it fit.

first is that any words in the picture will be backward, as has happened to the woman's jersey and the signs in the background in Figure 13.12. The second problem is that right-handed people are suddenly signing things with their left hands, or men who part their hair on the right are given a new hairdo. The third—and most important—reason not to flip pictures is that it is not truthful storytelling. This woman did not come down court wearing her shirt inside out and dribbling the ball with her left hand, as the picture seems to be reporting.

CREATING GRAPHICS

At well-run newspapers, graphics and photographs are the result of teamwork. Some newspapers hold what they call "maestro" meetings in which reporters, photographs, editors and graphic artists decide how a major story will be covered. The "maestro" is the editor in charge of coordinating the project. Whether a newspaper uses these

Figure 13.10.
Original picture.

Figure 13.12.
Picture flipped.

Figure 13.11.
Picture stretched vertically to
make it fit.

formal meetings or less formal conversations, the so-called "visual people"—the graphic artists, photographers and page designers—are involved as soon as reporters and editors begin to develop the story.

Let's follow the production of a news package at the *South Florida Sun-Sentinel* in Fort Lauderdale. The paper sells about 260,000 copies daily and 371,000 on Sundays. The staff covers an 80-mile strip along the Atlantic Coast. The area includes three of Florida's most populous counties: Miami-Dade, Broward and Palm Beach.

Journalists at the *Sun-Sentinel* were confronted with a monstrous amount of data in May 2002 when the U.S. Census Bureau began to release its analysis of American lifestyles, using data gathered in the 2000 census. Editors knew they needed to report findings for the region as a whole and for each county. And they knew that in an area growing so dramatically, they needed to compare the new census data with that of 10 years ago. It was too much for one story. They decided on a series that would look at each of the major issues raised by the census figures.

The package for tomorrow's paper would begin on Page One and fill an open page on the inside. Reporter Ken Kaye began to analyze the data using the Microsoft Excel spreadsheet program.

Editors did not want stories that were just numbers. They wanted the points made by the numbers to be illustrated with real-life examples. So, eight reporters began to find and interview people; three of them would collaborate on writing the final piece. Three photographers were assigned to shoot pictures for the package.

The job of presenting the data visually was given to David Horn, a copy editor/designer. Horn usually designs the paper's front page, but editors thought the package needed a detail-oriented person such as Horn. He has been at the *Sun-Sentinel* for about three years after stints at the *Florida Times-Union* in Jacksonville and *The Jersey Journal* in Jersey City. Horn discovered copy editing on his college newspaper and has worked on the desk ever since.

Horn met with Charles Jones, a senior graphics reporter, and they made some preliminary decisions about how to present the data visually. Jones would produce a series of bar graphs; Horn would arrange the numbers in tables that accompany the bar graphs. As Kaye began to make sense out of the census data, he e-mailed his findings to everyone involved in the project. Horn and Jones conferred several times throughout the evening to keep any statistics from falling through the cracks.

Meanwhile, Jim Rassol, a staff photographer acting as that day's photo editor, was going through the pictures that were being sent to the downtown newsroom from photographers in the field. Rassol selected one picture that he thought might be used on Page One and others that might go on the inside page. Later in the afternoon, Rassol took that potential Page One picture along with pictures of other news stories to a meeting of top editors who decide what will be on the front page. They decided the top story of the day—and the one that would receive the biggest picture—would not be the census story.

Throughout the evening, Horn and Jones sorted through Kaye's e-mails and worked on the graphics. Photographers continued to file photos for the package, and reporters and editors began to prepare the story. Horn would usually design pages, but tonight other copy editor/designers took over so that he and Jones could begin working on graphs for future stories based on the census numbers.

The next day's *Sun-Sentinel* had a census package with four pictures, a dozen bar graphs, rows of tables, a 70-inch story and four infographics that presented the highlights of the findings. The package was the result of the cooperative effort of reporters, copy editors, graphic reporters and photographers.

SMALLER, SIMPLER GRAPHICS

The trend in newspaper graphics is toward simpler charts and graphics. Here's a sample of Horn and Jones' work, which ran on the inside page:

In the 1980s and 1990s many newspapers used much more elaborate graphics, often embellished with little drawings. If a study said women had higher IQs than men, the chart would have a drawing of a woman next to a smaller drawing of a man. Often these pictures did

Foreign languages and origins

Number of foreign-born

■ 2000 ▨ 1990

Broward	Palm Beach	Miami-Dade	State
410,379	196,852	1,147,756	2,670,794
189,430	100,505	837,124	1,589,453

SOURCE: U.S. Census Bureau   Staff graphic/Charles W. Jones

Proportion of the foreign-born population from various regions.

	Year	Broward	Palm Beach	Miami-Dade	Florida
Pct. of foreign-born	2000	71.6%	64.2%	92.7%	72.8%
from Latin America	1990	54.0%	49.4%	90.4%	67.5%
Pct. of foreign-born	2000	7.7%	8.6%	2.5%	8.7%
from Asia	1990	7.2%	7.6%	2.4%	7.3%
Pct. of foreign-born	2000	14.1%	20.2%	3.8%	13.3%
from Europe	1990	29.4%	34.2%	6.0%	19.0%

little to help readers understand the point that was being made. Worse, occasionally the relative sizes of the drawings were not proportionally correct and therefore distorted the statistics.

EDITING GRAPHICS

Although everyone concedes that informational graphics are an important part of a newspaper, many editors do a poor job of editing them, giving them only a cursory check and then sending them into the paper. The result is likely to be a correction or clarification in the next day's paper. Mary Holdt, design director for The New York Times Company's regional newspapers, told *Design* magazine (Spring 1994) that she had scolded the chain's city editors for treating graphics as if they were works of art and not news. "You wouldn't put an unedited reporter's story in the paper," she told them. "Why would you put an unedited graphic in the paper?"

Some graphics obviously make it into print without being edited. They contain misspelled words and bad grammar. A Florida paper recently ran a locator map showing where "Maimi" was.

Sometimes the facts in the graphic are not the same as the facts in the story. One publication ran a clever graphic showing how many calories are burned by various types of exercise. The numbers in the graphic were higher than those in the story. The reporter and the artist had used different sources that gave different estimates.

Other graphics are just flat-out wrong. One paper used outlines of submarines for a story about reductions in the number of battleships in the Navy; another paper used an out-of-date drawing of an Air Force jet. A major newspaper recently ran a correction after it identified Europe as Africa on a locator map. For a graphic about the 9-11 attacks, one newspaper illustrated a story about the planes involved with a schematic showing the dimensions of Boeing 737. The planes involved were Boeing 767s and 757s.

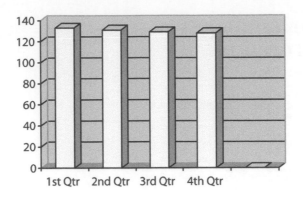

Figure 13.13.
The graph suggests that the company's stock is stable.

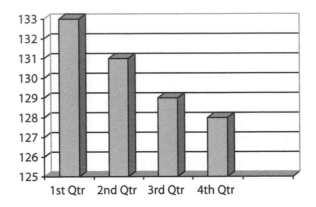

Figure 13.14.
The same data can suggest a rapidly falling stock price, depending on the baseline used.

Graphics can be technically accurate but still misleading. The graphs in Figures 13.13 and 13.14 are based on the same data. Yet the one in 13.13 suggests that stock price of the company is quite stable; the one in 13.14 shows that a company's stock is falling fast.

The difference is the result of graphic artists' decisions on what the appropriate starting point for the graph should be. The one in Figure 13.13 begins at zero and works its way up in increments of 20; the one in Figure 13.14 begins at 125 and goes up in increments of one.

Decisions on where the zero point should be are often based on practical considerations or the context of the story. Usually, graphs beginning at zero are more accurate representations. However, space limitations sometimes make that difficult: The stock-market graphs in most papers start at 8,000 or higher so that the graphs can be small yet still communicate to the reader whether the market is heading up or down and by how much.

Other graphs may not have zero as their baseline because they represent data in which small differences are very important: To business people, changes of 1 percent or less in many key economic indexes are major events. A graph that minimizes those seemingly small changes might not convey to readers the significance of the story.

Most copy editors aren't statisticians. They may not be sure whether the graph should begin at zero or some other number. But they can make sure that the information in the story jibes with the impres sion readers will get from the chart. If copy editors are editing a story about a company with a long history of stability, and the graphic shows the company taking a nosedive, copy editors have to speak up.

Which graphic should be used, the one in 13.13 or 13.14? Read the story. If the company is doing everything it can to stop its falling stock price, the graph in Figure 13.14 may be better. If the story talks about how investors buy the stock because it is so dependable, then the one in Figure 13.13 may be the right choice.

For a *Design* article (Spring 1994, pp. 34–37), W. Daniel DeJarnette, a journalism instructor and former copy editor, studied a variety of informational graphics. He found all kinds of errors, including graphics that said just the opposite of what the reporter had written in the story. He offered these 10 tips:

1. Assume nothing. A reliable publication once placed the Grand Canyon in New Mexico.

2. Double-check any sequence of numbers or letters. Sometimes numbers or letters are transposed or omitted.

3. Check all endnotes, footnotes, tables, charts and graphs. Make sure text and references correspond and agree in all particulars.

4. Reread all headlines—letter by letter.

5. Use a calculator to check numbers in tables and charts.

6. Use an atlas or map to double-check the location and spelling of countries, states, cities, counties, rivers, roads and so on.

7. Don't skip anything: Footnotes, precedes and shirttails (notes that come before or after copy blocks) and credit lines are easily overlooked—and potentially damaging. An endnote in one publication referred to an instructor in public relations as an instructor in pubic relations.

8. Be extra careful with the first title, headline, sentence and paragraph. These are the places where uncaught errors are especially noticeable to readers and embarrassing to publishers.

9. Read every word. If the story has only a little text, read it letter by letter—out loud even. If the story has a lot of text, read it syllable by syllable.

10. Familiarity breeds contempt. If you've seen the same text several times, you're likely to miss mistakes. Get another set of eyes to look it over.

THE BASICS OF PAGE DESIGN 14

Editors and page designers in the 1800s had it a lot easier than we do. They assumed that readers wanted to read every word in the paper. To them, layout and headlines didn't matter much. They would put a one-column head in the upper left and run a story as far as it would go in the first column. Then they would place the second headline and the second story. If the story filled the first column, they would place the rest of the story at the top of the second column. Stories snaked across the page, one after another.

Today's editors know they can't assume that readers will read every word in their papers. They use design to draw attention to stories and often to help explain the story. We'll talk a little about the general approaches to newspaper design and then offer some step-by-step tips.

BASIC UNDERSTANDING I: DOMINANT IMAGES

Every page needs a dominant image, usually a large graphic or picture. These images create what designer Mario Garcia calls "centers of visual interest." Readers' eyes are drawn to these pictures. They give the page focus.

The *Seattle Post-Intelligencer* in Figure 14.1 has a strong CVI. When readers open the paper, they see the giant picture of the ferry pulling into the dock. Their eyes are drawn to it. In addition to giving the page focus, the picture makes readers wonder what's going on with the ferry and why it's so important. Most of them will then read the cutlines and headlines, and many will be drawn into the story.

The page also has several "secondary centers of visual interest." The picture of the murder trial will draw readers to the stories at the bottom of the page. The *Post-Intelligencer* also uses typography to create centers of visual interest. The "Murder conviction" story at the bottom of the page has a boldface pull-quote, and the "Poverty breeds

Figure 14.1.

Post-Intelligencer has a dominant image. Courtesy of *Seattle Post-Intelligencer.*

Figure 14.2.
Poorly designed page.

terror" story in the upper left has a boldface refer. These refers (pronounced REEF-ers) serve at least two purposes. The obvious one is that they refer readers to related stories inside. But the bold type surrounded by white space also attracts readers' eyes as they scan the page. The boxes at the top of the page have both pictures and typographic effects. This *Post-Intelligencer* page works because the dominant and secondary images give the page focus.

On the other hand, the State and Local page in Figure 14.2 fails for many of the reasons that the *Post-Intelligencer* page succeeded. The page loses impact because:

- It lacks dominant art to give the page focus. The two large pictures are roughly the same size.

- The page has no focus. It's difficult for readers to know where to look first.

- All three pictures are the same basic shape. The lack of variety makes the page more static and therefore a little less interesting.

- The pictures seem poorly cropped with lots of wasted space. These bad crops also contribute to a feeling that the page isn't very newsy.

- The pictures are arranged in a stair-step formation. Instead of emphasizing the pictures, this arrangement tends to draw attention to itself rather than to the content on the page.

BASIC UNDERSTANDING II: MODULAR DESIGN

Most American newspapers are modular. That means that related stories, graphics and pictures are in one rectangle on the page. (See Figure 14.3.)

The *San Jose Mercury News* is a modular paper. On the right side of Figure 14.3, we drew boxes around each of the modules. Notice that some modules can include several related items. The centerpiece package about strife in Palestine contains several elements:

- A large picture that serves as the dominant art on the page.

- A large headline and drop head above the fold.

- A story and headline about the fighting in Palestine.

Figure 14.3.
Mercury News is a modular paper. Copyright © 2002 *San Jose Mercury News.*
All rights reserved. Reproduced with permission.

- A sidebar story about a local athlete who is from that region and the concern he has for friends and family back home.

- A picture of the athlete.

On the right side of the page are two vertical modules. The top one, "Jury: Texas mother guilty" has a picture, and the bottom one, "Consumers disregard," has a cutout of an auto. The "Airport checks" module is horizontal and includes an information graphic.

ARGUMENTS AGAINST MODULAR DESIGN

Modular design is used at an overwhelming majority of American newspapers, primarily because it presents the news in an orderly, easy-to-use fashion. But not all newspapers are modular, and not all designers believe modular designs are best. There are perhaps three arguments against modular design:

Figure 14.4.
Story is not in a rectangular module.

Figure 14.5.
Two ways to make the story modular.

- Some say that modularity is one reason American papers, particularly midsize newspapers, look so much the same.

- Modular designs sometimes cause editors to put design concerns ahead of news judgment. To get stories to fit into rectangles, sometimes copy editors have to cut important stories and let unimportant stories go longer than needed.

- Because all the shapes on a page tend to be similar, the pages sometimes lack contrast.

A few recent designs have not followed strict modular frameworks. Of course, many papers, like *The New York Times* and *USA Today*, have never been modular.

MAKING THINGS MODULAR

Papers that use modular design are modular throughout the paper, even on inside pages that are filled with ads. Modular papers will not have pages designed like the one in Figure 14.4. When you try to draw a rectangle around the "Strip-searches" story, you discover you can't.

The page can be made modular in many ways. Figure 14.5 shows two of those ways.

Remember that all related items, including stories, headlines, pictures and graphics, must be in the module. The page in Figure 14.6 is not modular because the story and the related picture are not in a rectangle.

The page would need to be redesigned so that the picture and the related story are in the same module. Figure 14.7 shows two ways that could be done.

County bans personal watercraft

WSB is assessing what disciplinary action to take after award-winning TV reporter Tom Regan "uttered a horrible obscenity" into a live microphone while a taped segment aired during Tuesday's 6:00 p.m. newscast.

Regan, a weekend anchor and general assignment reporter for the ABC affiliate "knows he made a terrible mistake," said WSB News Director Ray Carter.

Regan said his comment was "incredibly stupid, and I make no excuses for it. I would be offended if I heard that on television. I sincerely apologize to everyone offended by it."

The WSG crew was doing a story for the 6:00 p.m. newscast on rising natural gas prices and was on location in downtown Tipton.

"There were some kids who were trying to distract Tom," during the piece, Carter said. "Unfortunately, Tom let the anger get the best of him."

Regan's tape was running, and he "was not seen on the air at the time. ... He was in the live truck with the microphone open and, unfortunately, uttered a horrible obscenity," Carter said.

Added Regan: "I just assumed my mike was dead. That still doesn't excuse that kind of language. It was not directed to viewers in any way. I was just kind of muttering to myself."

Carter was undecided what disciplinary action would be taken. Regan joined the station in April 1989 and has received ten Emmy

John Jones gets one last ride on jetski

7 Brownie scouts given major award

A tornado ripped through the Elmwood Community college campus Sunday night and destroyed the library and damaged several other buildings.

About a dozen students were treated for minor injuries.

Officials said that if the storm had hit a couple of day later the injury list would have been much longer. Freshmen orientation was scheduled for Monday and classes were to start Wednesday.

Orientation has been rescheduled for next Monday with classes to start the following Wednesday. Officials are asking that all students and faculty stay away from campus until they receive further notice.

U.S. Weather Bureau officials confirmed that a twister touched down on campus, traveled about 100 yards on the ground and then lifted back into the sky.

ECC Pres. Mildred Haynes

Figure 14.6.
Story and picture are not in a module.

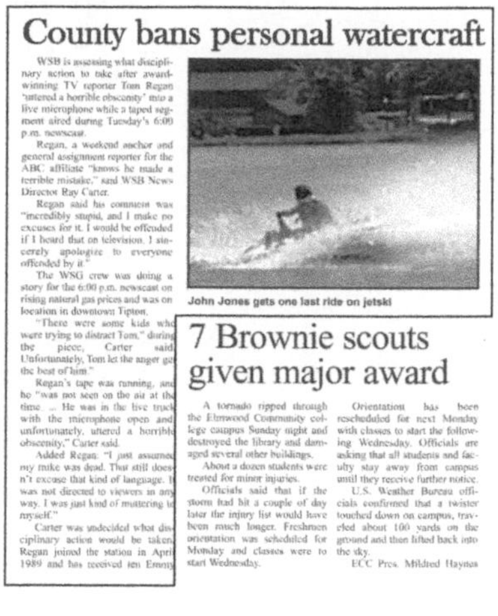

BASIC UNDERSTANDING III: NEWS JUDGMENT

At one time, design at many newspapers was so heavily formatted that the front pages looked pretty much the same every day. Usually, a banner headline ran across the top of the page set in 72-point type—regardless of the news value. Some editors even had a few designs drawn ahead of time. They would use the one that best suited the sizes of the pictures and stories.

Today designers recognize that design helps readers understand the news. Instead of preconceived notions about what the page will look like, designers look at the quality and complexity of the day's news and find ways to tell that news. In the examples from the *San Jose Mercury News*, the designers have preserved enough common elements that you can recognize it's the same paper. But the designs themselves vary so they can tell the day's news.

Page 7, *Daily Times*

County bans personal watercraft

WSB is assessing what disciplinary action to take after award-winning TV reporter Tom Regan "uttered a horrible obscenity" into a live microphone while a taped segment aired during Tuesday's 6:00 p.m. newscast.

Regan, a weekend anchor and general assignment reporter for the ABC affiliate "knows he made a terrible mistake," said WSB News Director Ray Carter.

Regan said his comment was "incredibly stupid, and I make no excuses for it. I would be offended if I heard that on television. I sincerely apologize to everyone offended by it."

The WSG crew was doing a story for the 6:00 p.m. newscast on rising natural gas prices and was on location in downtown Tipton.

"There were some kids who were trying to distract Tom," during the piece, Carter said. "Unfortunately, Tom let the anger get the best of him."

Regan's tape was running, and he "was not seen on the air at the time. ... He was in the live truck with the microphone open and, unfortunately, uttered a horrible obscenity," Carter said.

Added Regan: "I just assumed my mike was dead. That still doesn't excuse that kind of language. It was not directed to viewers in any way. I was just kind of muttering to myself."

Carter was undecided what disciplinary action would be taken. Regan joined the station in April 1989 and has received ten Emmy

John Jones gets one last ride on jetski

7 Brownie scouts given major award

A tornado ripped through the Elmwood Community college campus Sunday night and destroyed the library and damaged several other buildings.

About a dozen students were treated for minor injuries.

Officials said that if the storm had hit a couple of day later the injury list would have been much longer. Freshmen orientation was scheduled for Monday and classes were to start Wednesday.

Orientation has been rescheduled for next Monday with classes to start the following Wednesday. Officials are asking that all students and faculty stay away from campus until they receive further notice.

U.S. Weather Bureau officials confirmed that a twister touched down on campus, traveled about 100 yards on the ground and then lifted back into the sky.

ECC Pres. Mildred Haynes

Page 7, *Daily Times*

County bans personal watercraft

WSB is assessing what disciplinary action to take after award-winning TV reporter Tom Regan "uttered a horrible obscenity" into a live microphone while a taped segment aired during Tuesday's 6:00 p.m. newscast.

Regan, a weekend anchor and general assignment reporter for the ABC affiliate "knows he made a terrible mistake," said WSB News Director Ray Carter.

Regan said his comment was "incredibly stupid, and I make no excuses for it. I would be offended if I heard that on television. I sincerely apologize to everyone offended by it."

The WSG crew was doing a story for the 6:00 p.m. newscast on rising natural gas prices and was on location in downtown Tipton.

"There were some kids who were trying to distract Tom," during the piece, Carter said. "Unfortunately, Tom let the anger get the best of him."

Regan's tape was running, and he "was not seen on the air at the time. ... He was in the live truck with the microphone open and, unfortunately, uttered a horrible obscenity," Carter said.

Added Regan: "I just assumed my mike was dead. That still doesn't excuse that kind of language. It was not directed to viewers in any way. I was just kind of muttering to myself."

Carter was undecided what disciplinary action would be taken. Regan joined the station in April 1989 and has received ten Emmy

John Jones gets one last ride on jetski

7 Brownie scouts given major award

A tornado ripped through the Elmwood Community college campus Sunday night and destroyed the library and damaged several other buildings.

About a dozen students were treated for minor injuries.

Officials said that if the storm had hit a couple of day later the injury list would have been much longer. Freshmen orientation was scheduled for Monday and classes were to start Wednesday.

Orientation has been rescheduled for next Monday with classes to start the following Wednesday. Officials are asking that all students and faculty stay away from campus until they receive further notice.

U.S. Weather Bureau officials confirmed that a twister touched down on campus, traveled about 100 yards on the ground and then lifted back into the sky.

ECC Pres. Mildred Haynes

Figure 14.7.
Two ways to design the page so that it is modular.

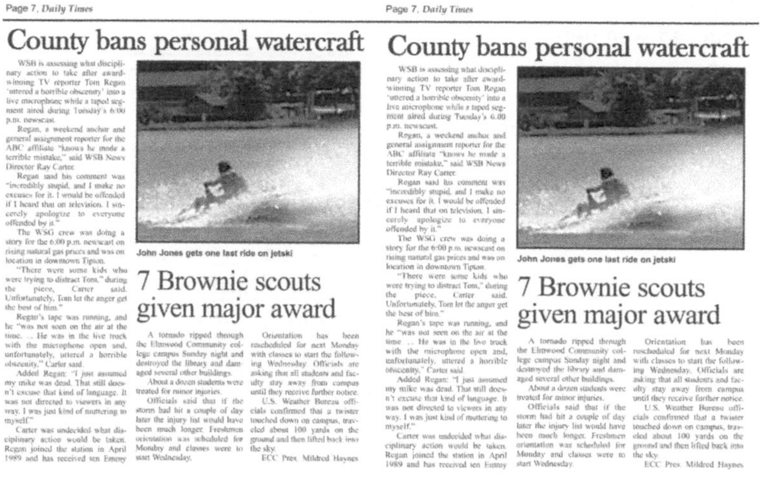

In Figure 14.8 are two front pages from typical news days, when no dominant news event happens. The story counts (meaning the number of stories on the page) are high, and many stories are placed above the fold (the middle of the page where it is folded). The space above the fold is generally considered prime real estate where only the best stories are played.

The page on the left has five stories. This page has three stories above the fold: A profile of a relatively unknown candidate for governor, a suicide bombing in the Mideast, and the Microsoft antitrust trial, a major story in technology-rich San Jose. In addition to the boxes over the nameplate, the page has a large block of type referring to two inside stories. The page on the right is a six-story front. The Mideast package and three other stories are above the fold. The front

Figure 14.8.
Two *San Jose Mercury News* front pages. Copyright © 2002 *San Jose Mercury News*. All rights reserved. Reproduced with permission.

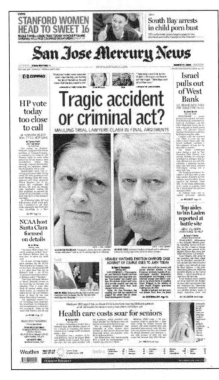

Figure 14.9.
Major area stories are dominant packages. Copyright © 2002 *San Jose Mercury News*. All rights reserved. Reproduced with permission.

pages of these editions of the paper tell readers there is news today, but there's no one major development.

When there is a major story, designers want the front page to shout that to the reader. A local story is major news on the pages in 14.9. A

couple was prosecuted for murder after their dog killed a neighbor. It
was the first time a murder charge had been filed against a dog owner,
and it was news throughout the nation. Because it happened in
California, it was even bigger news in San Jose. The large mug shots of
the expressions on the faces of the couple help give the coverage depth,
as does the look on the woman's face when the verdict is read. Both of
these fronts have six stories, but the trial story dominates them. On the
day of the verdict, only two stories are above the fold: the verdict and,
on the right, over the nameplate, the first four paragraphs of a sports
column about the NCAA basketball tourney.

Like most metro papers, journalists at the *Mercury News* often produce major investigative and enterprise stories. Designers want to give
these stories as much impact as possible. The front pages in Figure
14.10 contain major centerpieces.

When reporters uncovered a story that ski resorts were making big
profits by using government-owned land, the front-page design helped tell
the story with a dramatic picture of a government-owned mountainside, a
skier and the art headline "Cold Cash." The picture runs the full length of
the broadsheet page. The page still has five stories, including a key development in the Mideast. But the centerpiece dominates the news.

Six months after the 9-11 attacks, the paper put together a package
about how life had changed. For the West Coast and much of the nation,
the most direct impact was in air travel. The front page, in Figure 14.10,
again used a full-length picture, this one showing a jet taking off into a deep
blue sky at dusk from a local airport. This front has only three stories.

Figure 14.11.
The Virginian-Pilot uses design to help tell the news.

Efforts like these led the Society of News Design to put the *Mercury News* on its list of the world's best-designed newspapers.

The Virginian-Pilot in Norfolk is another paper that SND considers one of the world's best-designed. The paper is known for designing pages so that they help tell the news, as in Figure 14.11. When the man who bombed the Murrah Federal Building in Oklahoma City was executed, *The Virginian-Pilot*'s front page told both of the execution and the enormity of the man's crime. To tell the story of 9-11, *The Virginian-Pilot*, like many papers, used graphics and large headlines.

Sometimes designers can tell the news in very direct ways. When a prisoner escaped by crawling through narrow heat ducts, the *Savannah Morning News* in Georgia used its front page to show readers the exact size of the ducts. The dotted line around the story in Figure 14.12 shows clearly how small the ducts were.

This practice of using design to help tell the news is one of the more exciting changes in newspaper journalism. As newspapers continue to emphasize substance and context and leave breaking news to TV and the Internet, the role of news judgment in designing pages will grow.

BASIC UNDERSTANDING IV: BALANCE

Several years ago, newspaper editors thought balance was incredibly important. Many of the pages were symmetrical, much like the one in Figure 14.13. The page was divided in half vertically. The right side was a mirror image of the left.

Today's designers still use symmetry occasionally, often for the same reasons that made it popular before. Symmetry can be used in

Figure 14.12.
The designer at *Savannah Morning News* helped the reader visualize the story.

Figure 14.13.
Symmetrical page seems orderly and serious.

packages to create order and stateliness. Designers at *The Virginian-Pilot* used a symmetrical design in their coverage of the 9-11 tragedy. The symmetry adds to the seriousness and the impact of the page.

But designers no longer routinely use symmetry to get balance. Today's balance is considerably less formal. Designers make sure that the pages are not top-heavy, meaning all the big headlines and pictures are above the fold. They also make sure that big headlines and pictures are not on one side of the page. As you can see from looking at the examples of well-designed papers in this chapter, designers combine informal balance and contrast to create exciting pages.

BASIC UNDERSTANDING V: CONTRAST

Look at the four European newspapers in this section and the center-piece from an American paper in Figure 14.18. Unless you're multilingual, you probably cannot read all of them. Yet, you probably react to them differently. Does one seem more serious? Does one seem friendlier? More trustworthy? More sensational? You are making judgments about the papers' personality traits based on their design.

Figure 14.14.
Design helps develop a paper's personality.

The amount of contrast on a page is a major way for newspapers to display their personalities. The *Darlington Evening Gazette* (see Figure 14.15), a British paper, has lots of contrast, including:

- The variety of headline fonts.

- Headlines that are underlined.

- Some headlines that are capitalized and others that are not.

- Use of arrows.

- Use of boldface body type.

- Variety of shapes of stories and pictures. Draw lines around the stories. You will see that the "Young Braves" and "Trevor's a hero" stories are oddly shaped, while the "Bravery of Fred" story is a rectangle.

The Sun, a British tabloid, adds contrast in other ways:

- Headlines are at angles. Note the "Dido Love Split" and "Moulin Minogue" heads.

Figure 14.16.
Design of London tabloid *The Sun* emphasizes contrast.

Figure 14.15.
A British regional paper.

- Headlines have a variety of formats. Some are centered, some flush left. Some are white on a black background.

- Pictures are of varied shapes. The dominant image is a large cutout.

- Strongly contrasting colors are used. The right side of the page is bright red with green headlines. The box in the center of the page is bright green with red lettering.

These British pages have so much contrast that many Americans have trouble taking them seriously. That's not the case in England. *The Sun* is a daily paper with about 3 million readers, more than any newspaper in the United States. A former prime minister, Margaret Thatcher, once said that *The Sun*'s endorsement gave her campaign the boost it needed.

Denmark's *Frederiksborg Amts Avis* is tamer than the *Gazette* or *The Sun*, but it still has lots of contrast. The top picture of the sailboats is strongly horizontal and the middle picture is almost square. The paper uses serif type for most of its heads, but sans serif type in the left column. The left column has a slight color tint, which adds more contrast. Some of the headlines are in very large type; some are in small type.

FISHERMAN WAITS | 'NOT WORTH MY TIME'

Allan Peterson passes the time at the dock of Cahoon Seafood in Swan Quarter. 'It's just not worth my time to go out,' Peterson says of the prospects for catching crabs.

STAFF PHOTO BY MEL NATHANSON

FISHING FUNK

North Carolina's seafood catch lowest in 28 years

BY JERRY ALLEGOOD
STAFF WRITER

SWAN QUARTER – The harvest of blue crabs, the most valuable shellfish on North Carolina's coast, fell for the second year in a row in 2001, helping to push the state's total seafood catch to the lowest level in 28 years.

At docks along North Carolina's coast, commercial fishermen unloaded 137.1 million pounds of fish and shellfish last year, a drop of 17.1 million pounds from the year before, according to the state Division of Marine Fisheries' annual report on commercial fishing.

Not only did the total harvest drop, but the value of the catch dipped to $88 million, a drop of $20.3 million, the report said.

State officials and industry observers blamed the decreases on lingering damage from flooding in 1999, fishing restrictions and poor market conditions partly due to the Sept. 11 terrorist attacks. Destruction of the World Trade Center in New York forced a major New York fish market to temporarily close and relocate, dampening demand for seafood.

"I've seen some bad years, but I've never seen anything like the last two years," Claudia Cahoon, operator of a small seafood busi-

SEAFOOD HARVEST

Commercial fishermen in North Carolina landed 137.1 million pounds of seafood last year, the lowest amount in 28 years.

Pounds of seafood landed
IN THOUSANDS

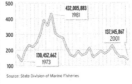

Source: State Division of Marine Fisheries

ness in the Hyde County community of Swan Quarter, said Friday.

Cahoon, who buys crabs, fish and oysters, said that good prices for blue crabs last year saved fishermen from disaster but that many

SEE **FISHING**, PAGE 16A

SEE **FISHING**, PAGE 16A

Figure 14.17. Layered package from *The News & Observer* in Raleigh, N.C. Reprinted by permission of *The News & Observer*.

General-Anzeiger has the least amount of contrast. At the bottom of the page are four stories that are the same size and shape. Above them are two stories, which are also the same shape and size. The top story is vertical; however, it is the same basic shape as the accompanying picture. The headlines on the bottom four stories in the *General-Anzeiger* are the same size and shape. The headlines in the middle two stories are also the same size. This lack of contrast makes the page seem authoritative. Many American designers are borrowing the look and feel of the German papers. They believe readers want newspapers that are more traditional and serious. The Society of News Design has included German papers similar to the *General-Anzeiger* in its list of the world's best-designed newspapers.

The Raleigh, N.C., *News & Observer*, shown in Figure 14.17, has more contrast than the *General-Anzeiger*, but considerably less than the British papers. Among the contrasting elements in this centerpiece are:

- The main headline, "Fishing funk," is all caps; the drop head is in a smaller, italic font.

- The "Fisherman waits" headline over the picture is in a sans serif typeface; the rest of the heads are in a serif face.

- "Fisherman waits" is in bold, black type; the words "Not worth my time" are gray.

- The picture of the fisherman is vertical; the graphic about the seafood industry is square.

This variety of typography and shapes undoubtedly caused many readers to take notice of the centerpiece.

BASIC UNDERSTANDING VI: LAYERING AND POINTS OF ENTRY

Many of today's readers are people in a hurry. They want to understand the news, but they don't necessarily have a leisurely morning to spend with the paper. Designers have developed ways to help these people read the newspaper.

One way designers do this is by *layering* the news. In Chapter 13, we discussed how well *The News & Observer* used the picture of the fisherman to help tell the story of the decline of North Carolina's commercial seafood industry. (See Figure 14.17.) The package itself is also an example of effective layering. Even if readers only scan this package, there are enough layers of information that they will learn about the problem.

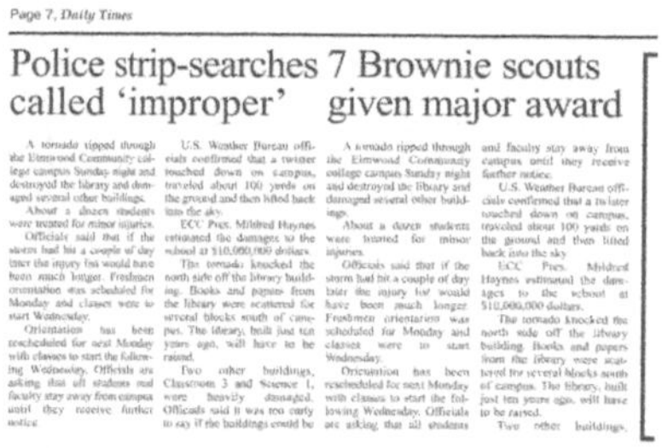

Their education begins with the picture. It is obvious that this man is sitting by the water looking forlorn. The headline declares what the picture suggests: Fishermen are in a funk. The drop head says, "North Carolina's seafood catch lowest in 28 years." The graphic shows that the seafood harvest is down. The cutlines (caption) under the picture read: "Allan Peterson passed the time at the dock of Cahoon Seafood in Swain Quarter. 'It's just not worth my time to go out,' Peterson says of the prospects for catching crabs." And the overline above the picture repeats that idea: "Fisherman waits: 'Not worth my time.'"

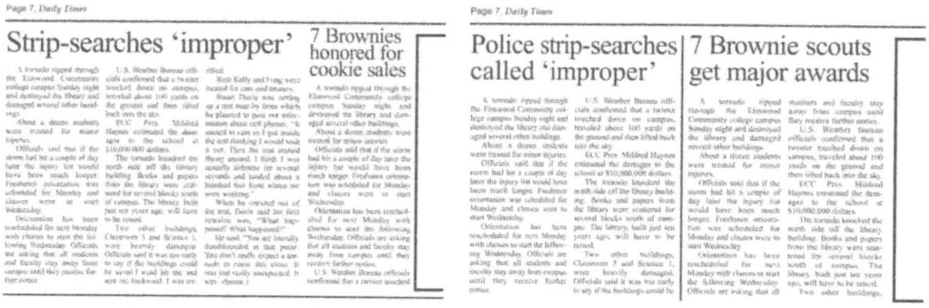

These items—the picture, graphic and headlines—also serve as *points of entry* to the story, meaning they may induce readers to read the story. Some readers will want to learn more about the plight of the fishermen in the picture. Or they may wonder about the "fishing funk." Others may be concerned about the ramifications of a poor seafood harvest on the state's economy, an issue raised in the graphic and the drophead. These points of entry probably increased the readership of the package.

PRACTICAL CONCERNS

In addition to major understandings about design, copy editors must deal with some practical concerns and accepted practices among designers. Most of these "rules" are really guidelines. Experienced designers know when to break them; beginners ought to follow them to the letter.

BUMPING HEADS

Placing two heads side by side is called *bumping heads*, as in Figure 14.18. The main problem with bumping heads is that readers might

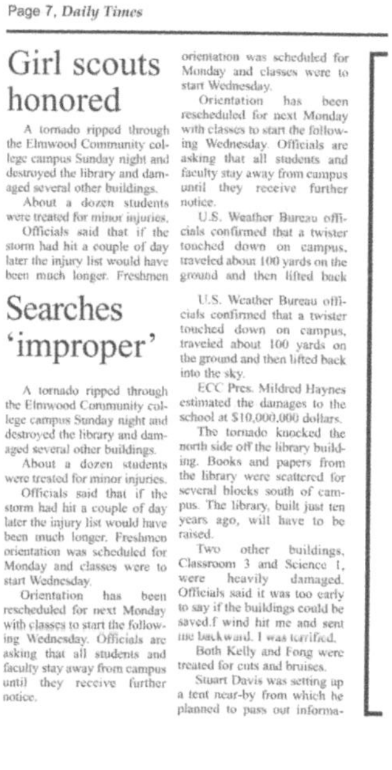

Figure 14.18.
Bumped headlines.

Figure 14.19.
Two ways to fix bumped heads.

Figure 14.20.
Raw wrap creates confusion.

Page 7, *Daily Times*

7 Brownies honored for cookie sales

A tornado ripped through the Elmwood Community college campus Sunday night and destroyed the library and damaged several other buildings.

About a dozen students were treated for minor injuries.

Officials said that if the storm had hit a couple of day later the injury list would have been much longer. Freshmen orientation was scheduled for Monday and classes were to start Wednesday.

Orientation has been rescheduled for next Monday with classes to start the following Wednesday. Officials are asking that all students and faculty stay away from campus until they receive further

notice.

U.S. Weather Bureau officials confirmed that a twister touched down on campus, traveled about 100 yards on the ground and then lifted back into the sky.

ECC Pres. Mildred Haynes estimated the damages to the school at $10,000,000 dollars.

The tornado knocked the north side off the library building. Books and papers from the library were scattered for several blocks south of campus. The library, built just ten years ago, will have to be raised.

Two other buildings, Classroom 3 and Science 1, were heavily damaged. Officials said it was too early to say if the buildings could be saved.

A small group of students were on campus when the twister hit. Kelly Stevens and Ada Fong were members of a

Figure 14.21.
Acceptable raw wrap.

Page 7, *Daily Times*

THS senior named top programmer

A tornado ripped through the Elmwood Community college campus Sunday night and destroyed the library and damaged several other buildings.

About a dozen students were treated for minor injuries.

Officials said that if the storm had hit a couple of day later the injury list would have been much longer. Freshmen orientation was scheduled for Monday and classes were to start Wednesday.

Orientation has been rescheduled for next Monday with classes to start the following Wednesday. Officials are asking that all students and faculty stay away from cam-

Girl scout wins computer award

pus until they receive further notice.

U.S. Weather Bureau officials confirmed that a twister touched down on campus, traveled about 100 yards on the ground and then lifted back into the sky.

ECC Pres. Mildred Haynes

Figure 14.22.
Wraps around pictures are generally accepted.

not immediately recognize that the page contains two distinct heads. Because gutters in modern papers are often small, bumping heads can be a problem.

The problem can be dealt with in two ways, as shown in Figure 14.19. One way is to use different size type in the headlines and different shapes for the stories. It's unlikely that any reader would not recognize that the page on the left has two headlines. Another way to deal with bumped headlines is to use gutter rules, lines in the space between stories as in the page above. As newspaper pages become skinnier, designers are using gutter rules much more frequently than they did just a few years ago.

RAW WRAPS

Most designers shy away from *raw wraps*. Other names include *naked wraps* and *dutch wraps*. Raw wraps are created when the text wraps into the next column without being under the story's headline. The problem is that readers may get lost. In Figure 14.20, does the "Girl scouts honored" story continue in the next column? Does the "Searches 'improper'" story continue at the top of the next column or half way down?

An experienced designer may use a raw wrap when the package is clearly designated on the page and readers are unlikely to be confused, as in Figure 14.21. If the story wraps around pictures, like the one in Figure 14.22, readers should be able to follow the story.

GRAY SPACE

Beginning copy editors are sometimes told to follow the "dollar bill rule." Here's the idea: Try to lay a dollar bill on your page so that the bill covers only text—no pictures, no headlines, no graphics, etc. If you can do that, your page may have too much gray space.

To be honest, it's not a very good rule. You can find lots of well-designed pages that would violate it. Think of it as a reminder that your pages should not have large blocks of gray space if you can help it.

The lower right portion of this State and Local page in Figure 14.23 is a large block of gray type. If designers had thought about the "dollar bill rule," they might have put a picture, pullquote or graphic somewhere in the lower right.

On this page, the gray space is not only dull, but it destroys the balance. The left side of the page has all the pictures. The right side has nothing but text and two headlines. While perfect balance is no longer considered good design, pages shouldn't be lopsided, as this one is. Although the designer may not be able to fix this page so that it follows the dollar-bill rule, rearranging the pictures and creating new graphics would certainly make it more interesting.

WHITE SPACE

The movement to narrower papers, discussed in Chapter 13, has caused designers to rethink how they use white space. The tall, skinny pages can create a dense feeling with type and pictures seeming to be squeezed. Perhaps that's why designers are emphasizing white space in their designs.

White space can be an effective way of grouping related items and separating unrelated items. White space around a package signals to the reader that the items in the package are related and that the contents are something special on the page—not just normal news stories. That's the effect designers wanted in Figures 14.24 and 14.25.

Designer Jon Blasco at the *Evansville (Ind.) Courier & Press* surrounded his "Butterfly Children" centerpiece with white space in Figure 14.24. To create more white space at the top of the package, Blasco centered the headline. He also *boxed* the package, meaning he put rules (lines) around it. The result is a centerpiece that stands out on the page.

"One thing I strive for is balance," Blasco says. "I try to make sure I have equal spacing between elements. I also try to balance the white space in the package. If I have white space at the top of the package, I'll create more white space at the bottom, as I did on this page."

Margaret Magee at the *Daily Breeze* in Torrance, Calif., used lots of white space around the "Blue Line" centerpiece, particularly along the sides of the package in Figure 14.25. Like many designers, Magee prefers setting the package off with extra white space rather than boxing the story.

To use white space effectively in packages, follow these three guidelines.

- Put the white space on the outside of the module. The white space in both the *Courier & Press* and *Daily Breeze* pages is on the edges of the module. Notice the extra space on the lower left of each of the modules.

- Don't "trap" white space, which means surrounding it by related text, pictures or graphics.

Figure 14.23.
This page has too much gray space and is poorly balanced.

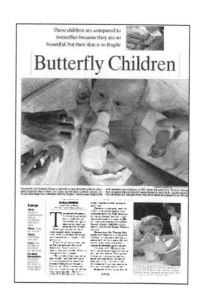

Figure 14.24.
The *Evansville Courier & Press* uses extra white space to set off centerpiece.

Figure 14.25.
The *Daily Breeze* uses lots of white space around centerpiece and on each side of the gutter rules. Copyright © *Daily Breeze*, 2002.

- Remember that white space should combine related items and separate unrelated items. Don't mistakenly put white space where it doesn't belong.

To make the pages seem more open, designers also put considerable white space around gutter rules (Figure 14.26) and cutoff rules (horizontal lines between stories). Most newspapers have design stylebooks that spell out exactly how much space must be used. Like many papers, the *South Florida Sun-Sentinel* specifies 1 pica around gutter rules and 2 picas between stories. When the *Daily Breeze* was redesigned in 2001, editors wanted a more open feel. Magee explained, "One of our major changes was the introduction of rules and adding the 2 picas of white space on each side of them to open up the page more and give it a more 'breezy' feeling."

The desire to maintain consistent use of white space has caused some newspapers to modify their basic grids—the underlying structure of the page. To simplify things for national advertisers, American newspapers standardized their pages at six columns. When copy editors begin to design a page on their computers—particularly an inside page—they begin with a six-column grid on the screen.

But for open pages (meaning pages without ads) many papers use grids with more columns. *The Tampa Tribune* has 11-column grids. Of course, no page would have 11 columns of type that skinny. Instead, designers place type in blocks that are two or three columns wide, creating a variety of column widths on the page and thereby adding more contrast. Another major use of the 11-column grid is to make it easy for designers to create uniform white space by leaving skinny columns blank around packages.

HIERARCHY OF HEADLINES

Many things determine the correct size of type to use for headlines. The paper's overall design plays a role. Papers with lots of street sales (as opposed to home delivery) often use bigger headlines so the headlines can be read more easily in news boxes. And some papers consistently use big heads to suggest to readers that they have big news.

Tabloids, like New York's *Daily News* and the *Post,* often use very large headlines to shout at readers. Other newspapers regularly use smaller headlines so they will seem more dignified. *The New York Times* rarely uses larger headlines. The fact that the *Times* has used big

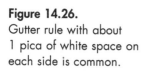

es | 7 E
er' | get

y from
ive fur-

au offi-
twister
ampus,
irds on
lifted

Aildred
dam-
ool at

ced the
library
papers
e scat-
s south
y, built
have to

ldings,

A
through
Commu
pus Su
destroye
damageo
building
Abou
were tr
injuries.
Offic
storm ha
day late
would
longer.
tion wa
Monday
to start V
Orie
reschedu
Monday
start

Figure 14.26.
Gutter rule with about
1 pica of white space on
each side is common.

Figure 14.27.
Chart suggests step-headline sizes for *Sun-Sentinel* designers.

headlines for a story is sometimes reported by other news outlets to drive home the magnitude of the day's events.

The importance of the day's news plays the biggest role in deciding the size of headlines. When terrorists destroyed the World Trade Center in New York City, many papers used very large type (and very large pictures) to indicate the monumental importance of that day's news. On slow news days, no story is worth more than a relatively small headline.

But some general observations can be made about headline sizes. Most newspapers have *stepped headlines*, meaning the bigger heads are on top and the smaller heads are on the bottom. Jeff Glick, the deputy managing editor/creative director at the *Sun-Sentinel*, prepared the page in Figure 14.27 to remind copy editors at his paper of the importance of using type size to establish a hierarchy of headlines. The sizes Glick suggests to *Sun-Sentinel* editors are fairly typical of the type sizes used by most papers on an average news day.

Figure 14.28.
Stepped heads in
Minneapolis *Star Tribune*.

But assigning sizes for headlines isn't mathematics. Editors at the Minneapolis *Star Tribune* in Figure 14.28 followed the general pattern of stepped heads. The top story, "Deal may be near . . ." has the most prominent headline. The type size is large, and the head is given additional weight by having four lines and a drophead. The second most important stories, "Chirac" and "Behind DFLers," have headlines that are about the same size. They are smaller than the headlines on the top story. The smallest headline is on the "Spiral of abuse" story, which is stripped across the bottom.

Type usually appears bigger when it's used in a one- or two-column headline with three or four lines than when it's spread across four or more columns. The "Behind DFLers" head has more impact than the "Chirac" head, even though the type size is about the same.

This page has one major exception to the stepped-headline rule. The type in the art head "Dome Rats" is the largest on the page. That's often the case with art headlines. Their job is to draw attention to the centerpiece, so editors make them bigger and often tinker with them so they don't look like the other heads.

On inside pages, the stepped headline rule is almost always followed. That's especially true if the page has lots of ads. The longest stories get the biggest headlines and are put at the top of the page. Shorter stories receive smaller headlines and are lower on the page. The page in Figure 14.29 does not follow the rule. Most editors would change it to something like the page in Figure 14.30.

ARRANGING PICTURES IN PACKAGES

Packages are collections of pictures, graphics and stories presented in a module. Designers almost always follow a proven and effective pattern in arranging the pictures and stories in those modules. They place the story so that it is immediately below the headline, as in Figure 14.31. They do not separate the headline from the story start. The arrangement in Figure 14.32 is less effective. The picture separates the headline from the story start.

The same general rule applies when the package is horizontal. The headline and the story start will be together as in Figures 14.33 and 14.34. However, few designers would float the picture in the story, as done in Figure 14.35.

There are exceptions. Many papers want to have the headlines above the fold on Page One so that the headline is visible in newspaper boxes and on newsstands. Often they will put the main headline above the picture and a smaller headline between the picture and the story start. Also, packages with art headlines may require special treatment.

Page 7, Daily Times

Girl scouts honored

A tornado ripped through the Elmwood Community college campus Sunday night and destroyed the library and damaged several other buildings.

About a dozen students were treated for minor injuries.

Officials said that if the storm had hit a couple of day later the injury list would have been much longer. Freshmen orientation was scheduled for Monday and classes were to start Wednesday.

Orientation has been rescheduled for next Monday with classes to start the following Wednesday. Officials are asking that all students and faculty stay away from campus until they receive further notice.

U.S. Weather Bureau officials confirmed that a twister touched down on campus, traveled about 100 yards on the

Police strip-searches called 'improper'

A tornado ripped through the Elmwood Community college campus Sunday night and destroyed the library and damaged several other buildings.

About a dozen students were treated for minor injuries.

Officials said that if the storm had hit a couple of day later the injury list would have been much longer. Freshmen orientation was scheduled for Monday and classes were to start Wednesday.

Orientation has been rescheduled for next Monday with classes to start the following Wednesday. Officials are asking that all students and faculty stay away from campus until they receive further notice.

U.S. Weather Bureau officials confirmed that a twister touched down on campus, traveled about 100 yards on the ground and then lifted back into the sky.

ECC Pres. Mildred Haynes estimated the damages to the school at $10,000,000 dollars.

The tornado knocked the north side off the library building. Books and papers from the library were scattered for several blocks south of campus. The library, built just ten years ago, will have to be raised.

Two other buildings, Classroom 3 and Science 1, were heavily damaged. Officials said it was too early to say if the buildings could be

Figure 14.29.
Not usually done: Longer story, bigger headline below shorter story and smaller headline.

Page 7, Daily Times

Police strip-searches called 'improper'

A tornado ripped through the Elmwood Community college campus Sunday night and destroyed the library and damaged several other buildings.

About a dozen students were treated for minor injuries.

Officials said that if the storm had hit a couple of day later the injury list would have been much longer. Freshmen orientation was scheduled for Monday and classes were to start Wednesday.

Orientation has been rescheduled for next Monday with classes to start the following Wednesday. Officials are asking that all students and faculty stay away from campus until they receive further notice.

U.S. Weather Bureau officials confirmed that a twister touched down on campus, traveled about 100 yards on the ground and then lifted back into the sky.

ECC Pres. Mildred Haynes estimated the damages to the school at $10,000,000 dollars.

The tornado knocked the north side off the library building. Books and papers from the library were scattered for several blocks south of campus. The library, built just ten years ago, will have to be raised.

Two other buildings, Classroom 3 and Science 1, were heavily damaged. Officials said it was too early to say if the buildings could be

Girl scouts honored

A tornado ripped through the Elmwood Community college campus Sunday night and destroyed the library and damaged several other buildings.

About a dozen students were treated for minor injuries.

Officials said that if the storm had hit a couple of day later the injury list would have been much longer. Freshmen orientation was scheduled for Monday and classes were to

start Wednesday.

Orientation has been rescheduled for next Monday with classes to start the following Wednesday. Officials are asking that all students and faculty stay away from campus until they receive further notice.

U.S. Weather Bureau officials confirmed that a twister touched down on campus, traveled about 100 yards on the

Figure 14.30.
More commonly done: Longer story, bigger headline at top of page, shorter story and smaller headline below it.

USE COLOR WISELY

Color stormed into American journalism in the 1980s and '90s. Color had been used before, but new presses and new emphasis on design led to papers that were a sea of color. Sometimes these seas got too wild. Newspapers were putting blue and yellow stripes in their nameplates. Front pages had pastel boxes and reverse type on bright blue and red backgrounds. And always a colorful picture, even if was the fourth picture of Rollerbladers this month.

Newspaper designers now use color much more effectively. They know that color can:

- *Make papers more interesting and exciting.* Readers, both young and old, like color in their newspapers. Studies have found that readers tend to think news on a page with color is more interesting than the same news on a page without color.

- *Help direct readers' eyes.* Studies done at the Poynter Institute have found that people look first at pictures on a page whether the pictures

Urban area or wild swamp? It's the new Big City State Park

New state park brings ← Head
nature to city-dwellers

Picture

Picture

Head

Story start

Story start

The former director of Northern State University's educational support department stole cash and took home thousands of dollars worth of electronic equipment, according to accusations in a university investigation report.

Belinda Marger, 49, resigned in April after Provost Marcella Jones recommended to the Regents she be fired after working 22 years for the university.

Details of the investigation was released Tuesday after a public records request by *The Blaster*, the NSU student newspaper.

The investigation into Marger's conduct was sparked by complaints from a employee in the department that he suspected illegal activities. Marger could not be reached for comment Tuesday.

According to the university report, the unnamed employee told a university official that Marger went with him to Home Depot in July of last year and purchased about $1,000 worth of supplies, most of which was taken to Marger's home. Among those items taken to her home, he said, was three ceiling fans. He said he hung one in her kitchen and two on an outside patio.

"She told me, Don't you say anything to anyone, because if you do, I'm through with you," the employee is quoted as telling officials.

When confronted by university officials, the accusations were denied. Marger said the employee was lying in an attempt to get back at her for telling him he needed to work harder, the report said.

"He wasn't a happy camper about that," she said in the

Figure 14.31.
Effective design.

Figure 14.32.
Less effective design.

are in color or black and white. Then their eyes are drawn to any color on the page, even if it is only a small bar.

- *Help show which stories are related.* Using the same color throughout a news package helps readers see the relationship between stories.

- *Help establish the paper's personality.* People react strongly to color. Research has shown that some colors make us hungry and some make us relaxed. A paper dressed in bright reds and greens is making a different statement from one dressed in dark blues and grays.

Color can also be abused. *Color screens* (also called *tint boxes* or *tint screens*) are one offender. These lightly colored backgrounds for short stories can be effective. But they must be handled carefully to make sure the type is still legible. Also, if overused, they make the page look like great-grandma's quilt. Tint boxes are banned at many newspapers. Other papers may allow editors to use one on occasion if the background color is a very light gray.

At one time, the choice of color was made by an editor who said something like, "Oh, let's put that in blue. No, let's use red." Today many papers establish color palettes. These are sets of standard colors

New state park brings nature to city-dwellers

The former director of Northern State University's educational support department stole cash and took home thousands of dollars worth of electronic equipment, according to accusations in a university investigation report.

Belinda Marger, 49, resigned in April after Provost Marcella Jones recommended to the Regents she be fired after working 22 years for the university.

Details of the investigation was released Tuesday after a public records request by *The Blaster*, the NSU student newspaper.

The investigation into Marger's conduct was sparked by complaints from a employee in the department that he suspected illegal activities. Marger could not be reached for comment Tuesday.

According to the university report, the unnamed employee told a university official that Marger went with him to Home Depot in July of last year and purchased about $1,000 worth of supplies, most of which was taken to Marger's home.

Among those items taken to her home, he said, was three ceiling fans. He said he hung one in her kitchen and two on an outside patio.

"She told me, Don't you say anything to anyone, because if you do, I'm through with you," the employee is quoted as telling officials.

When confronted by university officials, the accusations were denied. Marger said the employee was lying in an attempt to get back at her for telling him he needed to work harder, the report said.

"He wasn't a happy camper about that," she said in the report.

On another occasion the employee said an overhead TV projection system had been sent to a local shop for repairs. When the repairs completed, Marger told him to pick up the system and take it to her son-in-laws house. He said the device was listed on university records for months as being in the shop. "I know because we were getting lots of calls from pushy professors wanting to know

Urban area or wild swamp? It's the new Big City State Park

when that thing would be back in the lecture hall," the employee was quoted as saying. It was not returned until the start of classes in the fall, he said.

Once investigators began questioning Marger about such practices, she returned a 27-inch TV and a number of other school items, including a laptop computer, a digital camera, a scanner, a pager, a cell-phone, two Palm Pilots and a calculator, the report said.

Marger produced documents showing that she had signed out some of the items for temporary use. On the receipts were the initials of her secretary Mayra Hernandez. Hernandez later told district officials that Marger had her sign the receipts after the district started looking into Marger's activities, not before. Hernandez told her that she was 'trying out the equip-

---

New state park brings nature to city-dwellers

The former director of Northern State University's educational support department stole cash and took home thousands of dollars worth of electronic equipment, according to accusations in a university investigation report.

Belinda Marger, 49, resigned in April after Provost Marcella Jones recommended to the Regents she be fired after working 22 years for the university.

Details of the investigation was released Tuesday after a public records request by *The Blaster*, the NSU student newspaper.

The investigation into Marger's conduct was sparked by complaints from a employee in the department that he suspected illegal activities. Marger could not be reached for comment Tuesday.

According to the university report, the unnamed employee told a university official that Marger went with him to Home Depot in July of last year and purchased about $1,000 worth of supplies, most of which was taken to Marger's home.

Urban area or wild swamp? It's the new Big City State Park

Among those items taken to her home, he said, was three ceiling fans. He said he hung one in her kitchen and two on an outside patio.

"She told me, Don't you say anything to anyone, because if you do, I'm through with you," the employee is quoted as telling officials.

When confronted by university officials, the accusations were denied. Marger said the

employee was lying in an attempt to get back at her for telling him he needed to work harder, the report said.

"He wasn't a happy camper about that," she said in the report.

On another occasion the employee said an overhead TV projection system had been sent to a local shop for repairs. When the repairs completed, Marger told him to pick up the

system and take it to her son-in-laws house. He said the device was listed on university records for months as being in the shop. "I know because we were getting lots of calls from pushy professors wanting to know when that thing would be back in the lecture hall," the employee was quoted as saying. It was not returned until the start of classes in the fall, he said.

Once investigators began questioning Marger about such practices, she returned a 27-inch TV and a number of other school items, including a laptop computer, a digital camera, a scanner, a pager, a cell-phone, two Palm Pilots and a calculator, the report said.

Marger produced documents showing that she had signed out some of the items for temporary use. On the receipts were the initials of her secretary Mayra Hernandez. Hernandez later told district officials that Marger had her sign the receipts after the district started looking into Marger's activities, not before. Hernandez told her that she was 'trying out the equip-

Figures 14.33 and 14.34.
Acceptable picture placements. Readers can easily follow the story as it wraps under the picture.

New state park brings nature to city-dwellers

The former director of Northern State University's educational support department stole cash and took home thousands of dollars worth of electronic equipment, according to accusations in a university investigation report.

Belinda Marger, 49, resigned in April after Provost Marcella Jones recommended to the Regents she be fired after working 22 years for the university.

Details of the investigation was released Tuesday after a public records request by *The Blaster*, the NSU student newspaper.

The investigation into Marger's conduct was sparked by complaints from a employee in the department that he suspected illegal activities. Marger could not be reached for comment Tuesday.

According to the university report, the unnamed employee told a university official that Marger went with him to Home Depot in July of last year and purchased about $1,000 worth of

supplies, most of which was taken to Marger's home. Among those items taken to her home, he said, was three ceiling fans.

Urban area or wild swamp? It's the new Big City State Park

He said he hung one in her kitchen and two on an outside patio.

"She told me, Don't you say anything to anyone, because if you do, I'm through with you,"

the employee is quoted as telling officials.

When confronted by university officials, the accusations were denied. Marger said the employee was lying in an attempt to get back at her for telling him he needed to work harder, the report said.

"He wasn't a happy camper

about that," she said in the report.

On another occasion the employee said an overhead TV projection system had been sent to a local shop for repairs. When the repairs completed, Marger told him to pick up the system and take it to her son-in-laws house. He said the device was listed on university records for months as being in the shop. "I know because we were getting lots of calls from pushy professors wanting to know when that thing would be back in the lecture hall," the employee was quoted as saying. It was not returned until the start of classes in the fall, he said.

Once investigators began questioning Marger about such practices, she returned a 27-inch TV and a number of other school items, including a lap-top computer, a digital camera, a scanner, a pager, a cell-phone, two Palm Pilots and a calculator, the report said.

Marger produced documents showing that she had signed out

Figure 14.35.
Less acceptable placement of picture. Readers might think that the second column of story ends at the top of the picture and try to continue reading in the third column.

with instructions on how they are to be used. Designers choose the colors using color theory. Color theory is difficult to discuss in a black-and-white text like this. However, several Web sites, including Poynter's at www.poynter.org, have clear and reasoned introductions.

STEPS FOR LAYING OUT PAGES

How do you go about laying out a page? There's no clear answer.

At small papers, it's not unusual for copy editors to be given a page and a list of local stories and available pictures. They will then edit the stories, choose and crop the pictures, lay out the page and write the headlines. Decisions about what will go on Page One are usually made at a budget meeting of top editors, but the actual appearance of the front page is up to the copy editor/designer. For inside pages, wire editors use their own judgment in selecting stories. They then edit them, lay out the pages and write headlines.

At larger papers, these tasks may be divided among several people. Some larger papers have design desks. These designers are responsible for the final appearance of the page, but copy editors do the editing and headline writing. Often more senior editors make the news decisions.

However, even at large papers today, the movement is toward a more hybrid system. Often desk people are given the job title "copy editor/designer." They are expected to be able to handle design, editing and headline writing.

For these "Steps for Laying Out Pages," we'll assume you are working at a smaller or medium-size newspaper where copy editors are also expected to lay out pages and where they are also responsible for the content.

STEP 1: JUDGING THE NEWS

Design should help the reader understand the relative significance of the stories and, when possible, help tell them. Don't approach the page with any preconceived ideas of what you want the design to be. The content plays a major role in the design. To judge the news:

1. Read the stories and consider which are the most important and which will have the most impact on your readers. The best play should go to the most important story of the day.

2. Consider the relative importance of the stories. Some days have truly major news. Even inside pages may have strong stories. The design should show readers how important these news events are. Consider using big headlines or art headlines that use typography to draw even more attention to the story. Other days are slow news days. Nothing remarkably important happens. The design should reflect that, too. No story will dominate the page. The

story count (the number of stories on a page) may be higher than usual and the headlines smaller.

3. Look at the art you have available. In many ways, the decisions you make about pictures and graphics are going to play a key role in the design of the page. Also pictures can tell some stories better than words.

4. On most days, you will have one picture or one graphic that dominates the page. That's particularly true for open pages, meaning pages with no ads. Look for a picture that can be played big enough to grab the readers and tell the story effectively.
   a. Decide how big the picture needs to be to tell the news. Decide what shape the picture must be (vertical, horizontal, strongly vertical or strongly horizontal).
   b. You may need to do some additional cropping and resizing so the pictures will suit your needs.

5. Newspapers often feature packages on the front pages of sections and on open pages inside. These packages sometimes serve as centerpieces.
   a. Do you have stories and art that are related?
   b. Packages tend to draw lots of attention. Are the stories newsworthy enough to merit this attention?
   c. Do the photos and graphics provide a piece of art that could serve as a dominant image for the page?

6. Think about the relationships of stories. Readers have become accustomed to newspapers packaging related stories. Many papers will jump stories to inside pages and then put related stories on that page.

7. Be on the alert for unintentional packaging. You don't want to put perversely related stories together. Don't put a picture of cute toddlers eating cotton candy at the county fair next to a story about starving children in Bangladesh. Those kinds of mistakes happen even at the best papers. They are often featured in *Columbia Journalism Review*'s collection of silly newspaper errors.

STEP 2: HELPING TELL THE STORY

Copy editor/designers are part of the story-telling team. As you read through the stories and judge the pictures and graphics, consider what you can do to make the story easier to understand.

1. Look for lists. Depending on how important and interesting the information is, you may want to give it special treatment.
   a. Some papers use what they call pullout graphics for lists. The

list then helps layer the news and can serve as a point of entry. A story about the complicated negotiations at an international conference might include a pullout graphic "What the Russians want." Readers who scan the page will probably read the pullout and will learn something about the news. They may even decide to read the story.

b. Most papers use bullets (dots, squares, etc.) for lists in stories. Reporters sometimes present list in normal text fashion. If the list is important and interesting, copy editors might consider using it as bullet material.

2. Look for strong quotes.
   a. Pullquotes or liftout quotes are useful devices in two ways. First, like lists, they can help layer the news and serve as points of entry. Also they can break up gray areas of pages.
   b. Good quotes can be used in decks and labels.

3. Look for information that might be presented in charts or graphics.
   a. Ideally, graphic journalists are included early enough in the story process so that graphics don't have to be produced at the last minute.
   b. If a page designer sees an opportunity to present the information more effectively in a simple graphic, it's probably worth the effort.

4. Look for mug shot possibilities.
   a. Those half-column pictures of faces may be small, but they are valuable in helping tell the news, getting readers interested in the story and breaking up gray space.
   b. Most papers keep collections of mug shots of people who are frequently in the news. Often, usable mugs can be cropped out of larger pictures.

STEP 3: DESIGNING THE PAGE

Once you have judged the stories and collected the graphics and pictures for the page, you can begin the design.

1. Place any standard objects on the page. For instance, your paper may always run a 2-inch-deep nameplate across the top of Page One. An inside page may always have a column of briefs. If you place those items on the page first, you won't forget them.

2. If you have decided that some stories should be in a package or serve as a centerpiece for your page, you might want to design it first and then build the rest of the page around it.

    a. The package may include graphics, smaller pictures and sidebar stories. If the package is the centerpiece for the page, one of its pictures or graphics will probably be the dominant image on the page.

    b. Art heads that use typographic effects sometimes can be as effective as a picture or graphic at getting the readers' attention and helping tell the story.

3. If the dominant art is not part of the package, crop and size it.

4. Remember that you can't stretch pictures to fill spaces. The images get distorted. Decide the size and shape each picture will need to be now. Don't design a page and then try to shoehorn the pictures into it.

5. On more typical news days, most papers put the most important Page One story in the upper right corner. Researchers say there's no reason to put the main story there, but it is a custom that is widely followed.

6. If two or more stories are important, try to give them good play above the fold. In Figure 14.8, the *San Jose Mercury News* had three stories it wanted to give prominent, above-the-fold play.

    a. It stripped the "airport" story across the top of the page.

    b. The story about violence in Palestine is in a package with the dominant image.

    c. In the upper right corner—the traditional top spot on the page—is the story about a jury finding a Texas mother guilty of killing her kids.

7. If you are designing a front page or an open inside page, you will probably want at least one other photo or graphic to serve as a secondary image on the page.

8. Avoid large blocks of gray type. The dollar-bill rule is flawed, but it is worth considering, particularly on a front page.

9. Sketch a rough drawing—or even a dummy—of the page or check it for obvious problems in balance and focus.

INSIDE PAGES

Don't slack off when designing inside pages, even pages with lots of ads. These pages may not provide the same challenges as open pages, but often the stories are interesting and important. The design should help readers find these stories too.

1. The advertising department will already have placed ads on the page, leaving a news hole for you to fill. The ad lines will play a major role in how you lay out the page.

2. If the page is fairly open (meaning there are few ads), you will want a dominant picture or graphic. It will not be as big as the dominant image on the front page. But it will draw readers' attention to the page and give the page focus.

3. The most important stories go at the top of the page. They also receive the biggest headlines.

4. Less important stories go near the bottom of the news hole and get smaller headlines.

5. Use mug shots, graphics and pullquotes to create interest on the page. Research shows that even small pictures and graphics catch readers' eyes and draw them to stories.

EDITING AND DESIGNING WEB PAGES **15**

A few years ago, a noted Web designer made a list of the 10 worst things you can do when designing a page. Four years later, he revised his list. As you might guess, some of the former bad things had become acceptable. The designer, Jay Small, was asked what he had learned from his years of experience. He answered, "I'm certain of only this: No one yet knows how to design an ideal interactive service for a general news audience."[1]

The reasons? Here are a few:

- Software and technology are constantly improving. Each development in technology opens new ways to use pictures, animation and video.

- Readers are becoming more at ease with the Internet. A few years ago, research suggested that readers did not like to scroll down Web pages. They wanted longer stories to be broken into several one-screen takes. More recent research has found that readers have become more accustomed to scrolling. They will read fairly long pages if the content is compelling.

- Fashions change quickly on the Web. When software companies add a new trick or a new filter, Web designers can't wait to use it. In a few weeks, the new development is on dozens of Web sites, and in a few months, it looks terribly clichéd.

This constant change is why books about the Web—or even chapters in books, like this one—can become obsolete quickly. In this chapter, we stick to the stuff we think will be around for a while. But don't hold us to it.

THE WEB AND NEWS

Many news organizations, such as the *Atlanta Journal-Constitution* and *Washington Post*, were quick to begin offering news online. They saw that online news could combine the best of broadcast and print journalism.

Web sites have the immediacy of TV news. The BBC's Web site claims that it is "updated every minute of every day." Breaking news has become a staple of national Web sites such as MSNBC.com and CNN.com and of many local Web sites owned by newspapers and TV stations. When a fire broke out at a high school near Fort Lauderdale,

231

reporters from the *Sun-Sentinel* called details into the paper's Web staff. They updated the story whenever there were new developments. Meanwhile, a photographer flew over the burning classroom in a helicopter and took digital pictures, which were uploaded to the paper's computer system and quickly placed on the Web site.

In addition to having the immediacy of TV, the Web also allows for in-depth reporting and analysis, much like that of newspapers and news magazines. Multipart stories can be broken into effective news pages. Often these pages can feature more photos and graphics than could appear in a newspaper or magazine. After the Sept. 11 terrorism attacks, many news Web sites featured special coverage of a wide range of topics, including the nature of terrorism, explanations of the basic beliefs of Islam, the geography and history of Afghanistan, and the engineering behind "smart bombs."

As technology improves, the Web will become even better at delivering news. Today, most people use modems and dial-up Internet providers. The relatively slow speeds of these hookups limit the use of video and animated graphics. When broadband delivery services become the norm, journalists will be better able to tell their stories with words, high-quality video and interactive graphics. Some sites already have special pages for high-speed users.

EDITING FOR THE WEB

Today many newspapers simply dump stories from that day's newspaper onto their Web pages. Yet everyone agrees that reading a story on the Web is not the same as reading it in a newspaper: The size of the type, its distance from the eye, and the reader's sitting positions are all different. It's more difficult to curl up in a comfortable chair with a computer—even a laptop. Many people simply don't like to read stories online. Even Bill Gates, the tech-savvy founder of Microsoft, is said to prefer printouts of all but the shortest of articles.

As journalists and researchers learn more about how people read news online, they are finding similarities and differences in writing for the Web and writing for the printed page. Few journalists will be surprised by these recommendations gleaned from recent research reports:

- Keep sentences short. Limit them to one idea. Short sentences can be read and understood quickly. Given that many people are uncomfortable reading online, the short-sentence rule becomes even more important.

- Keep paragraphs short, even shorter than you might for a newspaper story.

Research suggests that Web editors and producers need to worry about the presentation of the story itself. Among the tips offered are the following:

- Use bullets and lists. They are easy to read, and they look good on the Web and draw the reader into the story.

- Write subheads (little one-line headings) every four or five paragraphs. Subheads can encourage readers to stay with the story, and they keep the screen from looking like a sea of gray words.

- Use a space between paragraphs and no indents. Readers are accustomed to seeing that on the Internet, so it's a good idea to stay with that. Also, the extra space keeps the page from getting too gray.

- Make links a different color and underline them. Stray from that Web tradition only if you are sure your new system will be readily understood.

Two versions of a story are shown in Figure 15.1. The version on the left is the story as it was written for the newspaper. The version on the right has received additional editing for the Web. The paragraphs have been shortened, lists have been broken out and given bullets, and subheads have been added. The result is a page that looks lighter and easier to read. It will probably attract and keep more readers.

Seminole County officials and a car dealership have been fighting over sign violations for so long one lawyer calls it "a story comparable to War and Peace." And the battle isn't over. County commissioners did not act Tuesday on an offer from Bob Dance Dodge to pay $3,000 on a $20,500 code violation, though the deal came with a promise to never again violate sign rules. County officials say the dealership, on U.S. Highway 17-92 near Longwood, has made similar promises before and didn't live up to them.

But commissioners didn't reject the offer. They simply postponed action while the county continues to work with Bob Dance on yet another sign issue. Since 1990, the county has repeatedly cited the dealership for violating rules designed to reduce clutter and garish business signs along roadways. The latest skirmish stems from violations in June, including balloons on cars. Balloons, pennants, streamers and similar displays are prohibited, except during grand openings, and the giant inflatable balloons car dealers love can be used only once a year for seven days. County attorneys recommend that commissioners reject the dealership's offer to settle.

In a September letter to the dealership's lawyer, deputy county attorney Stephen Lee said that, in the past decade, Bob Dance has been cited in four separate

Seminole County officials and a car dealership have been fighting over sign violations for so long one lawyer calls it "a story comparable to War and Peace."

And the battle isn't over.

Unkept promises

County officials say the dealership, on U.S. Highway 17-92 near Longwood, has made similar promises before and didn't live up to them.

But commissioners didn't reject the offer. They simply postponed action while the county continues to work with Bob Dance on yet another sign issue. Prohibited are:

- Balloons
- Pennants
- Streamers
- Giant balloon figures

Similar displays are prohibited, except during grand openings, and the giant inflatable balloons

Repeated citations

Since 1990, the county has repeatedly cited the dealership for violating rules designed to reduce clutter and garish business signs along roadways.

Figure 15.1.
Subheads, space and bullets make a page more accessible.

MULTIMEDIA REPORTING

Just as many newspapers are reworking stories for presentation on the Web, some are creating special reports just for their Web sites. These special reports have heralded the return of a long-lost journalist format: the photo essay. Years ago, newspapers and news magazines would run pages of nothing but pictures arranged to tell a story. As news holes became smaller, editors stopped running photo essays because they took up too much space.

The unlimited space of the Web has allowed newspapers such as the *South Florida Sun-Sentinel* and the *Herald-Sun* of Durham, N.C., to display photo essays. The *Herald-Sun* (www.heraldsun.com) often adds audio to its stories. When Duke basketball coach Mike Krzyzewski was inducted into the Hall of Fame, the paper's Web site had a photo essay of his career accompanied by audio of people talking about his life and accomplishments.

Because many major Web news sites are produced by TV networks, it is not surprising that they use video to help tell stories. CNN.com and MSNBC.com feature streaming video on many of their stories.

Many local newspapers also are adding video to their sites. As this was written, the online site of *The News Tribune* in Tacoma, Wash., combined still pictures, video, audio and words to explain the possibilities of an eruption of Mount Olympia, a nearby volcano. *The Philadelphia Inquirer*'s Web site used these multimedia techniques to explain the deadly rescue attempt by U.S. soldiers in Somalia. As the software improves, video images will be clearer, bigger and more useful as story-telling devices.

Converged news operations such as the one in Tampa described in Chapter 1 create even more of these multimedia packages. Tampa's TBO.com usually has four new multimedia presentations each day. TBO's staff combines stories and still pictures from the newspaper with video coverage by the TV station. Producers then add additional material such as the complete text of speeches and links to Web sites that have more information about the topic. These multimedia packages are one reason that TBO.com is one of the most popular news sites on the Web.

Interactive graphics—often produced with software programs such as Flash—are another way to tell the news online. After Florida's voting fiasco in the 2000 presidential election, Broward County adopted touch-screen voting. The *Sun-Sentinel*'s online version of the story included an interactive Flash movie showing voters how to use the new system. During the war in Afghanistan, England's *Guardian* newspaper created a Flash movie to explain the United States' military strategies if the war spread to Iraq.

The real promise of the Web is likely to be fulfilled when newspapers combine multimedia with nonlinear reporting. Mindy McAdams, a pioneer in online news who now teaches at the University of Florida, describes this new form of newswriting as "the inverted pyramid—broken apart." In a normal news story, reporters and editors decide which information will be read first, which will be at the bottom of the story and which will be left out because of space. Readers have little choice but to follow the story the way the reporter has organized it.

McAdams suggests that writing for the Web can be nonlinear. She means that reporters and editors use hyperlinks to give readers the opportunity to read the sections that interest them the most. Long stories are broken into a series of components. In a story about a proposed law, some readers may want to know the background of a bill. They might read that part first. Other readers may be more interested in the law's consequences and may start with that section. Still others might want to hear a tape of legislators arguing about the bill in committee. Or they might want to see a Flash presentation that explains the problem the law is meant to correct. In nonlinear reporting, readers can choose their own paths through stories.

Presenting the news this way will change the way reporters and editors organize the information. McAdams describes it like this:

> When an article is broken apart, the reader can move around at will within the text, choosing an order for reading that suits her or him.
>
> Two key aspects of these separate components:
>
> - Each component is tightly focused on a single idea, event, description, or problem.
>
> - No component of an article substantially repeats anything stated in another component in the same article.
>
> Each piece of an article will average about 250 words. Some pieces, or components, will be longer (up to about 350 words at most) and some will be shorter (usually no less than 150 words). These lengths are not arbitrary; an examination of most newspaper writing, and many other nonfiction texts, reveals that journalists (and others) already write naturally in blocks of similar size.[2]

Some journalists believe that writing stories this way will cause them to lose control of the story. They will not be able to emphasize what they believe is the most important information. McAdams and others argue this fear is unwarranted. They say that journalists will retain control of their stories by the way they select and write the components.

DESIGNING WEB PAGES

Just as writing for the Web is different from writing for print, designing for the Web requires new understandings and skills. Some of the apparent differences include:

- In a newspaper, large pictures can create impact. On the Web, they don't have as much impact, and they take forever to download. Research suggests that although most readers are drawn to pictures in print, they look at headlines first online.

- Bulleted lists are even more effective online than in print.

Figure 15.2.
"Salon" magazine.

- Newspaper readers are willing to turn pages to see what's inside. Web readers want to know immediately what information is on the Web site. They are much less likely to search a Web site in hopes of finding something to read.

- Newspaper front pages are often dominated by a few stories. A Web front page may give prominence to one or two stories but will provide links to dozens of others.

- Everything is smaller online. Although newspapers usually run their names across the top of the front page in inch-high type, online nameplates are often very small. "Big" graphics and pictures online are often only two or three inches wide.

- In one key way, Web design is much like newspaper design. Front-page designers worry about what is "above the fold" because that's the part of the page that is visible on newsstands. Web designers worry about what is "above the scroll" because that's what people see when they first visit the Web site.

The designer's task is to find functional yet appealing ways to create pages that meet these demands. The online magazine "Salon" (Figure 15.2) has won awards as the Web's best news site. Its home page features a very clean design. One story is emphasized. The rest are presented in lists. White space and color are used to make these lists easy to use.

HTML: THE LANGUAGE OF THE INTERNET

Web pages are written in a computer code called HyperText Markup Language. When you use programs such as FrontPage, Dreamweaver or Netscape Composer, they write the code for you. However, most Web designers learn the basics of HTML. They know that the software programs are not infallible. Sometimes the programs produce Web pages that don't work. So, the designer must tinker with the code. And sometimes the software doesn't create the effect the designer wants, so the designer writes—or rewrites—the code.

Mastering HTML can be a daunting task. But learning the basics is not difficult. Several Web sites have easy-to-use guides. A search of the Internet with Google, Yahoo or other search engines will yield dozens of sites. A favorite of many beginners is an interactive program at www.webmonkey.com.

HTML code is a set of directions that tell the computer what it should do. The computer recognizes it is being given an order when it sees words or letters in pointed brackets like this *<command>*. For example, <i> is the tag that instructs the computer to italicize. When you want the computer to stop italicizing, you enter a stop command, which looks like this: </i>. So, if you wanted to italicize a word, the code instruction would look like this: <i>*word*</i >.

Here's a simple Web page. The left column shows the HTML code and the right explains its meaning.

<html>	Tells the computer this page is written in HTML.
<head>	Indicates the start of the "head." The "head" is not seen when the reader views the page. Instead, it can be used to provide a variety of instructions to the computers. It can also contain "metatags" that help search engines find your page.
<title>My Page</title>	In the "head," we put a title of the page. Usually the title can be seen by the reader, so it should be something descriptive.
</head>	Indicates the end of the head.
<body>	Indicates the beginning of the body of our page. The body includes the words that will appear on the page.
<p>This is my <bold> first </bold> Web page.</p>	When readers look at this page, they will see this sentence. The word "first" will be in boldface type. The tags <p> and </p> show the beginning and end of a paragraph.
<p>I like to read <a href="http://www.cnn.com"> CNN</a>.</p>	Creates a link to CNN. CNN's URL address will not appear, but CNN will be underlined and in color.
<p>Here is my picture. <img src="pixofme .jpg"></p>	Tells the computer to place the picture here. The picture must have exactly that name and it must be uploaded separately from the Web page.
</body>	Indicates the end of the body.
</html>	Indicates the end of the page.

If you want to see how this works, type the code along the left side of the box in a word processing program such as Word or Write. Because computer codes such as HTML must be written in a basic text format, you will need to take two special steps. Use Save As instead of Save. In the Save As dialog box, name the file "mypage.html." In the Type window, select Text or Text Only. Notice that there are no spaces in the file name. Spaces won't work on many of the main Internet computers. And make sure that the name of the page is followed by a dot and the letters "htm" or "html."

You can see your page by opening a browser such as Microsoft Explorer or Netscape. Move the cursor over "File" in the top left of the screen and click. Select "Open" and find the page you just saved. If you want a picture to appear on the page, you will have to save it as a JPEG with the name "pixofme.jpg" and place it in the same folder where you saved the page.

UNITS OF MEASURE AND PAGE WIDTHS

Web designers use pixels to measure things. Pixels are the small squares of light that create images on a computer screen. The number of those dots determines the screen resolution. At one time, most monitors had screen resolutions of 640×480, meaning 640 pixels wide and 480 pixels tall. As monitor screens have become larger and video cards more powerful, screen resolutions have changed. Today, monitors can handle screen resolutions of 800×600, 1024×768 and higher.

The variety of monitor sizes and screen resolutions creates two considerations for Web designers. As odd as it sounds, designers never really know how big pictures and headlines will be when people see them at home. Two people could have identical monitors. But the screen resolution on one monitor may be set at a resolution of 800×600 and the other at 1600×1200. If a designer places a picture on a Web page that is 800 pixels wide, the picture will fill the screen on the first monitor, but it will go only half way across the screen on the other.

Web designers must take this into account when they decide how wide their pages will be. Suppose that the designer creates a great page that is 1000 pixels wide. And suppose that the reader at home has an older monitor with the screen resolution set at 640 pixels wide. Instead of a great-looking page, the reader will see a mess. About a third of the page will be off the screen to the right. In addition to scrolling down to see the page, the reader will have to scroll horizontally across the page to read each line of the story. That's a major inconvenience.

To prevent this problem, many designers set their page widths to satisfy as many readers as possible. HTML lets you create pages that will fit any screen, no matter what the resolution. Some news sites use this one-size-fits-all approach. However, this approach does not work well if the page design is very intricate. It causes at least two problems. One problem becomes obvious immediately: You lose control of where the graphics will appear in relation to the text on the page. A less obvious problem has to do with readability. Reading experts say that text is more difficult to read if it is in very narrow columns or very wide columns. Controlling the width of columns solves these problems.

WEB COLORS

Designers also don't know for sure what shades of color will appear on their pages when the reader sees them. That beautiful scarlet on the designer's screen may be a dull dark red on some readers' monitors. Several factors affect color. The browsers Netscape and Internet Explorer create slightly different shades of some colors. Also, colors can be different on a Macintosh than on a Windows computer. The quality of monitors and video cards also will affect the colors the viewers see.

Early in the history of the World Wide Web, the creators of Netscape and Explorer agreed to use a 216-color palette. This palette was designed to make viewing Web pages faster and to deal with limitations of the computer color technology of the day. Web designers accepted the notion that there are 216 Web-safe colors. A Web-safe color supposedly will appear pretty much the same on all monitors. Charts are available online that show the 216 colors. Photoshop gives users the option of working with only these Web-safe colors. (It's frequently called a 256-color palette, but some of the colors are not available to designers.)

As researchers learn more about computer technology, some of them have challenged the number of colors that are truly Web-safe. Some contend that only 22 colors are truly Web-safe. Others think the quality of computers is so high today that nearly every color is Web-safe. They argue that designers no longer need to worry about whether their colors are Web-safe.

Until the experts sort out these issues, you should be aware of the problem when you select colors for the Web. It's probably a good idea to check the box that limits you to the Web-safe color palette when you're working in Photoshop. And you'll probably get better results if you stay with basic colors. The professionals do. Spend some time looking at professionally designed Web pages, and you will see lots of solid reds, blues and greens.

TABLES

At first, HTML was used primarily by scientists who shared their research on a network of computers developed by the U.S. Department of Defense. Because scientists often reported their data in tables, it was imperative that HTML be able to create tables. Scientists used tables like this:

	Took experimental drug	Took placebo
Got better	73	14
Got worse	1	15
No change	6	91
Totals	80	120

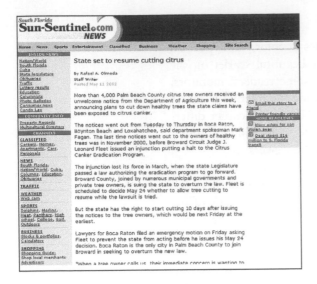

This table has three columns and five rows. Altogether it has 15 cells, which are not all the same size. The upper-left cell is blank.

Curiously, Web designers use tables in ways the HTML creators never imagined. Tables have become the basic element of design. Web designers use the same <table> command that the scientists used. But they no longer put numbers and headings in the cells. They put pictures, graphics and text.

On basic pages, the tables are obvious. Figure 15.3 shows a fairly typical news page of the online version of the *South Florida Sun-Sentinel*. We've drawn an outline of the page's basic framework. It is a table with three columns and two rows. The six cells are not the same size.

For more complex pages, tables are placed inside tables. A more complex Web page, also from the *Sun-Sentinel*, is shown in 15.4. The designer began the page by setting up a table that has four columns and two rows. (We've outlined this basic table with heavier lines in the drawing.) Next, the designer placed additional tables inside the cells of the original table. (We've outlined them and shaded them light gray.)

Look at the three bottom cells. The cell on the left contains a table that is 1 cell wide and two cells tall. The large cell in the middle has two tables. The cell on the right

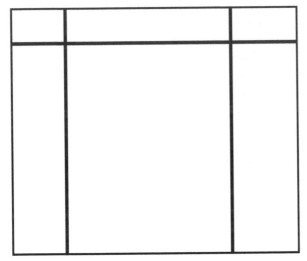

Figure 15.3.

A page from the *South Florida Sun-Sentinel* Web site and an outline of its tables.

has one table with four cells. The designer then placed the words and pictures in these cells. By arranging the size and location of the cells, the designer hoped to create a pleasing page. Because the table widths are set at 780 pixels, the page will appear the same on everyone's computer. (Except, of course, on those of people still using 640-pixel-wide screen resolution. Part of the page will be off their screens.)

Software programs such as FrontPage, Dreamweaver and Netscape Composer create tables for you. Always begin a page by creating a table of the standard width for your publication (usually 600 or 780 pixels). You can then build your page inside this table.

GRAPHICS, PICTURES AND THE WEB

Web graphics and photographs are usually created and edited in programs such as Photoshop and then saved in a format that can be used on the Web. Most online graphics and pictures are in one of the following formats:

- Photographs are almost always in the JPEG format. This format, pronounced jay-peg, usually reproduces good-quality pictures with fairly short download times.

- Graphics such as those used for nameplates or for typographic effects are almost always in GIF format. GIF, which some people pronounce with a hard *g* and others pronounce as jiff, like the peanut butter, is best for graphics with solid colors and for line art. GIF format has two advantages. GIFs can have transparent backgrounds. If a page has textures or a colored background, a transparent GIF will not cover up these effects. GIFs also can be used to produce simple animations.

- PNG, pronounced ping, is a newer format. It was expected to replace GIF. However, it has been slow to gain acceptance.

- Animated graphics produced with programs such as Flash are saved in SWF format.

Many Web design beginners forget a peculiarity about Web design. When you design a Web page with a picture, you are not really placing the picture on the page. You are placing *instructions* in HTML for the computer to find the picture and place it on the page. You have to upload both the page and the picture separately to the server. It's easier if you place the picture in the same folder as the page, but some designers prefer to put all the pictures in one folder. To upload pages and pictures, you will need a basic FTP (file transfer protocol) program. Some are available on the Web as freeware.

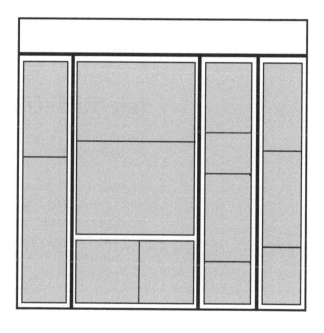

Figure 15.4.
More complex *Sun-Sentinel* page and an outline of its tables.

THINGS TO CONSIDER

The Internet has lots of sites that offer basic instruction in Web design. Unfortunately, often the advice on one contradicts the advice on another. As this was being written, one popular site was trying to teach good design by showing examples of really awful Web pages. The site has a feature called "The Daily Sucker," which selects and critiques a poorly designed Web site each day. The site, www.webpagesthatsuck.com, is a good starting point for beginning designers. Webmonkey at www.web-monkey.com also offers great advice. Keep in mind, though, that today's really great advice may produce a page that in a year might be "The Daily Sucker." You must constantly be learning new skills and new design techniques to keep your pages up-to-date. Here are three ways to do that:

- Review other sites. If a page has an interesting feature, add the technique to your repertoire. Don't steal the design. But use it as a starting point for your own creativity. If the site uses software you don't know how to use, perhaps it's time to learn.

- Keep up with the research. Good work is being done at the Poynter Institute (www.poynter.org). Another source for research is Online Journalism Review (www.ojr.org).

- Challenge yourself to find new and interesting ways of telling the news.

TEN GUIDELINES FOR BASIC WEB DESIGN

Although Web design is ever changing, here are 10 basic guidelines that we think will be around for at least as long as this book:

1. Set your page width with the tables command <tables width=760>. Software programs such as Front Page and Dreamweaver make it easy to do this. As this was written, the standard was approximately 760 pixels, although some sites still use 600-pixel widths. As monitors get larger and graphics cards more powerful, those standards will change.

2. Don't get carried away with technology. Rollovers, Flash animations and animated GIFs can make pages more fun for readers. Also, animations can explain some information more clearly than words and pictures. But don't use these rollovers and animations just to show how good your computer skills are. They can distract and even annoy readers. Worse, these fancy graphics slow download times.

3. Don't use clip art just for the sake of using clip art. The Internet is filled with sites that offer free clip art. Most of the time, clip art makes an otherwise good page look amateurish. Rarely does clip

art help tell the story. If your page has a story about football and a picture of a football player, adding a clip-art image of a football doesn't provide much additional information.

4. Don't steal graphics and photographs. It's easy to go to someone else's site and copy the pictures and graphics. But doing so is stealing and a violation of copyright law. Freelance photographers and graphic artists depend on selling their work to make a living. Copying their work and then giving them credit is not enough. A credit line or byline won't help them pay their bills. Contact the owner of the copyright before you take copyrighted graphics and pictures off the Web. And remember that a picture or graphic does not have to have the copyright symbol to be copyrighted.

5. Think about what readers will see when they first open your page. Chances are, they will see from the top of your page down about 400 pixels. To see the rest of the page, they will have to scroll. That top 400 pixels should sell the story to readers. Don't create your graphics and pictures so big that they are the only things readers see. Almost always, you will want a picture or graphic, the headline and the start of the story in the top 400 pixels of the page.

6. Keep things small. Readers will view your pictures and graphics on a bright computer screen. A small picture on the Web can have as much impact as a much larger one in a newspaper. Experiment with picture sizes. Smaller is often better.

7. Be cautious with background colors and textures. Make sure that backgrounds do not make the text hard to read. If you intend to place pictures on the page, make sure that the textures or patterns in the background do not clash with the pictures. White backgrounds are safe bets.

8. Avoid long columns of gray type. Long columns of type on a computer screen can be difficult for even the most computer-savvy reader. Find ways to break up long text passages. Drop caps, pullquotes and other design techniques can make a long story more appealing to readers. Add a subhead every five or six paragraphs so that the reader can see what's in the rest of the story.

9. Make sure that readers will have an easy time navigating from any one of your pages to the next. Readers need to know where to click and what will happen when they click there. If you use icons as navigation tools, make sure that they are clear. For example, arrows may work as navigation tools. But arrows and

the word *next* may work better. Also, make sure that readers can get back to your home page easily.

10. When you create links to other sites, tell readers why they should go to those sites. On a story about pets, you might write, "For more information, go to www.purina.com." But your readers will appreciate your page more if you tell them what they can find at these other sites. Currently, the Purina Web site has an interactive questionnaire to help people choose the right pet for them.

11. (A bonus guideline.) Nearly all Internet users expect links to be in a different color and underlined. If your links follow that pattern, you don't have to write, "Click here to read CNN." Also, if you want the reader to go to a specific page on a Web site, make the link go to that page. An example: www.sun-sentinel.com will take readers to the front page of the *Sun-Sentinel*'s Web site. But www.sun-sentinel.com/edge/santa.htm will take them directly to the *Sun-Sentinel*'s clever collection of Flash Santa Clauses.

REFERENCES

1. Jay Small, "Ideal Web design: No one knows what it looks like," *The Media Center* (americanpressinstitute.org/mediacenter), March 2002.

2. Mindy McAdams and Stephanie Berger, "Hypertext," *Journal of Electronic Publishing*, March 2001.

EDITING SYMBOLS

Over the years, copy editors have developed a set of symbols so that they can quickly mark copy for printers to set into type. With computers, of course, editors make the changes in the copy on the computer screen and don't need to use the symbols. But that doesn't mean the symbols are relics.

Occasionally you'll edit printouts of stories. More often, you'll read proofs, which are photocopies of the pages given to the copy desk before the page is sent to the pressroom. Copy editors go over these proofs in what is typically the last chance to catch mistakes before the presses roll. In addition, proofing offers another set of eyes because editors generally proof stories they didn't edit themselves. The markings used in proofreading are pretty much the standard editing symbols. Learning them is easy and well worth the 20 minutes it will take to commit them to memory.

Figure App 1.1.
Editing symbols.

Paragraph this.

But not this.

This is different.

We use a line to help.

Transpose two letters.

Transpose elements two.

Capitalize stanton.

Lower case Town.

Indicate bold face.

Indicate Italics.

Abbreviate: 105 Poi Street.

Spell out: Calif. man.

Spell out: 9

Use a figure: twelve dogs

Separate two words

Join words: week end

Join letters.

Delete one or more words.

Delete a letter.

Insert a missing letter.

Insert a word phrase

Put a period here

On this line try a comma.

Open quotes:

Close quotes:

Use a dash right here.

Restore this wrong deletion. *stet*

Underscore these in

handwriting: *a u w*

Overscore these in

handwriting: *m n o*

Insert apostrophe: Smiths.

Center this line.

Do not obliterate copy; mark

it out with a definite but thin

line so it can be compared with

the printed version.

Always use a sharpened pencil.

COUNTING HEADLINES

Traditionally, copy editors were told how many units they could use in each line of the head. They would write a head and then count the number of units. Note the use of the word *units* rather than *letters*. All letters are not created equally. Some, such as *M*, are wide; others, such as *i*, are thin. So editors assign more units to wide letters than to thin letters.

Here, we describe the *flirt* system. In this system, the thin *f*, *l*, *i*, *r* and *t* are counted as 1/2 unit. Most other lowercase letters count 1 each, except *m* and *w*, which are fatter and therefore count 1 1/2. Most capital letters count as 1 1/2, except for the capital *M* and *W*, which are even fatter, so they count as 2. Small punctuation marks count 1/2 each; the fat ones count 1 1/2. Spaces usually count 1, although some newspapers count them as 1/2. In chart form, we have:

1 count	1/2 count	1 1/2 counts	2 counts
abcdeghjk	flirt l	ABCDEFGH	MW
nopqsuvxyz	, . ; ! _ : ( )	JKLNOPQR	
s (space)	1{ }[ ]=	STUVXYZmw	
		@#$%&— ¢?	

You may have seen count lists that differ a little from our flirt system. That's because in some typefaces the letters *j* and *r* are very thin and need to be counted as 1/2. In other faces, the *j* and *r* are fatter and get a full count. It's the same for spaces. Papers that begin each word in a headline with a capital letter don't need much space between words for ReadersToBeAble to separate words. But papers that don't capitalize all words needmorespace.

Now try your hand at counting a headline. Count spaces as 1:

Yarber calls president a liar

This headline counts 24 1/2 by the system outlined above. Note that if we just counted letters and spaces, it would count 29.

Beginners find it convenient to make marks on the copy to keep track of the count:

Yarber calls president a liar

247

The marks below the letters count 1, and the marks above the letters count 1/2. Count the number of marks below the letters (19 of them here) and then count them above the letters (11 of them here). Because the marks above the letters count 1/2, divide that count in half and add it to the count below the letters. You get 5 1/2 plus 19, or 24 1/2.

Count these heads, excluding the identifying numbers.

1. Prune pie is plum good
2. Prune pudding wrinkles noses
3. Quick brown foxes jump
4. Illicit Illinoisan is illiterate

Answers: 1. 21; 2. 26 1/2; 3. 22; and 4. 22 1/2.

SIZING PICTURES WITHOUT COMPUTERS

In Chapter 13 we go into some detail about cropping pictures, that is, making editorial decisions about pictures. These editorial judgments are made much the same way whether you are editing pictures on a computer or from a print. The advantage of the computer is that you can see exactly what your cropped picture will look like.

But the next step in handling pictures—we've called it sizing—has changed. The computer takes care of the math for you. But before computers came along (and in newsrooms that don't yet have computer systems that handle graphics well), editors relied on two methods to size pictures. They used either a mathematical procedure or a proportion wheel.

Remember that we are trying to find the dimensions of the picture as it will appear in the newspaper. We can measure the size of the original picture. That's the easy part. And we can decide how wide we want the picture to be in the paper. But here's the math problem we're trying to solve. If we enlarge the width of our original picture to the size we want it to be in the paper, how tall will the picture become? (Remember that pictures must be enlarged proportionally.) If we write this problem as an equation, it looks like this:

$$\frac{\text{Width of Reproduction}}{\text{Width of Original}} = \frac{x}{\text{Height of Original}}$$

In this equation, the width and height of the original are what you measure your picture to be after you've cropped out the unneeded parts. Then you make an editorial decision about how wide you want the picture to be when it appears in the paper. That's the width of reproduction. The x indicates the height (some call it depth) of the reproduction, which is what you have to figure out. If you remember your basic algebra class back in high school, you'll recall that you can cross-multiply to solve for x.

Let's do this with real numbers. We're using a picture that is 3 by 2 inches (width is always given before height). Your equation will start like this:

$$\frac{\text{Width of Reproduction}}{3 \ (\text{Width of Original})} = \frac{x}{2 \ (\text{Height of Original})}$$

Say that we want to run the picture so that it is 3 columns wide, which is just over 6 inches (we'll round it to 6 to make the math easier). So we plug the 6 in as the width of reproduction:

$$\frac{6 \text{ (Width of Reproduction)}}{3 \text{ (Width of Original)}} = \frac{x}{2 \text{ (Height of Original)}}$$

We know enough math to cross-multiply and see that $6 \times 2 = 3x$, so $12 = 3x$; therefore, $4 = 1x$. Look at it another way: If repro width (6) is twice as large as copy width (3), then repro depth (x) must be twice as large as copy depth (2), that is, 4.

Question: Copy width is 3, copy height 2, repro width 4 1/2, and repro height x. How would you set up your formula?

$$\frac{4 \ 1/2}{3} = \frac{x}{2}$$

Question: With that formula, what size will the picture be when it appears in the paper?

Answer: If you cross-multiply, you get $2 \times 4 \ 1/2 = 3x$, so $9 = 3x$. Divide 3 into 9 for the answer, 3.

For most problems you'll find it easier to measure your original picture, both width and height, in picas. Otherwise, you can end up multiplying 4 11/16 by 5 3/8, which would be a true test of how good you were in fifth-grade arithmetic. Using picas, you'll rarely have tricky fractions to multiply.

Lots of people prefer using proportion wheels to size figures. A proportion wheel consists of two circular pieces of plastic clipped together. The wheels are labeled "original size" and "reproduction size." Say that you intend to enlarge a picture that is 24 picas by 40 picas. You want the width of the reproduction to be 48 picas. You operate the wheel by putting like on like, that is, lining the width of the original (24) up with the width you want the reproduction to be (48). Now find the depth of the original on the "original size" wheel (40). The number just above or below 40 is the depth the picture will be when it appears in the picture—in this case, 80.

Wheels are clearly labeled and most have the directions printed on them. With a little practice, you'll do fine. (By the way, most wheels you buy will be labeled in inches. Don't worry about that. The wheel is just plastic and does not know whether you're thinking in inches, picas, centimeters or furlongs.)

INDEX

Note: Boldface numbers indicate illustrations.

Copy editing marks

Paragraph this.

No ¶ But not this.

This is different. No ¶

We use a line to help.

Transpose two letters.

Transpose elements two.

Capitalize stanton.

Lower case Town.

Indicate bold face.

Indicate Italics.

Abbreviate: 105 Poi Street.

Spell out: Calif. man.

Spell out: 9

Use a figure: twelve dogs

Separate two words

Join words: week end

Join letters.

Delete one or more words.

Delete a letter.

Insert a missing letter.

Insert a word phrase

Put a period here.

On this line, try a comma.

Open quotes:

Close quotes:

Use a dash right here.

Restore this wrong deletion. stet

Underscore these in

handwriting: a u w

Overscore these in

handwriting: m n o

Insert apostrophe: Smiths.

Center this line.

Do not obliterate copy; mark

it out with a definite but thin

line so it can be compared with

the printed version.

Always use a sharpened pencil.